Slipping Backward

LAW IN THE AMERICAN WEST

Series Editor

John R. Wunder

University of Nebraska–Lincoln

Volume 8

Slipping Back

ward

A History of the
Nebraska Supreme Court

James W. Hewitt

UNIVERSITY OF NEBRASKA PRESS • LINCOLN AND LONDON

© 2007
by the
Board of Regents of the University of Nebraska
All rights reserved
Manufactured in the United States of America
⊗
Library of Congress Cataloging-in-Publication Data
Hewitt, James W.
Slipping backward : a history of the Nebraska Supreme Court / James W. Hewitt.
p.   cm.
(Law in the American West)
Includes
bibliographical references
and index.
ISBN-13: 978-0-8032-2433-9
(hardcover : alk. paper)
ISBN-10: 0-8032-2433-8
(hardcover : alk. paper)
1. Nebraska. Supreme Court.
2. Nebraska. Supreme Court—History.
I. Title.
KFN512.H49 2007
347.782'03509—dc22
2006029781

Set in Quadraat.
Designed by R. W. Boeche.

Contents

Illustrations

Following page 84

Tables

Preface

I began practicing law in 1956 and made a number of appearances before the Nebraska Supreme Court, beginning in 1957. I lost my first case, won my last, and pretty much broke even in between. But in the forty-five years that I appeared before the court, I formed an abiding respect for it, for most its members, and for the whole system of litigation as a method of settling disputes.

From the fall of 1985 until the fall of 1986, I was privileged to serve as president of the Nebraska State Bar Association. Nebraska's bar is a unified bar, which means that all lawyers practicing in Nebraska must belong to it. As president, I was privileged to meet frequently with the chief justice and to learn of the problems and concerns of the court.

I spent six years, from 1983 until 1989, as a member of the American Bar Association's Committee on the Federal Judiciary. The committee was charged with the responsibility of investigating every candidate for a federal judicial post, including appointments to the U.S. District Court, the Court of Appeals, or the Supreme Court, and reporting its findings with a recommendation to the Senate Judiciary Committee.

While I was on the committee, I had the task of investigating all the candidates within the Eighth Circuit (containing Nebraska, Iowa, Minnesota, Missouri, South Dakota, North Dakota, and Arkansas), and all committee members worked on Supreme Court nominations. The nomination of Robert Bork, whose choice kicked off a firestorm of partisan wrangling that has not abated since, came before the committee during my tenure.

These experiences gave me a very substantial interest in the work of appellate courts and in the politics of judicial selection. When it came time for me to select a topic for my PhD dissertation, my thoughts naturally turned to something about appellate courts and the way they work. And this book is based on that dissertation.

I began my graduate studies in history while still serving as vice president and general counsel of Nebco, Inc. I realized that the time would come when I would need to step aside for someone younger, and so I indulged a long-standing interest in history and took classes early in the morning, during the noon hour, late in the afternoon, and through individual reading. I received my master's degree in 1994 and then embarked on a PhD candidacy. I completed my coursework, took my comprehensives in 1998, and then began writing my dissertation. I had a two-year hiatus from my dissertation because of an unsuccessful candidacy for Nebraska's legislature. I finally finished the dissertation and received my degree in the spring of 2003. I retired from Nebco, after forty-one years of service, at the end of 2002.

In concert with my advisor, Professor John R. Wunder, I chose the Nebraska Supreme Court as my dissertation topic. Dr. Wunder felt that there was a great need for histories of all of America's state supreme courts, and no one had ever attempted a history of the Nebraska court. I decided that modern-day jurisprudence in Nebraska really coincided with the arrival of Chief Justice Robert G. Simmons, who took office in November 1938. I end my study with the court of Chief Justice William C. Hastings, who left in 1995. I thought that an analysis of the more recent history of the supreme court would lack historical perspective and objectivity. Therefore, I focus on the chief justiceships of Simmons (1938–63), Paul W. White (1963–78), Norman Krivosha (1978–87), and Hastings (1987–95).

I read 14,335 cases, every decision handed down by the court under the four chief justices. I have attempted to analyze many of the decisions herein. I have concentrated more on what the court said, and how the public and the bar reacted to its statements, than I have on how earlier decisions inevitably influenced later decisions. I have tried to write for the general public as well as for the bench and bar.

Many lawyers have helped me with suggestions for this book. But I rate the judges who served from 1938 to 1995, and the ratings are mine, and mine alone. I have tried to rate them without bias, but I am quite sure that some will disagree with my conclusions. However, if the work in general adds to public knowledge about the court, what it did, and how it functions, I will be quite satisfied.

Acknowledgments

I am deeply indebted to Professor John R. Wunder of the University of Nebraska–Lincoln history department, a wise lawyer and wide-ranging scholar whose suggestions and attention to detail pointed me in the right direction and spurred me onward.

Chief Justices Norman Krivosha and William Hastings, and Justices Leslie Boslaugh and Hale McCown, all from the Nebraska Supreme Court, consented to be interviewed and offered many helpful insights and analysis, for which I am most grateful.

Former court administrators Jim Dunlevey and Joe Steele, Chancellor Harvey Perlman of the University of Nebraska–Lincoln, and former *Lincoln Journal* editorial page editor Dick Herman all contributed many nuggets of fact that made this work much richer for their recollections. Shannon Doering, a former supreme court clerk, offered much helpful information concerning the inner workings of the court.

I am grateful to Leslie Boslaugh, the Nebraska State Historical Society, and the Nebraska Supreme Court for use of their photographs in these pages.

But most of all, I must recognize the tremendous contributions of my wife, Marjorie, who typed innumerable copies both of the dissertation from which this book sprang, and draft after draft of the manuscript; who offered many valuable suggestions; and who graciously allowed me the time to read and write and study over a period of almost ten years. Without her help, this book would never have been written, and I can never repay her.

Slipping Backward

1. An Introduction to the Nebraska Supreme Court
The Past is Prologue

A Little Lower Than The Angels

To lawyer and nonlawyer alike, the words *supreme court* summon the image of a huge marble pile, high on Capitol Hill, with Corinthian columns and fifty-three steps leading from the street up to the huge bronze doors. Few think of the Alaska Supreme Court, the South Dakota Supreme Court, or the Utah Supreme Court. People think of Justice Benjamin Cardozo, never realizing that he spent three times as long on the New York State Court of Appeals as he did on the U.S. Supreme Court; or Justice Willis VanDevanter, never knowing that he was chief justice of the Wyoming Territorial Supreme Court; or Oliver Wendell Holmes, never appreciating that he wrote two hundred more opinions as the chief justice of the Supreme Judicial Court of Massachusetts than he did as an associate justice of the U.S. Supreme Court.

The federal courts are the Olympians of American jurisprudence. Everything else seems to pale into insignificance, with the U.S. Supreme Court offering thunderbolt rulings that often appear to have come directly from heaven. But to the knowledgeable observer, that picture is as complicated as the stories of the Parthenon or the Acropolis; the grandiose legend is hardly reflective of what is actually transpiring today. The mighty nine in Washington may issue the more oracular pronouncements, but the less prominent figures in the state courts really dispense the meaningful, everyday judicial opinions. Grand issues involving free speech or religious freedom may be few and far between, but every day state court justices issue important decisions affecting real property, the disposition of a decedent's estate, or public policy exceptions to the doctrine of employment at will. State courts are, and have been for a century, the catalytic agent for laws that affect America's citizens in their everyday lives. Because of their impact, the state courts are worthy of a more careful examination than they have received to date.

The types of cases heard by state supreme courts have changed over the years, just as America itself has changed. Studies by such scholars as Lawrence M. Friedman, Morton Horwitz, and Kermit L. Hall examining the work of the state courts from 1870 to 1970 show how the nation has gone from "horse-and-buggy" days to the era of the space shuttle, from telegraph lines to satellite transmissions.[1] Cases involving debt collection and real property, exceptionally prevalent a century ago, have all but vanished from supreme court dockets, while tort cases, criminal cases, and cases involving public law (especially taxes, licensing, eminent domain, zoning, and elections) have increased exponentially.

There are a number of reasons for this change. Many, if not most, state supreme courts now have an intermediate appellate court interposed between them and the trial courts of general jurisdiction. The supreme courts are thus in a position to regulate their own dockets and pick and chose only cases of legal significance, leaving the dross of litigation and correction of errors to the intermediate courts. Much of the law governing debt collection and real property has been well developed for years and can be relegated to the mid-level courts, while newer, more intriguing issues can occupy the energy of the highest benches. State supreme courts need not worry about the nuances of adverse possession, for example. That law is clear, and only the desperate bother to litigate such issues.

The development of the criminal law in the states has occurred out of necessity, as federal courts have adopted new rules of substantive law and due process, thereby opening the gates for multitudinous criminal appeals and post-conviction hearings.[2] The U.S. Supreme Court, starting early in the 1920s, held that many of the protections of the federal Bill of Rights were available to defendants in state criminal trials because these rights were incorporated into the Fourteenth Amendment and were therefore applicable to the states. This line of interpretation brought a huge increase in criminal appeals by defendants. Congressional action, especially in the area of unfunded mandates, has resulted in much new state legislation, which must be interpreted by the courts. The creation of new governmental benefits is especially galling to those who have been denied such benefits, and their grievances often result in litigation.

The Nebraska Supreme Court offers a valuable case study of the efficacy of the judiciary at the state level during a period of federal transformation, especially through the terms of four chief justices: Robert G. Simmons (1938–63);

Paul W. White (1963–78); Norman Krivosha (1978–87); and William C. Hastings (1987–95). An assessment of this nearly sixty-year period can shed light on the development of jurisprudential ideologies, the composition and selection of the courts, the evolution of judicial leadership, and the role of dissent on the court. In many ways, the twentieth century set the stage for the modern evolution of the legal system of Nebraska. I will explore the achievements of the Nebraska state courts—including the development of the state appellate court system, an integrated (unified) bar, and an evolving jurisprudential intervention on the part of the state supreme court, reaching beyond traditional legal formalism—while examining each of the four courts.

It is important to scrutinize the courts as entities and the members as individuals to determine how each court functioned and how the court, and the jurisprudence it authored, changed over time. Judges in appellate courts do not decide legal cases by lot. They argue and wrangle over what the decision should be, and the background, experience, and mindset of a judge are critically important to his or her position on any given issue. Automatons cannot produce opinions, which are the output of a judicial mind, expressing the result in a case from the perspective of the author. And as leaders, or members, of a court change, one can detect subtle or even overt shifts in direction of a judicial body when it is compared, over time, to the opinions of its predecessors.

If the personality and beliefs of a judge were not vitally important, no one would really care who occupied the seats on a supreme court, be it on the federal or state level. Presidents would not pledge to appoint only judges who believed in "the intent of the founders." There would be little concern over whether a judicial aspirant were pro-choice or pro-life. But such views do matter, and supreme court judges, who are infallible because they are final, issue opinions that shape the course of our country, our states, and our society. In our democratic system, citizens obey those opinions, whether or not they accept them intellectually. For that reason alone, it is important that we know who has occupied the courts, what they said, and when and hopefully why they said it.

I have utilized a variety of sources in this work, including oral interviews, newspaper articles and editorials, and bar association polls, to gauge the subjective opinions of bar leaders, court functionaries, and some judges. I analyzed every one of the judicial opinions of the Nebraska Supreme Court during the incumbency of the four chief justices from 1938 to 1995 for summary data and for jurisprudential emphasis. I also examined secondary literature, particularly political science studies and the legal history of other state courts.

The modern history of the Nebraska Supreme Court contains an anomaly. While the court appeared to function adequately during the twists and turns of the twentieth century, it also declined in public acceptance and public influence. This decline owed in part to the court's own actions and, no doubt, partially to external influences—it is hard to imagine any set of circumstances more damaging to public respect for law and the judicial system than the Watergate scandals of the early 1970s, which brought the Nixon administration crashing to earth—but a careful examination of the court itself illuminates the reasons for its changing relationship with Nebraskans.

As a practicing lawyer with fifty years of experience in the courts (1956–2006) and as a past president of the Nebraska State Bar Association (1986), I have known and have practiced before all four of the chief justices who are evaluated in this history. Personal feelings or unconscious bias may have crept into this work. I have tried to write as a historian rather than as a lawyer. Most, if not all, of my conclusions are based upon a historian's standard of proof and should meet the preponderance of evidence test applicable in civil cases, but I do not argue that they have been proven beyond a reasonable doubt. Especially in the evaluation of members of the court, my own personal experiences and conversations with colleagues have contributed to the conclusions I have drawn. As James Madison wrote to Edward Everett in March of 1823, "It has been the misfortune of history that a personal knowledge and an impartial judgment of things rarely meet in the historian."

How Judges Decide Cases

Most of America's leading legal historians suggest that early American judges decided cases using the common law in order to promote the growth of the American economy and did more than merely protect property and the established order. "Law," writes Morton Horwitz, "was no longer conceived of as an eternal set of principles expressed in custom and derived from natural law. . . . [I]nstead, judges came to think of the common law as equally responsible with legislation for governing society and promoting socially desirable conduct."[3]

Broadly construing their role in society, judges apparently did not feel bound by any rigid rules of precedent. If, indeed, they were intent on helping America switch from a barter system to a market economy, they had to make new and innovative rules, much as the maligned Roger B. Taney did in 1839 when he conjured up the doctrine of substantive due process in the *Charles River Bridge v. Warren Bridge* case.[4] Taney narrowly construed a legislative charter for a toll bridge across the Charles River near Boston, when, several years later, the legislature chartered a competing bridge. He felt that competition between the old and the new bridge was a desired end. Taney's decision contained the first appearance of the concept known as substantive due process, where the court evaluates the wisdom of legislative activity.

But as the American economy established itself and developed, new and innovative doctrines became less necessary. The westward expansion of the country led to greater numbers of cases. As workloads increased and the market economy flourished, judges began to move from legal innovation to a system in which flexibility and imagination were replaced by rules that appeared to be immutable, inevitable, and inexorable, a system in which precedent and the mechanical application of the rules were designed to yield a readily predictable result and comfort all who dealt with the system.

Such a system became known as legal formalism. Judges who ascribe to legal formalism rely extensively on precedent, believing that legal rules, values, and principles have all been determined and will not change. They only have to select the right precedent and apply it to the facts of a given case.[5]

Legal formalism held sway in the United States during the latter half of the nineteenth century. As the twentieth century dawned, adherents to formalism were challenged by a new concept, "sociological jurisprudence," so named by Roscoe Pound, a Nebraskan who served as the dean of Harvard Law School. He preached that judges should not interfere when the legislature adopted a rational policy.[6] Oliver Wendell Holmes Jr., in his famous work *The Common Law*, propounded the position that judges had to take social and economic consequences into account in determining the result of any litigation. Both Pound and Holmes believed that judges should consider evidence of the social and economic impact of a particular case so they could weigh it as they made the decision.[7]

In the 1930s scholars Jerome Frank and Karl Llewellyn promulgated a philosophy called "legal realism." Proponents of realism were opposed to legal formalism. The realists questioned every legal rule, and they demanded that courts admit that the law was simply a utilitarian device to achieve social or economic ends. They also felt that those who believed in realism had to acknowledge that the law was fundamentally a set of tools used to attain a certain goal.[8]

State supreme courts undoubtedly worked from all these philosophies at one time or another. Gradually, courts decided more questions of law, and the states became more sedate, no longer part of a changing frontier. The state courts did not have the same incentive to reach innovative solutions to legal problems that they had when the whole jurisprudential canvas was blank, awaiting the artist's stroke.

Norman Krivosha, chief justice of the Nebraska Supreme Court from 1978 to 1987, acknowledged that his court based its decisions on legal formalism rather than on sociology or legal realism primarily because most of the issues that his court considered had been previously decided. He felt that if social and economic considerations motivated his judges as they considered new and unique issues, such motivation was subconscious and was not openly discussed by the judges as they worked toward a consensus.[9] Krivosha's position is not unusual. Most judges see themselves as followers of precedent; not following precedent would be to violate the doctrine of separation of powers by encroachment on the legislature.

Nebraska did not have an intermediate appellate court during Krivosha's regime. The Nebraska court did not therefore have at that time the luxury of picking and choosing the cases it heard. The supreme court was constitutionally required to hear every appeal, which put a premium on legal formalism. It was designed to correct error by lower courts, not to become an innovative policy-making body.

Judicial Selection

When America was a British colony, colonial governors appointed judges in the name of the king. When America became an independent nation and the colonies were transformed into states, governors or state legislators appointed judges.[10] But shortly after the United States was founded, democratic practices began to spread even to the judicial system. Some states held popular elections for judges, including Ohio in 1802, Georgia in 1812, and Indiana in 1816. In 1832 Mississippi decided that all its judges would be elected. New York followed suit in 1846. California's 1849 constitution made all judges elective, and in 1850, both Michigan and Pennsylvania made their supreme courts elective.[11]

In his comprehensive work *American Law in the 20th Century*, Lawrence

Friedman discusses the rationale for the election of judges: "For all its irra-
tionality, the American system did recognize a fundamental fact: judges have
power, and exercise power; and they do it in ways that have political meaning. How else, then, could you control your judges, except by electing them?"[12]
Friedman pointed out that judicial elections became the norm in the nineteenth century, but that some groups, such as the Progressives, were not fond
of the elective system, a sentiment that gained in popularity as corrupt judges
were placed in office by big-city political bosses.

The zeal of reformers seeking to end the elective judiciary became even
more pronounced in the twentieth century. Many states switched to the so-
called Missouri Plan, a system wherein the state's governor appoints judges.
Governors are not given the same free hand that the U.S. president enjoys.
Judicial nominating commissions comprised of laymen and lawyers select
finalists from among the applicants and forward a list to the governor. The
governor must chose from this list. Appointees then have to face the electorate within a fairly short period of time (in Nebraska, at the next election after
having served three years), but the judge does not run against an opponent. The
voters simply decide if he or she should be kept. As Friedman puts it, "Because
you cannot fight somebody with nobody, sitting judges under the Missouri
plan rarely lose. . . . In 4,588 retention elections between 1964 and 1999, only
fifty-two judges lost out. And in 1998 not a single judge lost a job because the
voters said no."

The U.S. Supreme Court has recently ruled unconstitutional a Minnesota
statute prohibiting candidates for judicial election from stating their views on
disputed legal or political issues such as partial-birth abortion or stem cell research. Nine other states had statutes virtually identical to Minnesota's, and
all have been invalidated. The case has aroused a great deal of criticism, as it
has caused critics to argue that judicial candidates will be forced to seek votes
by suggesting how they might rule in future cases.[13]

Most judges prefer the appointive rather than the elective system. Former
chief justice Krivosha believes that judges are subconsciously concerned about
retention elections and that their opinions in the year preceding their election
are reflective of their awareness of public opinion. He prefers a system like the
federal judiciary, where judges are appointed for as long as their behavior is
good—in effect a lifetime appointment.[14]

Judges are at a disadvantage in elections: they have no platform and cannot tell what they will do in the future. They can only defend their past. Some commentators argue that state supreme courts are less resistant to imposing the majority will than the federal courts. Legislatures can reverse decisions interpreting the state constitution by constitutional amendment and can overturn judicial interpretations of statutes. Neither process is as burdensome as it can be on the federal level.[15]

The tension between judicial independence and public accountability is not likely to be resolved soon. At the very least, if the public wants the right to remove judges because of their performance, it must remain fully informed of the judges' performance and not simply respond to key words or catch phrases.

Bar association involvement in election campaigns poses problems, but it can have salutary aspects. Political scientist Charles Sheldon found that the public was quite willing to follow the bar's lead in judicial endorsements, reasoning that the lawyers knew the candidates better than anyone else.[16] Nebraska has allowed the bar's involvement in elections since 1984, and it has worked well. But in states where bar association membership is not mandatory, competing interest groups, such as the plaintiff's bar and the insurance-defense bar, might give widely divergent endorsements. And in states where membership is mandatory, the association might find itself in serious difficulty if one or two supreme court judges whom it had opposed decided to exercise the court's role of oversight and regulation of the bar association.

Scholars who have written on judicial selection and election have divergent views on some points but all agree that it is very difficult for a judge to remain independent and objective when his continuation in office may well depend on the type of vote he casts in a certain case. Should judges face the electorate and account for their performance? Or should they be carefully selected, appointed for good behavior, and allowed to issue opinions freely, restrained only by conscience and not by fear of voter retribution? This debate might rage on, unabated, for years to come.

Court Leadership

The Romans had a phrase for it: *primus inter pares*—first among equals. On a court composed of seven or nine well-educated men or women who are trained to be disputatious, a chief justice must proceed gingerly in order to avoid angering the other judges, whose votes are just as important as the chief's. Many chief justices do no more than their brethren except for exercising certain administrative chores. But those who do more can exercise considerable influence for good or ill.

John Vile contrasted the presidential selection of the chief justice of the United States for life with the procedure used in many states, where the chief justice seat is rotated among the members of the court.[17] State procedures for selecting a chief justice vary greatly. Before 1920 the member of the Nebraska Supreme Court with the least amount of time remaining in his term was chief justice. Since the constitutional amendments of 1920, Nebraska's chief justice is specifically selected for the position and remains in the post throughout his or her service on the court.[18] Vile concludes that appointing the chief justice for life is the preferable method of selection because it "lends a prestige to the office and to the institution the chief justice serves, insures greater continuity and experience in the office, and reduces incentives for justices to jockey for this position."[19]

G. Alan Tarr and Mary C. A. Porter specifically studied the supreme courts of Alabama, Ohio, and New Jersey in their *State Supreme Courts in State and Nation*.[20] They found that the personality and leadership style of a chief justice could have a profound effect on collegial relationships on the court and, consequently, on the work of the court. The chief justice is responsible for establishing the atmosphere in which a court works, and a lack of harmony will be attributed to a failure of leadership.[21] Charles Sheldon states that no court can tolerate a high level of dissonance over an extended period of time and remain viable. Cohesion is a necessary goal of any stable group and is especially needed on a supreme court.[22]

Dissent as an Element of Leadership

Craig Ducat and Victor Flango, in *Leadership in State Supreme Courts: Roles of the Chief Justice*, argue that unanimity in judicial decisions is a desirable goal and that chief justices accepted unanimity as desirable.[23] They set out to determine what leadership qualities chief justices needed to have to promote unanimity, focusing on dissent rates, both those of the court as a whole and of the chief justice as an individual member of the court. They concluded that the most successful chief justices were those whose dissent rates declined as the dissent rate of the entire court declined. An increase in both types of dissents signaled a leadership deficiency in the chief justice.[24]

Ducat and Flango confined their study to state supreme courts. The U.S. Supreme Court is sui generis. Scarcely a case goes by in that high court that does not spawn a dissent or, at the very least, a withering concurrence.

Because dissent creates uncertainty as to the law and reduces the impact of judicial decisions, and because it can lead to conflict resulting from the explicit criticism of a colleagues' work, Ducat and Flango believe that an effective chief justice will strive to promote unanimity whenever possible.[25] To promote consensus, the chief justice might have to suppress his or her own tendency to dissent, even if the decision runs counter to the chief's own value preferences. This study will examine in part the dissent rates of the Nebraska Supreme Court, considering each court as a whole and the chief justice individually, in order to evaluate the leadership of the chief justice. However, dissent rates are not the only measure of leadership, and many other factors must, and will, be included in the leadership equation.[26]

Political scientists have found that dissent rates are much higher in states that have intermediate appellate courts than in states that have no such court. With an intermediate court available to correct errors, a state supreme court is free to consider novel and highly charged issues.[27] Sheldon noted that the Washington court had a high dissent rate, regardless of who sat as chief justice.[28] He quoted Charles Evans Hughes to the effect that a dissent was an appeal to the brooding spirit of the law and to the intelligence of a future day. He also opined that dissents performed the symbolic function of showing the litigants and their counsel that the case had received considerable study and discussion. Nonetheless, he acknowledged that dissents are indicative of a lack of cohesion on the bench. Sheldon also assumed that those judges who wrote the most unanimous opinions were exercising another form of leadership.[29]

There are other, somewhat tangible methods for measuring the success of a chief justice's incumbency. The volume of newspaper coverage of the court is one, including editorials for or against specific opinions. In Nebraska the bar association polls its members every two years to determine how they rate the work of the individual judges. Evaluating the leadership of the chief justice is a subjective undertaking, but there are some objective criteria that can be applied to the process. These evaluations are important to a public understanding of the direction in which the court is heading and the acceptance or rejection of that directional pattern.

The Early Years of Nebraska Law

Nebraska became a territory with the passage of the Kansas-Nebraska Act by Congress in May 1854 and a state with Andrew Johnson's presidential proclamation on March 1, 1867. As in other frontier states, Nebraska's new government needed new statutes, regulations, and forums to resolve disputes. Courts and judges had to interpret the laws, adjudicate the conflicts, and lend an aura of dignity, permanence, and acceptability to the governmental scheme while managing the problems of the newly created region and its inhabitants. Fifteen men served as territorial judges in Nebraska. Michael Homer relates that five of the Nebraska judges, one-third of the total, stayed in Nebraska even after their terms had expired and they had left office. Of the fifteen appointees, three never assumed their offices. Of the twelve who did serve, five resigned, two died in office, two were removed, and the remaining three were still serving when Nebraska became a state. Only two of the fifteen had been Nebraska residents prior to their appointment, a sore point for residents of the territory.[30]

One of the appointees, Edward R. Harden, brought a black slave named Sam with him. Harden served for two years but went back to Georgia because his wife refused to join him in Nebraska. He became the station agent for the Western and Atlantic Railroad at Dalton, Georgia, hardly a promotion.[31]

The Nebraska territorial judges brought some political experience with them, and some went on to further political careers. Four of them had been state legislators elsewhere before their appointment, and three had been U.S. congressmen who secured their appointments after losing their bids for reelection. One of the judges, Samuel Black, became the governor of the Nebraska Territory after resigning from the court.

Two of the judges were Democrats who were removed from office by Abraham Lincoln after he became president. He appointed two Republicans in their stead. One of the deposed Democrats, Eleazer Wakely, challenged his removal in a case that went all the way to the U.S. Supreme Court, where his claim was rejected. Wakely subsequently served as a state district court judge in Omaha from 1883 to 1892, and after finishing as a judge he went on to become one of Nebraska's most distinguished lawyers. He served as the first president of the Nebraska State Bar Association when it was founded in 1900.[32]

Homer discovered only a few opinions by the territorial supreme court, as the judges were not required to write opinions outlining the reasoning behind their rulings. In the opinions he was able to study, he found that both the judges and the lawyers who appeared before them cited judicial decisions from other states and legal texts as authority for propositions of law. Almost all the territorial judges in Nebraska had some legal ability, and they attempted to decide cases with fairness and in accordance with the legal standards they brought from their home states. They were largely successful in organizing the Nebraska judicial system, getting the settlers to bring disputes to court rather than resorting to the doctrine of self-help.[33] One of the territorial judges, Elmer S. Dundy, became Nebraska's first federal district judge, serving from 1868 to 1896.[34]

Thirty-seven men served as judges of the Nebraska Supreme Court from the time of statehood until the commencement of this history, in November 1938. Five of them—William B. Rose, George A. Eberly, Bayard H. Paine, Edward F. Carter, and Frederick W. Messmore—were on the court when Robert Simmons assumed the role of chief justice and the modern era of Nebraska's justice system began. The court consisted of three judges until Nebraskans amended the constitution in 1908 to increase the membership to seven.[35]

Early judges were elected on partisan ballots after having been nominated at party conventions. This method of judicial election persisted until the constitution was amended in 1908 to make their election nonpartisan.[36] In 1962, a half century later, legislators constitutionally changed judicial selection in Nebraska to a modified Missouri Plan, where candidates are appointed by the governor after having been approved by a nominating commission.[37] They then face a retention election periodically, running against their own record, with no opponent on the ballot.

Railroads controlled Nebraska politics during Nebraska's formative years and influenced the state supreme court. From 1870 to 1907 the railroads bribed many political office holders by offering them free passes for intra-state travel.[38] Because there was hardly any competitive form of transport, the free pass for railroad travel was a munificent gift indeed. As a consequence, railroad influence in political conventions was substantial, and woe to the hopeful who incurred the wrath of the railroad bosses. Judges being adroit politicians, and as capable of reading the political tea-leaves as the next man, it is no wonder that much of Nebraska's early law involved the railroads and that almost all of it was favorable to the bosses' cause.

But transportation was not the only issue to occupy Nebraska's early supreme court. Cases involving probate, real estate, and contracts all frequently came before the court. Tort law, divorce law, corporate law, and zoning law cases showed up on the docket, but with much less frequency. Taxation was much less of an issue then than it is presently in Nebraska. Nebraska had no sales or income tax until the 1960s, and real estate taxation was the principal source of revenue for both the state and municipal governments. The welfare state did not exist, and early judges could not have imagined the output of regulatory prose that has inundated the nation in the twentieth and twenty-first centuries. Cases before the premodern Nebraska Supreme Court dealt mainly with private economic matters between citizens. The court seldom discussed cases involving relationships between the three branches of government or between the government and citizens.

Occasionally, however, governmental involvement could not be avoided, and over the years, two of the court's most famous cases involved governmental action. In the first, in 1891, the court became embroiled in the contest of a gubernatorial election. James Boyd, an Omaha Democrat, won the 1890 gubernatorial nod over a Populist candidate, with the Republican candidate finishing third. The Populists contested the election on the grounds that many of Boyd's Douglas County votes were fraudulent. During the contest, outgoing governor John M. Thayer refused to surrender the office.[39] He called out the state militia to keep him in the governor's office. After the legislature decided the election in favor of Boyd, Thayer surrendered the office but then filed a *quo warranto* action in the state supreme court.

Thayer challenged Boyd's eligibility for office on the grounds that Boyd was not a citizen of the United States. Boyd's father, an Irish immigrant, had taken out naturalization papers many years before but had never completed the process. Boyd's father did not secure full citizenship until 1890, long after Boyd had reached the age of majority. Thayer argued that the father's attainment of citizenship status did not confer that status on his non-minor children, including Boyd. The Nebraska Supreme Court agreed and restored Thayer to office.[40] Boyd appealed to the U.S. Supreme Court, and nine months later the Court reversed Nebraska's court, holding that Boyd was a citizen.[41] The Nebraska opinion was superior in style, content, and reasoning. Boyd should not have been restored to office, but the U.S. Supreme Court was reluctant to overturn the election result, a position from which it has subsequently retreated.[42]

Much later, in 1922, the Nebraska Supreme Court issued an opinion deficient in style, content, and reasoning, an opinion subsequently reversed by the U.S.

Supreme Court. In *Meyer v. Nebraska*, a teacher in a Lutheran parochial school taught the German language to a young student who had not yet entered the eighth grade. Nebraska had a statute barring the teaching of foreign languages to students below the eighth grade. The language appeared in a book of Bible stories, and Meyer argued that he was teaching religion, not language. The Nebraska court disagreed and upheld Meyer's conviction, holding that banning a foreign language fell within the police power of the state.[43] The dissent of Judge Charles B. Letton, in which Chief Justice Andrew M. Morrissey joined, recognized that the law banning the teaching of a foreign language was the result of mob psychology and a product of the passions engendered by World War I. Letton said, "I am unable to agree with the doctrine that the legislature may arbitrarily, through the exercise of the police power, interfere with the fundamental right of every American parent to control, in a degree not harmful to the state, the education of his child, and to teach it, in association with other children, any science or art, or any language which contributes to a larger life, or to a higher and broader culture."[44] The U.S. Supreme Court agreed.

The Law Governing the Law

The Nebraska Constitution provides the key to understanding how the state supreme court functioned in its formative years, how it bogged down in a morass of litigation in the late nineteenth and early twentieth centuries, and how it functions today. Nebraska has a somewhat unique constitutional structure. Its 1875 constitution still serves as the basic constitutional document of the state. It was amended after a constitutional convention in 1919–20, where delegates adopted over forty amendments instead of writing an entirely new document.

In the 1875 constitution, Article V, Section 4 provided that the judge of the supreme court with the least amount of time remaining in his term should serve as chief justice. This law remained the rule until the adoption of the 1920 amendments, which established a separate position of chief justice.[45]

With only three judges serving at the time of statehood, the court was soon inundated by the number of appeals being filed, even though Nebraska's case load was quite light. The problem was exacerbated by the fact that under the original statehood constitution of 1867, the judges of the supreme court also served as district court judges, trying cases throughout the parts of the state that were populated. The 1875 constitution eliminated their trial jurisdiction, but by that time the supreme court was far behind in cases. The 1875 constitution also provided that every case, no matter how much money was involved, could be appealed to the state supreme court (this section has now been amended to include the Nebraska Court of Appeals, after its creation).[46] In the late 1880s and 1890s the state grew in population and diversity, and a casual review of the published reports of the supreme court reveals a number of cases involving corporate and commercial matters.

In an attempt to alleviate the congestion on the docket, the legislature passed a statute in 1893 that allowed the supreme court to appoint three commissioners to assist it in its work. Each commissioner was to serve for three years and come from a different political party, including the Populist party, at the height of its influence in Nebraska in the 1890s. In pursuance of the act, the court appointed three commissioners and issued a general order that the opinions of the commissioners, when filed, would stand as judgments of the court. But the commissioners filed no opinions. They instead submitted them to the supreme court, which examined the opinion and the proposed syllabus. If it approved of the opinions, the court filed each one as the opinion and syllabus of the court. The commissioners did not sit with the court but sat as a separate court. The commission operated for three more years after 1895, but when the final act expired in 1899, it was not at that time extended further.[47]

However, by 1901, the court was losing even more ground with the cases, and so the legislature went back to the drawing board, creating a commission of nine members to be appointed by the court.[48] Six of the members were chosen for one year terms, and three for two years terms. The nine commissioners sat in three groups of three, in effect giving the state four appellate courts. The statute was renewed in 1903 and 1905, although the 1905 act reduced the number of commissioners from nine to six.[49]

The constitution was amended in 1908 to increase the size of the supreme court from three to seven judges, and there were no commissioners from 1909 to 1915.[50] However, another legislative bill created a commission that served from 1915 to 1921.[51] Those commissioners were appointed by the governor with the approval of the supreme court, a procedure that might have raised separation of powers issues. A final commission served from 1925 to 1931, even after the constitution was amended in 1920 to allow the court to sit in two divisions of five judges each by bringing up district judges. This provision was to be enforced "when necessary for the prompt submission and determination of causes."[52]

Commissions served simply as a temporary expedient, but they did do a good job of relieving the docket backlog. In 1926 the judiciary committee of the Nebraska State Bar Association recommended the creation of an intermediate appellate court, but the idea found little favor, and Nebraska would not have an intermediate appellate court until 1990, when a constitutional amendment established one.

Still needing assistance, the supreme court, from 1931 on, frequently called district judges to Lincoln to sit with the court. Sometimes five members of the court sat with two district judges, and sometimes six sat with one district judge. Because the district judges were hearing cases, one or two supreme court judges were released from hearing cases and could concentrate on opinion writing.

Laying Down the Law

In virtually all cases the Nebraska Supreme Court generates a written opinion, telling the parties, the bar, and the public why the court reached the result that it did. The appeals court, after its creation in the early 1990s, issued opinions as well, although not in every case. The precedental effect of court of appeals decisions is determined by the panel deciding the case, under criteria established by the supreme court. During the tenure of Norman Krivosha, when the supreme court was swamped by undecided cases, many opinions consisted of the terse comment, "Affirmed. See Rule 20."

As of 2006, and for many years past, cases before the supreme court begin with the filing of a notice of appeal. The clerk of the trial court prepares a transcript of the pleadings and orders in the case below, from which the appeal is taken and sent to the supreme court. If the case below involves testimony and exhibits, the trial court reporter prepares and sends forward a verbatim account of the testimony and all the offered exhibits. After considering the pleadings and the testimony from the trial of the case and hearing oral argument, the supreme court then issues an opinion, affirming or reversing the trial court.

The Nebraska Supreme Court by rule allows oral argument in all cases, but in most cases the arguments are very brief, lasting only ten minutes per side. The court hears arguments during the first week of each calendar month except in July and August. After the day's arguments are concluded, the court adjourns to its conference room and discusses the day's cases. The judges make tentative votes on each case, and the judge assigned the task of writing the opinion begins work. By one of its internal rules, the supreme court assigns opinions to its judges on a rotating basis unless special circumstances intervene, and the court usually knows before hearing oral argument in a case which member will be writing the opinion.

After a judge and any law clerks have crafted an opinion, they circulate it to the other members of the court and hold a second conference in which the judges discuss the draft opinion. If at least four members of the seven member court approve the opinion, it becomes the opinion of the court. Those judges who do not agree with the opinion are then free to write dissenting or concurring opinions. They may also remain silent. Cases that appear to be unanimous decisions are not always so. They may have been approved by the slimmest of margins—four votes to three—but the three judges not in accord with the majority may have concluded that there was little to be gained by writing a dissenting opinion.

Nebraska's court did not have law clerks until the 1970s, which is one reason why it fell so far behind writing and issuing opinions before this time. Judges had to hear argument, research the law, and write their opinions, all time-consuming tasks. Now each judge has two law clerks who perform much of the research that goes into opinions, and in many instances the clerks draft part or all of a judge's formal opinion. Judges rely on their clerks—usually young lawyers who graduated with law school honors—to different degrees, but unquestionably the clerks have aided immeasurably in reducing the workloads of the individual court members.

If an opinion does not receive four affirmative votes at the opinion conference, the author may go back to the drawing board in an effort to craft language more palatable to those judges who oppose his or her draft, or the opinion may be reassigned to one of those in opposition. In some instances, the judge who prepared the first draft may write the opinion as a *per curiam* opinion, or opinion of the court, because the defeated author would not approve of the changes required to placate the majority and would not want his or her name attached to the opinion.

After the opinion finally wins a majority, it is transmitted to opposing counsel and released to the public. It is then published in the Nebraska Supreme Court *Reports*, the official record of all judicial activity. Cases decided by the Nebraska Court of Appeals are handled in much the same way, although opinions of the court of appeals are published under certain constraints laid down by the supreme court, constraints that are mainly of interest only to appellate lawyers.[53]

The Effect of the Opinions

Courts can act only when confronted with a case or controversy. They cannot issue advisory opinions on potential cases. An appellate court must issue an opinion that not only decides the controversy but also articulates rules of law that will guide the conduct of the populace in days to come. And it is those rules of law that characterize an appellate court as good or bad, liberal or conservative, hide-bound or visionary. The opinions of the Nebraska Supreme Court that set out rules of law, especially in the court's modern era, beginning with Chief Justice Robert G. Simmons, offer penetrating insights into what the court thought, how it dealt with new social problems, and whether it was successful in its task of guiding the behavior of Nebraska's citizens. In my judgment, as will be revealed throughout this book, the Nebraska Supreme Court from 1938 to 1995 was a sober, hard-working, very conservative body that made some errors, showed little willingness to embrace new legal theories, seemed in many instances to be unaware of the societal impact of its rulings, and often took itself much more seriously than mere mortals should.

Not all the court's decisions shed great light on Nebraska's jurisprudence. I emphasize cases involving the death penalty and other crimes, governmental relationships, water law, tort law, and major civil issues. My decision to focus on these areas of law was entirely subjective and based primarily upon my fifty years of practicing law.

2. "The Judicial Mowing Machine Thus Cuts a Wide Swath"
The Simmons Court, 1938–63

Robert G. Simmons of Lincoln was elected chief justice of the Nebraska Supreme Court at the general election held November 8, 1938. The office had been vacant since August 13, 1938, when Chief Justice Charles A. Goss died. Simmons defeated former attorney general C. A. Sorensen in a race for the seat of chief justice by a vote of 241,664 to 185,165.[1] On November 12, 1938, Governor R. L. Cochran appointed Simmons as chief justice, and he assumed office immediately.

Simmons's arrival began the longest tenure of any chief justice in Nebraska. He held the position until he retired on January 2, 1963, after serving just over twenty-five years in office. During the tenure of Simmons, the supreme court moved from a "horse-and-buggy" court concerned mainly with real property, will contests, and an occasional felony to a court dealing with thorny criminal issues—many of which existed because of pronouncements of the U.S. Supreme Court—and a veritable explosion of cases involving divorce, sophisticated tort litigation, and problems associated with the burgeoning state government.

Simmons and his court set the standard for judicial probity and dignity in Nebraska. The public and the bar compared succeeding courts to the Simmons court and its accomplishments as well as to its approach to adjudication. The Simmons court faced little public scrutiny or criticism. It experienced one brief period of intramural quarreling, but only the bar was aware of the problem, and for the most part the court rendered its judgments quietly and unobtrusively, which is how courts should work. The public generally accepted what the court brought forth as its work product.

Simmons became Nebraska's chief judicial officer at a time when the state was still suffering from the combined effects of the Great Depression and the drought of the mid-1930s. During the thirties, Nebraska approached having average precipitation in only two years out of ten.[2] Despite the fact that farm production was drastically curtailed during the entire ten-year period, the price structure for virtually all farm prices collapsed. In 1932 corn was worth only 20 percent of its 1929 price, while hogs and beef brought only a quarter of their 1929 value.[3] Farmers dumped milk in roadside ditches to keep the commodity off the market, and in 1934 they marched to the capitol in Lincoln and successfully cowed the legislature into enacting a two-year moratorium on the foreclosure of farm mortgages.[4]

Nebraska's rock-ribbed Republicanism went by the boards during the thirties. Democrat R. L. Cochran won the governorship in 1934, 1936, and 1938.[5] Most state constitutional officers were Democrats, as were many in Nebraska's congressional delegation. Republican Senator George W. Norris of McCook, facing strong opposition from members of his own party, ran as an independent in 1936. Aided by the endorsement of President Franklin Roosevelt, who visited the state during the campaign to stump for Norris, the aging senator defeated Simmons, the GOP candidate, and Terry Carpenter, the Democratic standard-bearer.[6]

Norris had successfully led the fight for Nebraska's unique, nonpartisan unicameral legislature in 1934. Adopted in large part because it would save money, cutting the number of paid legislators from 133 to somewhere between thirty and fifty, the new unicameral opened for business in January 1937 with forty-three senators sitting.[7] The tensions between the new body and the other two coordinate branches of government would occupy Simmons and his court for some time to come.

During the 1930s Nebraska was still basically an agricultural state, but manufacturing and processing were beginning to have an impact on the state economy. Nebraska began moving toward public power in 1933, when the legislature authorized the creation of public power and irrigation districts. In 1946 Nebraska completed the transition to public power, becoming the first state in the country where all the power companies were publicly owned.[8]

Nebraska was struggling toward modernity, still trying to escape the awful financial strictures of the Depression and drought, when Simmons won his seat as chief justice and assumed the job in 1938. His political experiences and acumen would serve him well as the court began to consider new and innovative issues and legislation.

For most of his tenure, Simmons appeared to be in firm control of his court. For one eighteen year period, from January 1943 until January 1961, six of the seven judges of the Nebraska Supreme Court, including Simmons, served together without interruption, a period of collegial longevity virtually unprecedented in modern jurisprudence, and most certainly in Nebraska. However, for one brief period during the late 1950s it appeared that a schism had developed on the court, with acrimonious dissents and concurrences filling its advance sheets. The discord seemed to have cooled by the time Simmons retired. Judges being as close-mouthed as they traditionally are, it is virtually impossible to determine what finally ended the internecine warfare, although advancing age of all the jurists and an increasing workload may have contributed to the cessation of hostilities.

Simmons the Man

Simmons was born in 1891 on his father's farm in Scotts Bluff County, Nebraska. The family moved into the town of Scottsbluff in 1900, where Simmons's father was appointed postmaster. Simmons graduated from Scottsbluff High School in 1909 and attended Hastings College in Hastings, Nebraska, for two years. He then entered the University of Nebraska College of Law in 1912 and graduated in 1915. He supported himself during his law school years by washing dishes in a Lincoln boarding house.[9]

He returned to western Nebraska, to Gering, after graduation from law school and served as the Scotts Bluff county attorney in 1916 and 1917. In October 1917 he enlisted in the U.S. Army and was discharged as a second lieutenant in January 1919. He went back to Scottsbluff and practiced law until November 1922, when he was elected as a Republican to Congress from Nebraska's sixth district, replacing Moses P. Kincaid. Simmons was subsequently elected four more times, ending his congressional career when he was defeated in the Democratic landslide of 1932. He ran for the U.S. Senate in 1934 but lost in another Democratic sweep. He ran again for the Senate in 1936 but was defeated by the revered George W. Norris, a Republican running as an independent, although Simmons did defeat the Democratic candidate, Terry Carpenter of Scottsbluff.[10]

While serving as chief justice, Simmons was also an arbitrator for the National Mediation Board and a referee for the National Railroad Adjustment Board. During the Truman administration the Department of State appointed him as an emissary to Middle Eastern and African nations, and he chaired the legal group of the People-to-People program during the Eisenhower administration, working in Indonesia, India, and the Philippines.[11] Simmons was a former president of the University of Nebraska Alumni Association, a former commander of the American Legion in Nebraska, a very active Mason, one of the founders of Boys' State in Nebraska, a member of the American Bar Association's House of Delegates, and a member of the editorial advisory board of the American Bar Association Journal. He received honorary degrees from Hastings College and Creighton University.[12]

Colleagues

When Robert G. Simmons came to the court in 1938, his associates were William B. Rose, George A. Eberly, Bayard H. Paine, Edward F. Carter, Frederick W. Messmore, and Harvey M. Johnsen. Johnsen left the Nebraska Supreme Court in 1940, when President Roosevelt appointed him to the U.S. Court of Appeals for the Eighth Circuit. John W. Yeager replaced him on the Nebraska court. Rose and Eberly chose not to run in 1942, both having served several terms, and were replaced by Elwood B. "Jimmy" Chappell and Adolph E. Wenke, respectively. Neither Rose nor Eberly faced the voters after Simmons became chief justice. Paine retired rather than run again in 1948 and was succeeded by Paul E. Boslaugh. Carter and Messmore were still on the court when Simmons retired, as was Yeager. Chappell and Boslaugh left the court after the 1960 election, choosing not to run again. Wenke died in office in March 1961. So, from January 1943 until January 1961, six of the seven members of the court—Simmons, Carter, Messmore, Yeager, Chappell, and Wenke—served together without interruption. Boslaugh joined them for twelve years, from January 1949 to January 1961.

Carter, Rose, and Leslie Boslaugh, who succeeded his father in January 1961 and served until he retired in 1994, were the three longest-serving judges in the history of the Nebraska court, and all served with Simmons at one time or another. Carter's tenure was thirty-six years, Rose's thirty-four, and Leslie Boslaugh served thirty-three years.

The six members of the Simmons court who served together for eighteen years were remarkably alike. All but Simmons had been district judges before joining the supreme court, as had Bayard Paine, who served until 1948. Simmons was the only member of the court without district court experience until Paul Boslaugh replaced Paine in January 1949. All but Paine, including Simmons, had served in the military during World War I. Carter, Chappell,

Wenke, and Simmons had all been extremely active in the American Legion, and Carter and Simmons remained very involved during their service on the court. Simmons and Wenke had been presidents of the University of Nebraska Alumni Association, and Chappell had been very active in the group as well. Carter, Chappell, Wenke, Eberly, Paine, and Simmons were all members of various Masonic bodies.

All of the five district judges, with the exception of Yeager, had been elected to some political or organizational office before being elected to the district bench. Simmons had served ten years in Congress. These were men who were members, who were politically active, who had been intimately involved in community and organizational life. Yet they traded it all for the cloistered atmosphere of a state appellate court. Neither their opinions nor their infrequent public comments give any clear reasons for why they would make the commitment they did.

During Simmons's incumbency, he and eight other judges were Republicans, while four were Democrats. Although the Republicans were clearly in the majority, the court was almost always balanced four to three in favor of the Republicans because of the differing terms of the various members. During the eighteen-year period when the court membership remained virtually the same, Simmons had the most trouble with Carter, leader of a conservative bloc on the court, and Wenke, the leader of the liberal wing.

Simmons had a challenger in 1944, when he defeated Paul Manhart by a count of 347,842 to 97,342. He was unopposed in 1950 and 1956. Paine was unopposed in 1942. Yeager was unopposed in 1940 but drew a challenger, L. D. Carter, in 1946. Yeager prevailed, gaining 51,257 votes to Carter's 21,006 votes. He was unopposed in 1952 and again in 1958.[13]

Chappell had an opponent only in his initial run for office in 1942, when he defeated F. C. Radke by 30,901 to 15,902 votes. He faced no one in either 1948 or 1954. Wenke barely won his first election, defeating Frederick T. Spear of Fremont by a vote of 30,715 to 30,308 in 1942. However, no one entered the race against him in 1948, 1954, or 1960.[14]

Paul Boslaugh defeated Fred Hanson of McCook by a vote of 31,689 to 24,167 in his first try for the court in 1948. In 1954 he was unopposed. His son, Leslie Boslaugh, defeated John Bottorf of Sutton by 34,519 to 26,059 votes in 1960, and he faced only retention elections thereafter during his long service on the bench. Harry Spencer, who succeeded Chappell, defeated Doane Kiechel by

62,309 to 17,899 votes in 1960. Paul White won the final judicial election for the post of chief justice before the advent of the Missouri Plan in 1962, defeating former Nebraska attorney general Clarence S. Beck of North Platte by a vote of 225,073 to 175,551.[15]

Serious Schism or Peevish Power Play?

Although the Simmons court confronted a number of significant issues in the years following 1938, it did so without apparent conflict among the jurists. But all was not always rosy. Simmons, as chief, was the nominal head of the court, but it was Carter who led the usually vocal conservative bloc and who was recognized by bench and bar alike as the court's intellectual leader. Although Carter's position had to be galling for Simmons, the chief justice did not openly attempt to denigrate him. Their relationship in chambers or behind the scenes may well be another story.

The first real evidence of a Simmons-Carter problem appeared in 1956 in the case of *Ruehle v. Ruehle*.[16] A divorce action, the case involved questions about the effect of a stipulation of the parties concerning child support. But the real import of the case was a question raised by Carter in a dissent that concerned the court calling up a district judge to sit with it. Judge Frederick Messmore, who participated only on briefs, authored the opinion. Carter dissented, and Simmons joined in his dissent on the merits. Carter then went on to question whether a district judge could sit on any case except those four instances provided for in Article V, Section 2 of Nebraska's Constitution: (1) when the court sits in two divisions of five judges in each division; (2) when determining the constitutionality of a statute; (3) when hearing an appeal from a conviction of homicide; and (4) when reviewing a decision rendered by a division of the court.

When *Ruehle* first came to the supreme court, Chappell disqualified himself, so the case was heard by Simmons, Carter, Messmore, Yeager, Wenke, and Boslaugh. Mesmore wrote an opinion reversing the trial court, but he could not get a majority of the six hearing judges. Simmons then wrote an opinion affirming the trial court, and it also failed to get a majority. The supreme court set the case down for reargument and asked District Judge H. Emerson Kokjer of Wahoo to join it for the reargument. Subsequently, Carter challenged the right of Kokjer to vote on the case and implied that Simmons had appointed Kokjer to achieve the result Simmons desired. Messmore, Yeager, and Wenke (the liberal bloc), together with Simmons, held that Kokjer could sit. Carter and Boslaugh voted that he could not. Chappell had disqualified himself. The vote was four to two in favor of Kokjer's right to sit. His place on the court settled, Kokjer then voted in favor of the Messmore opinion, reversing the ruling of the trial court. Carter argued that without Kokjer, the court was equally divided and affirmance was required. Boslaugh concurred in Carter's total dissent, not just the segment on the merits.[17]

Kokjer wrote a concurrence, in which Yeager joined, explaining his vote on the merits. He said nothing about his position as to whether he could legitimately sit with the court. Simmons dissented in part and concurred in part. He first reaffirmed that he joined with Carter's dissent on the merits, and he then spent eleven and a half pages explaining why he agreed with the trial court. He next wrote an additional twenty-nine pages showing why he believed Carter was wrong to oppose calling up a district judge. He began with the interesting statement: "Although it is probably unnecessary, in doing so I wish to assure the bar that there is no personal acrimony involved at any stage of these proceedings. Language used by Judge Carter, coming from another's pen might be 'fightin' words,' but from Judge Carter's it is not so."[18]

Simmons went on to point out that Carter's challenge did not come before Kokjer sat but months later, when Messmore announced at an opinion conference of the court that Kokjer had informed him that he (Kokjer) supported the Messmore opinion that had failed of adoption. That news set Carter off and provoked the controversy. Simmons reviewed the Nebraska Constitutional Convention proceedings of 1919 and 1920 in great detail and argued that the convention recognized that district judges could be called up to sit with the court while it was sitting *en banc*, as it had since 1921, following the adoption of the 1920 constitutional provisions. He pointed out that Carter, while a district judge from 1927–34, sat with the court on several occasions when the court was not sitting in divisions. He concluded by stating that calling up district judges to sit was done to keep the docket current and that the decision had full constitutional authority. Simmons therefore won the debate, and Carter was vanquished in what appeared to be an open fracture of collegiality.

One year later, in *Capitol Bridge Co. v. County of Saunders* (1957), Carter, writing for the majority, granted a *quantum meruit* recovery to a plaintiff selling bridge lumber to a county, even though the contract of sale violated a statutory provision.[19] He held that the findings of fact were supported by the evidence and that the seller was allowed a recovery. Simmons, the sole dissenter, wrote fifty-four pages criticizing the court's adoption of the rule because the trial court had not made specific findings of fact but had in fact made only a general finding in favor of the plaintiff. He made the revealing comment about the court's decisional process, "We have no way of knowing, under a general finding, what facts or law the trial court acted upon. We are completely in the dark as to the facts or law that were deemed controlling by the trial court. So we reverse the process and take a proper rule of law and hunt for facts that will sustain the finding."[20] Nothing in either the majority or dissenting opinions indicated that the case was anything other than ordinary, or why it would engender a fifty-four page dissent. Perhaps Simmons felt that he needed to point his brethren in the right direction. Or perhaps he felt that Carter and the others were straying from established procedure.

The pace of controversy picked up substantially in 1958. In *Commonwealth Trailer Sales, Inc. v. Bradt* (1958), Wenke wrote for the majority that the defense of usury is a personal defense of the borrower and can be asserted only by him or his sureties.[21] Simmons, again the sole dissenter, criticized the court for adhering to a judicially declared rule of law that, in his opinion, no longer made sense: "It is a rule declared and controlled by the court. The court needs no legislative permission to do justice in this case."[22]

Carter and Chappell concurred: "[I]n view of the dissent we desire to point out the fallacy of its reasoning. . . . [T]he rule that the defense of usury is available only to the debtor and his privies has not been changed. Such a change is a proper subject of legislation and not one that properly can be made effective by judicial pronouncement."[23] The concurrence did not engage Simmons's argument that the rule was a judge-made rule and thus could be changed by the judges, which of course is entirely correct. One can only surmise that the majority of the court did not see the same pressing need for judicial activism that Simmons recognized.

Two weeks later Simmons wrote the majority opinion in *Hartman v. Drake* (1958), involving an issue of partition when a life tenant fails to object. The case appears to have been correctly decided. There were no dissents. However, Carter, Wenke, and Boslaugh concurred, criticizing Simmons for not setting out his reasoning in the opinion, an ironic twist to the arguments he raised in his dissent in *Capitol Bridge*.[24]

In *Gillespie v. Hynes*, decided in 1959, Carter wrote the opinion for a six-member majority, holding that where there is no equitable relief granted, a court of equity will decline jurisdiction to enter a money judgment on a legal cause of action, for to do otherwise would be to deprive the defendant of his constitutional right to a jury trial. Carter cited four cases that he said ran counter to this rule and specifically disapproved them, stating, "We disapprove the holdings of these cases, and others of similar import, which conflict with the federal rule that equity jurisdiction will not be retained to grant legal relief where no right to equitable relief is established."

Simmons, dissenting alone, spent fifty-five pages in excoriating the majority, not without justification, especially in regard to what, precisely, the majority disapproved of: "The court now disapproves four of them directly, without pointing out the extent of the disapproval. It disapproves all other 'cases of similar import' without seeking to find or cite them to trial courts or members of the legal profession." He continued, "The mistake of the trial court in this case was that it followed the rules of law repeatedly stated in the judicial precedents of this state. That, so holds the court, was prejudicial error." He then added a blistering indictment of the majority's activism, writing that the "judicial mowing machine thus cuts a wide swath through the established precedents of this court cutting down those that stand in its way, and weakening, if not effectively destroying, many others."[25]

It is difficult to reconcile Simmons's position in *Gillespie v. Hynes* with his call for judicial activism in *Commonwealth Trailer Sales, Inc. v. Bradt*, but as Ralph Waldo Emerson acknowledged, a foolish consistency is the hobgoblin of little minds. Furthermore, lawyers are equipped by training to make fine distinctions between factual situations and the rules of law. None of the majority saw fit to respond to Simmons's dissent, so whether or not they perceived an inconsistency in his argument will remain shrouded in mystery. But when Simmons was deserted by all of his brethren, he was quick to take up his pen and point out the error of their ways.

While he was engaging Carter in a war of words, Simmons was also exchanging verbal jabs with Wenke. In *Lutcavish v. Eaton* (1958), Messmore decided a will case involving a claim against a decedent's estate.[26] Simmons was the sole dissenter. He began: "The result of this decision is compounded confusion. The confusion rests on two premises. The first is a failure to analyze and find the reason of a rule of law as a guide to its application. The second is a failure to confine the scope of the decision to the issue presented." He went on to review at length past decisions of the court and to criticize the majority for not adhering to them. Chappell and Wenke, in a concurring opinion, took issue with Simmons: "We agree with the majority opinion. This concurrence is filed to respectively alleviate any misconceptions that may be engendered by the dissent filed in this case."[27] They went on to point out that the cases cited by Simmons did not support his conclusion. Suggesting that the chief justice did not understand the issue is certainly not deferential acceptance of his leadership.

In *Baker v. Baker* (1958), a case decided the same day as *Lutcavish v. Eaton*, Carter affirmed the trial court's grant of a divorce to a cross-petitioning defendant upon the grounds of the plaintiff's adultery.[28] Simmons dissented, again on the basis that the court was not properly following its earlier precedents. In a concurring opinion, Wenke again took up the cudgel against Simmons: "[B]ecause I feel the dissenting opinion comes to erroneous conclusions as to certain principles of law involved and fails to properly and sufficiently set out the conduct of appellant as it relates to the charge of adultery made against her, I deem it desirable to express my views in regard thereto." He went on to criticize Simmons for recounting many of the lurid facts of the adulterous conduct, facts that Carter, in the majority opinion, had said were not necessary to be recited. Wenke argued, "Ordinarily a statement of our conclusion reached in regard thereto would be sufficient as a recitation of such facts serves no useful purpose and only leaves a permanent record to possibly embarrass the three small children here involved after they grow up. The dissent eliminates the basis of this restraint exercised by the writer of the majority opinion in dealing with the sordid facts recited in the evidence."[29] In the button-downed, conformist days of the 1950s, accusing someone of a prurient interest in salacious material was harsh treatment indeed.

Shortly after Simmons wrote his lengthy dissent to Carter's opinion in *Gillespie v. Hynes*, he cranked out another lengthy effort in *Wischmann v. Raikes* (1959), a Wenke opinion reversing a trial court judgment in favor of the plaintiffs. The defendant had built dikes and levees that caused flood waters to flow across the plaintiff's lands. The court had written an earlier decision in *Wischmann v. Raikes* but withdrew it, changing the result. Wenke obviously anticipated a dissent, because his opinion was quite lengthy, and he spent a great deal of time reviewing applicable Nebraska cases. In his dissent Simmons again criticized the court for departing from long-standing precedent. This time he was not alone, for Yeager joined in dissenting, concurring in the Simmons dis-

Table 1. Chief Justice Simmons dissents, 1938–63

Total Simmons dissents	75
Dissents as % of total cases heard by the court	1.84
No. of dissents in which Simmons wrote an opinion	60
% of dissents in which Simmons wrote an opinion	80
Total Simmons sole dissents	33
Sole dissents as % of total Simmons dissents	44
Total Simmons dissents in battle period, 1955–58	18
Battle period dissents as % of total Simmons dissents	24
Total Simmons sole dissents in battle period, 1955–58	16
Sole dissents as % of total Simmons dissents, 1955–58	88.8
Sole dissents (1955–58) as % of total Simmons sole dissents	48.4

sent and writing separately to emphasize the anticipated consequences of the majority opinion.[30]

After this last dissent by Simmons, the verbal battle ended as unexpectedly as it began. Simmons dissented only six more times in his remaining years on the court. It seems fair to say that the skirmishing began when Simmons and Carter did battle in *Ruehle v. Ruehle*. Why it ended when it did, and what caused the parties to sheathe their verbal swords, cannot be definitely ascertained, because both Carter and Wenke continued to lead the conservative and liberal blocs on the court, and Carter continued on the court beyond Simmons' retirement. Wenke, reelected in 1960, would have outlasted Simmons on the court but for his death in 1961.

As table 1 demonstrates, Simmons dissented only seventy-five times in his twenty-five-year career on the bench, or 1.84 percent of the total cases decided by his court. He was the sole dissenter thirty-three times out of those seventy-five, or 44 percent of the cases. During the three-year period in which Simmons, Carter, and Wenke did battle, the chief justice wrote eighteen dissents, equal to 24 percent of all the dissents in his career. During the same period, he was sole dissenter in sixteen of his eighteen dissents, or 88.8 percent of the time. Some 48.4 percent of the dissents in which Simmons was the sole dissenter occurred during the battle period. Obviously, something was afoot to stimulate Simmons to such an output of lengthy criticism of his colleagues. One reason for the frequent dissents almost had to be a struggle on the part of Simmons to remain the leader of the court in the face of challenges from the two intellectual leaders of it.

Carter and Wenke may also have felt that they had a wounded lion in their sights. Simmons had recently expressed a desire to move on to other venues. When U.S. senator Dwight Griswold died in April 1954, Simmons asked Governor Robert B. Crosby for an appointment to fill Griswold's seat. Crosby declined to appoint Simmons and instead appointed Eva K. Bowring in Griswold's stead.[31] It is doubtful that such political maneuvering remained a secret to Carter and Wenke, who perhaps felt no obligation to grant Simmons obeisance if he wanted to leave the court.

The Jurisprudential Dimensions of the Simmons Court

The Simmons court, during its twenty-five year span, decided several cases of more than casual interest. These cases ranged from complex government relations and capital punishment to other criminality and the wrongful death of fetuses. All the cases foreshadowed social and political controversies that America would face in the late twentieth century.

Government Relations

As part of one of the three branches of state government, the Simmons court acted forcefully when it came to issues concerning its own power. It made that quite clear when, in *State ex rel. Ralston v. Turner* (1942), it went to war with the state legislature and won.[32] In 1937 the court had provided, by rule, that no one could take the Nebraska bar exam except graduates of reputable law schools, which the court defined as schools approved by the American Bar Association. In 1941 the legislature passed LB114, which declared all law schools operating in Nebraska to be reputable law schools, and which also declared all graduates of those law schools to be eligible to take the bar exam. Ralston, a graduate of the University of Omaha Law School, which was within Nebraska but not approved by the ABA, applied to take the bar exam. His application was denied, and he brought a mandamus action against George Turner, clerk of the supreme court, to force Turner to accept his application.[33]

The court, speaking through Justice Messmore, held that "LB114 is unconstitutional in that it directly usurps the inherent power of this court to fix and determine the qualifications of an applicant for admission to the bar in this state on a subject which naturally falls within the orbit of the judicial branch of government."[34] Messmore quoted from prior decisions of the court that the "claim of inherent judicial power is no novelty. There are many cases in which it has been invoked over the membership of the bar. It has been invoked in the admission, suspension, discipline, and disbarment of attorneys and in these no legislative permission is considered requisite, and, if a statute exists, it is regarded as declaratory of the inherent power of the judiciary and not exclusive in its provisions." The court had utilized the inherent power of the judiciary to integrate the Nebraska State Bar Association in 1937, before Simmons became chief justice. In *Ralston*, Justice William B. Rose, who as a member of the court had not dissented in the integration case, and Justice John Yeager, who was not on the court in 1937, both dissented.

The legislature was not the only governmental body to receive a firm "hands-off" message from the court. The U.S. Supreme Court received the same treatment from a Nebraska court that was very jealous of its prerogatives. The first salvo was fired in the case of *Johnson v. Radio Station WOW* (1944), which appeared before the Nebraska court on three occasions.[35] In *Johnson I*, an aggrieved policy-holder brought suit to keep the Woodmen of the World Life Insurance Society, a fraternal insurance company, from transferring the society's radio station and license to a group of insiders for grossly inadequate consideration, pre-dating Enron by almost three-quarters of a century. The Nebraska court, on a 4–3 vote, found constructive fraud on the part of the Society and invalidated the transfer.

The Society filed a motion for rehearing, which was granted. After the second airing, the court issued a new opinion, which adhered to the former ruling.[36] The Society had raised a new argument, claiming that the court lacked jurisdiction because the matter was within the sole jurisdiction of the Federal Communications Commission. Carter wrote the opinion on rehearing and conceded that the FCC had the sole power to license the station, but he held that a state court could hear and decide all the property rights involved in station ownership, which the Nebraska court had done in this case.

Johnson III came back to the Nebraska Supreme Court in 1945, having gone to the U.S. Supreme Court in the interim.[37] The U.S. Supreme Court issued a mandate requiring the Nebraska court to withhold the portion of its decree requiring the station property to be transferred back to the Society until the FCC could review new applications for the station's license. Carter, again writing for the Nebraska court, bristled: "The mandate of the Supreme Court of the United States directing this court to withhold its mandate on a matter solely within the jurisdiction of the state courts encroaches upon the plenary powers of this court and tends to undermine the autonomy and destroy the independence of the state courts in a field where they are admittedly supreme."

In conclusion, he thumbed the collective nose of Nebraska's jurists at their colleagues in Washington, remarking, "The mandate of this court will therefore issue on order by this court *without reference to the advisory directions* contained in the mandate of the Supreme Court of the United States. So ordered" (emphasis supplied).[38] Take that!

Yeager, who dissented in both *Johnson I* and *Johnson II*—as the holder of the Omaha seat on the court, he was aware that the Society was a powerful force in Omaha—dissented again and chastised Carter's chauvinism:

> It was on the ground that the state court had invaded the federal jurisdiction by its direction with regard to the radio license that the United States Supreme Court accepted jurisdiction. In its opinion, that court recognized the full and complete jurisdiction of this court over the entire subject matter except the radio license. Over the license it held this court had no jurisdiction, and properly so. . . . [D]irection was given to this court to withhold its mandate a sufficient length of time to allow for action by the Federal Communications Commission on an application for transfer of the license. . . . It appears to me that the majority opinion is but a volunteer discussion upon a subject whereon no opinion is required at the hands of this court, and that by it no useful purpose is served.[39]

Yeager thus displayed a more prescient understanding of the concept of federalism than his thin-skinned colleagues in the majority.

Simmons inveighed against the U.S. Supreme Court again in *Hawk v. Olson* (1946), a criminal case wherein Hawk had been before the Nebraska court several times and finally managed to get a favorable ruling out of Washington.[40] The federal court had remanded Hawk's cause for a hearing on whether or not he had been denied due process. Hawk moved to enforce the U.S. Supreme Court order and asked Nebraska's high court to issue a mandate to the district court of Lancaster County for a hearing. The Nebraska Supreme Court denied his motion.

Simmons explained that Nebraska was not bound to follow the mandate of the U.S. Supreme Court because that court had erroneously concluded that certain facts could be litigated in a Nebraska habeas corpus proceeding, when in fact they could not. Simmons held that Nebraska was the supreme authority on what could and could not be heard in a Nebraska habeas corpus proceeding: "In full accord with our decisions we are required to hold that petitioner's issues which the Supreme Court of the United States said he is entitled to have an opportunity to prove are issues which are not justiciable in a habeas corpus proceeding in this state."[41]

The Nebraska court also upheld the peace and dignity of Nebraska's inferior courts in *Reller v. Ankeny* (1955).[42] Reller, a bombastic curmudgeon who was the bête noire of the defense bar, sued District Judge Harry Ankeny for libel, claiming that Ankeny had libeled him in a written memorandum and order that Ankeny had filed in a case he was hearing. Ankeny had accused Reller of lying and dereliction. Those who knew Reller could have contended that he could not be libeled because anything he was accused of was likely to be true. Be that as it may, the one district judge in Lancaster County who might be inclined to libel anyone was Ankeny. He was generally regarded as snide, sharp, and sour.[43] He also wore a toupee, casually taking it off and putting it on as his fancy dictated, and lawyers in his court were often non-plussed when he wore it in the morning of a trial and took it off in the afternoon, or vice versa.[44]

Reller's suit was thrown out after Ankeny's lawyer filed a motion to dismiss. Reller appealed, contending that a demurrer, rather than a motion to dismiss, would have been the proper procedure. His position was eminently correct, but the supreme court ruled against Reller, holding that he had acquiesced in the procedure in the district court and that he could not raise the issue for the first time on appeal. More importantly, the court held that any comments made by a judge about a lawyer during a trial were absolutely privileged.[45]

The court not only dealt with the legislative branch and other courts in the judicial branch but also with the executive branch and its agencies. In *Johnson v. Johnson* (1942), the lieutenant governor sued the state treasurer for a pro rata share of the governor's salary, after he had performed the governor's duties when the latter was out of the state. Article IV, Section 16 of Nebraska's constitution provides that when the governor is out of the state, the powers, duties, and emoluments of the office shall fall to the lieutenant governor. Judge Rose wrote the opinion of the court and denied the lieutenant governor a share of the governor's salary, holding that Nebraska could not have two governors at the same time and that unless the governor's absence from office is permanent, the lieutenant governor is still only the lieutenant governor.[46]

In *State ex rel. Johnson v. Hagemeister* (1958), the court faced an original action in *quo warranto* involving two gubernatorial appointees who wanted the same seat on the board of education of the then state normal schools.[47] Johnson had been appointed by Governor Crosby to fill a vacancy on the board. He was confirmed by the legislature and served out the balance of the term. In October 1954, Crosby, by then a lame-duck governor, appointed Johnson to a full six-year term, beginning January 1, 1955. He was confirmed by the legislature on January 28, 1955. On January 31 a senator who had voted in favor of confirmation moved to reconsider the confirmation. The legislature reconsidered and voted not to confirm Johnson. The next day, the new governor, Victor E. Anderson, appointed Hagemeister to the six-year term. In a unanimous opinion written by Wenke, the supreme court, obviously at the request of the new governor, held that the legislature had the right to reconsider the confirmation, thus preserving peace among the three branches of government.

In dealing with other branches of state or federal government, the court showed itself to be protective of its power (as, for example, in *State ex rel. Ralston v. Turner*), and it was quite unwilling to take orders from the U.S. Supreme Court, as demonstrated by *Johnson v. Radio Station wow* and *Hawk v. Olson*. In areas not involving its power and prerogative, the court was somewhat deferential to the executive branch, as was apparent in *Johnson v. Johnson* and *State ex rel. Johnson v. Hagemeister*.

Capital Cases

In the 1940s and 1950s Nebraska's high court became involved in several cases regarding capital punishment. These cases required either the issuance of death warrants or appeals alleging trial court errors. On all occasions the court moved expeditiously to facilitate the execution of the convicted murderer.

The Simmons court issued death warrants for four murderers who met their end in "Old Sparky," the colloquial name for Nebraska's electric chair. Joseph MacAvoy, a twenty-three-year-old soldier at Harvard Army Air Base during World War II, raped and killed a sixteen-year-old girl in 1943. MacAvoy, whose home was in New Jersey, confessed to the crime and was convicted by a Clay County jury. The supreme court unanimously affirmed both his conviction and sentence in an opinion written by Justice Carter.[48] The court's opinion was dated June 6, 1944. It fixed the date of MacAvoy's execution on September 19, 1944. MacAvoy was in fact executed on March 23, 1945, a few months after the scheduled date, but still sooner than could be expected with the decades-long maneuvering in capital cases today. The strictures of war-time undoubtedly worked against MacAvoy, but the legal climate was very different then than it is now, especially with regard to the death penalty. Newspapers that carried accounts of MacAvoy's death did not mention any picketers protesting outside the penitentiary.[49]

Timothy Iron Bear, a Native American, killed a rancher for whom he was working and then, to avoid detection, killed the rancher's wife as well. The killings took place on July 24, 1947, and Iron Bear was tried and sentenced to death on September 30, 1947.[50] Iron Bear killed both victims with an axe, stole their car, and drove to his mother's home in South Dakota. He had been out of prison only two days at the time of the killings.

Iron Bear's counsel failed to file a timely appeal with the supreme court, which held that it had no jurisdiction to hear the appeal because of the late filing, and the court fixed the date of execution on July 9, 1948.[51] Iron Bear then filed a petition for a writ of habeas corpus against the warden of the penitentiary because of an error in the sentence in district court, which had set the date of execution for ninety days from sentencing. On appeal the supreme court held that the date of execution was not an essential part of the sentence.[52] Iron Bear was executed on December 1, 1948.

Roland Dean Sundahl, a young rapist from far northwest Nebraska, killed his sixteen-year-old victim and attempted to conceal his crime. The crime was committed on August 27, 1950. The trial took place almost immediately. Sundahl appealed the conviction and death sentence to the Supreme Court, which issued a Simmons opinion affirming both the conviction and sentence on July 5, 1951, less than eleven months after the crime was committed.[53] Sundahl was executed on April 30, 1952, twenty months after the crime. No one could make the claim that justice delayed is justice denied in this instance.

The final murderer to meet his fate in the Nebraska electric chair by action of the Simmons court was Charles Starkweather, whose name will always live in infamy in Nebraska. The teenaged Starkweather embarked on a homicidal spree, accompanied by his fourteen-year-old girlfriend, Carol Ann Fugate, in January 1958. In little over a week they killed nine persons in and around Lincoln and one in Wyoming. They were captured in Wyoming and tried separately in Nebraska for the murders. Both were convicted, and Starkweather was executed in the electric chair on June 25, 1959. The supreme court affirmed Starkweather's conviction in December 1958, less than a year after the killing spree occurred.[54]

Harry Spencer, who was elected to the supreme court in November 1960 to replace E. B. Chappell, was the district judge who tried both Starkweather and Fugate. He was quite concerned about the press coverage of the trials, which brought in media from all over the country because of the sensational nature of the cases. Spencer imposed stringent restrictions on the media while reserving courtroom space for them. He did not allow photographs to be taken in the courtroom or on the staircase leading up to the courtroom.[55]

Prior to the trials, Spencer appointed T. Clement Gaughn, Lincoln's most experienced criminal lawyer, and William Matschullat, a former government investigator, to represent Starkweather. He also appointed John McArthur, an experienced Lincoln trial lawyer, to represent Fugate, primarily at the urging of Edmund O. Belsheim, then dean of the University of Nebraska College of Law, who was quite concerned at the prospect of a young woman of Fugate's tender years being tried for murder in adult court.[56] McArthur tried unsuccessfully to have Fugate tried as a juvenile, but he was successful in keeping her out of the electric chair.

The main issue in Starkweather's appeal was his mental capacity. He was clearly of subnormal intelligence, but in a unanimous opinion written by Simmons, Nebraska's supreme court held that the jury had heard all the psychiatric evidence and had concluded that Starkweather had sufficient capacity to be aware of the nature of his acts and that there was ample evidence to support the jury's verdict.[57]

Two other killers were sentenced to death with the approbation of the Simmons court, but their sentences were subsequently commuted by the board of pardons, an agency of the executive branch. In *Griffith v. State* (1953), a husband shot and killed his wife on June 20, 1952. He was tried, convicted, and sentenced to death.[58] The supreme court affirmed his sentence in July 1953 and decreed the date of execution to be October 16, 1953. Griffith was not executed, however, and his sentence was commuted to a fifty-five-year term in January 1954. Griffith served his sentence and was released from prison in 1992.

Grandsinger v. State (1955) was one of the more celebrated murder cases to reach the Simmons court. Loyd Grandsinger, a twenty-one year old Native American transient, shot and killed Marvin Hansen, a Nebraska state patrolman, in a shootout as he tried to avoid capture on a felony burglary charge. The trial took place in northwest Nebraska, just south of Pine Ridge Indian Reservation, and white public sentiment in favor of Grandsinger's death was open and obvious. The killing took place on April 8, 1954, and Grandsinger's trial followed during the summer of 1954. Grandsinger was convicted and sentenced to death. The supreme court handed down its opinion affirming the sentence on December 16, 1955, with his execution fixed for March 30, 1956. But the sentence was commuted and the execution never took place.[59]

The board of pardons never stated any obvious reason for commutation, but the prevailing sentiment against a Native American who killed a highway patrolman could have contributed to a jingoistic result, raising the specter of a lack of due process. The supreme court brushed past an error on the part of the prosecutor, who during the course of Grandsinger's trial implied that the defendant should be executed because at some subsequent time he might be pardoned or paroled. Perhaps the board of pardons was concerned about this statement. The supreme court had conceded that it was a prosecutorial error but said that it was not prejudicial because undoubtedly all the jurors were already aware of the possibility of pardon or parole.

Still another problem in the *Grandsinger* case was the action of the defendant's trial counsel, Charles Fisher of Chadron, who intentionally altered an exhibit during a recess in the trial. Critical pieces of the evidence against Grandsinger were a Sam Browne belt and a trousers belt that Hansen, the murdered policeman, was wearing at the time of the shooting. The bullet that killed him passed through both belts. One of the issues in the case was whether Grandsinger's weapon, a .22-caliber handgun, had been the murder weapon, and the size of the hole in the belts was an important factor in determining the caliber of bullet, which had exited the victim's body and was never found.

When an expert witness for the prosecution was testifying about the size of the holes, the witness attempted to insert a wooden dowel the size of a .22 bullet into the holes. Fisher, as attorney for Grandsinger, objected on the grounds that insertion of the dowel could alter the size of the holes. The trial judge sustained Fisher's objection. The next day, before the trial reconvened, Fisher picked up the trousers belt and the dowel, both of which were exhibits admitted into evidence, inserted the dowel into the belt, and began twisting the dowel. The county attorney prosecuting the case caught Fisher in the act.

Fisher was immediately taken before the trial judge, a record was made, and Fisher admitted to his act. Fisher continued to represent Grandsinger throughout the rest of the trial, and after the trial was over, the Nebraska State Bar Association brought disciplinary proceedings against Fisher for unprofessional conduct.[60] When the appeal from those proceedings reached the supreme court, the court entered a judgment of a one-year suspension, acknowledging that Fisher had a large practice and a good reputation in Chadron, where he had practiced for twenty-seven years. The court's judgment, in light of the fact that Fisher knowingly altered the evidence in a first-degree murder case, seems in retrospect far too lenient, and its discussion of the gravity of the offense too limited.

Other Criminal Matters

The court displayed its ability to give careful scrutiny to criminal cases when it decided *Schluter v. State* (1949).[61] The case involved a jury instruction in which the trial judge told the jury that it could not reject the testimony of any witness unless it had a good reason for doing so. The supreme court disapproved the instruction and reversed the defendant's conviction. Simmons wrote the majority opinion, and Yeager concurred in a written opinion. Messmore and Boslaugh concurred, but without writing an opinion. Wenke dissented, in a written opinion, and Carter joined in Wenke's opinion. Thus, six of the seven judges were moved to publicly state their position on the issue, a rather unusual occurrence.

The court disapproved of criminal prosecutions for adultery in *Armstead v. State* (1955).[62] Hall County had prosecuted one of its citizens for adultery. No direct proof of intercourse, lawful or otherwise, was adduced, and the defendant was convicted solely on circumstantial evidence. On appeal, the supreme court reversed. Reviewing the evidence extensively, the court reiterated the rule that "mere disposition and opportunity to commit adultery are not alone sufficient to justify a conviction, but there must be circumstances inconsistent with any other reasonable hypothesis."[63] Hundreds of errant spouses must have breathed a sigh of relief.

Courts sometimes make mistakes, and the Nebraska high court certainly did in *Peery v. State* (1957).[64] Wesley Peery, one of the most hardened criminals ever to live in Nebraska, was tried and convicted in Sarpy County for forcing a woman driver off of the highway and raping her. The supreme court reviewed the evidence in detail, implied that the testimony of the alleged victim lacked credibility, pointed out that there was no other meaningful corroboration of the victim's testimony, and reversed the conviction. Wenke and Chappell dissented, and under any rational view of the evidence, they were clearly right.

When Peery was sentenced in the district court on the Sarpy County rape, undoubtedly the sentencing judge had Peery's criminal record before him. In 1947 he was convicted of an escape from custody. In 1948 he was convicted of armed robbery. In 1955, after being released from prison, he burglarized the home of Lincoln's deputy chief of police, E. H. Masters, and stole a .38 Colt Detective Special Revolver. Peery used this stolen gun to threaten the rape victim in Sarpy County. She was called as a witness in the burglary trial in Lancaster County, and she identified the gun as the one Peery used to stop her. She also identified photos of his car. This time the supreme court found her testimony to be admissible and credible and affirmed Peery's conviction of the burglary.[65]

In 1957, while out of jail on bond, Peery stole a car in Columbus, Ohio, and committed three armed robberies. He robbed and raped a woman who was seven and a half months pregnant. He attempted to escape from an Ohio prison and assaulted a courthouse librarian in the attempt.

Eventually, Peery was convicted of the brutal murder of a Lincoln coin shop owner in 1975 and was sentenced to death.[66] He went back to the Nebraska Supreme Court on four occasions seeking post-trial relief and was denied relief each time. He died in prison while on death row. When Peery was sentenced for the murder in 1975, the sentencing panel found that he was fifty-one years old and that he had spent thirty-three years and ten months in prison. Between 1947 and 1975 he had been out of prison for only two years and eight months.

Peery also played a role in another criminal case of note, the conviction of Darrel F. Parker, Lincoln's assistant city forester, for the murder of his wife. In *Parker v. State* (1957), Parker was found guilty of the murder of his wife, Nancy, in December 1955.[67] Parker was sentenced to life imprisonment in the Nebraska penitentiary.

In 1964 Parker brought a writ of error *coram nobis*, seeking a new trial. At the hearing on whether the writ should issue, Parker and one of his attorneys both testified that in 1956, Peery, who at the time was also a prisoner in the Nebraska penitentiary, told both Parker and the attorney that if the attorney or Parker's parents would guarantee Peery's bond, Peery would tell them where Nancy Parker's suitcase and wristwatch, both missing since the day of her murder, could be located. Peery also said that he would name Nancy Parker's killer.

Parker cited testimony by Kenneth Hamilton and Charles Sedlacek, former Nebraska prisoners, in which they claimed that Peery had told each of them on several occasions that he had killed Nancy Parker. Peery testified by deposition from the Ohio prison where he was lodged that he had lied to Parker's attorney and that he did not know or kill Nancy Parker.

In *Parker v. State II* (1964), the supreme court affirmed the denial of the writ of error, saying, "Under oath, Peery either denies that the declarations were made, or testified that the declarations were false when made."[68] Such a statement appears to give some credibility to Peery's testimony, which would clearly seem to be untrustworthy. The court obviously felt it was dealing with felons on both sides of the issue, all of whom, because of their records, were not worthy of belief. It said as much when it characterized Peery, Hamilton, and Sedlacek as "convicted felons." *Falsus in unis, falsus in omnibus*. So, showing disdain for all concerned, the court refused to grant the writ, declaring in conclusion, "Without further discussion or analysis, we think that it is apparent that the evidence in the case is, for the most part, not substantial or credible."[69] A bias against convicts is sometimes more helpful than analysis, but it is rare that a court will actually say so, as the Simmons court did here.

The Cult of Domesticity

The Simmons court did nothing meaningful in the area of family law, but two rather interesting decisions in divorce and adoption, however, serve as a footnote to long-established Nebraska law in domestic relations. The court also weighed in on the controversy regarding the definition of life.

In *Kroger v. Kroger* (1950), the court decided against a long-time and well-regarded district judge whose wife had sued him for divorce.[70] In the trial court, the judge had been granted a divorce on his cross-petition, but the supreme court, on the wife's appeal, found that he was not entitled to a divorce on his cross-petition and granted her a divorce on her petition. This action occurred before Nebraska enacted a no-fault divorce law. In addition to that rebuff, the court surprisingly doubled the alimony due the wife from ten thousand dollars to twenty thousand dollars, a very considerable sum in 1949.

In re *Petition of Ritchie* (1951) involved an attempt by an adult (a lawyer and political figure) to adopt another adult, invoking the equitable powers of the district court.[71] The supreme court held that adoption was statutory and that the adoption of an adult was not permitted. The court also held that equity courts had no power to overrule statutory procedures, thus preserving the sanctity of the legislative procedure for adoption.

In light of recent efforts both in Nebraska and in the U.S. Congress to define an unborn child as a person, *Drabbels v. Skelly Oil Co.* (1951) is very instructive as to the judicial mindset of the time.[72] In *Drabbels*, a canister of bottled gas exploded and caused injury to a woman who was eight months pregnant. Three days later her child was born dead. The father brought suit for the wrongful death of the child. The defendant demurred on the ground that an unborn child could not be subjected to wrongful death.

A unanimous court, in an opinion written by Carter, agreed with the trial court's sustaining of the demurrer. Carter spelled out the court's position, one antithetical to the arguments of twenty-first-century pro-life advocates: "In our opinion a child born dead cannot maintain an action at common law for injuries received by it while in its mother's womb, and consequently the personal representative cannot maintain it under a wrongful death statute limiting such actions to those which would, if death had not ensued, have entitled the party injured to maintain an action and recover damages in respect thereof." The court put its stamp of finality on the question, stating, "We adhere to the rule that *an unborn child is a part of the mother until birth, and, as such, has no juridical existence*" (emphasis supplied).[73]

Lincoln senator Mike Foley, a devout Roman Catholic and staunch pro-life supporter, changed Nebraska's law concerning the unborn after he was elected to the unicameral in 2000. In 2000 he took the first step in fetal protection with LB824, which created the crime of motor vehicle homicide of an unborn child. In 2003 Foley's LB294 authorized wrongful death action for the tortious death of an unborn child in utero at any stage of gestation, thus adopting for Nebraska the Catholic doctrine that life begins at conception, legislatively overruling *Drabbels* and *Smith v. Columbus Community Hospital*, a subsequent decision that followed the rule set forth in *Drabbels*.[74]

A United Front, Usually

In reviewing the significant cases decided by the Simmons court, it is strikingly apparent that the court's jurisprudence was generally cohesive, except for the brief feud between Simmons, Carter, and Wenke. Dissent and concurrence rates were very low. The *Ruehle* case and its progeny showed that the court wanted to abide by its prior decisions, and any attempt to invoke new rules or change established patterns of *stare decisis* would arouse fierce criticism from within the court.

In criminal capital cases, the arguments of convicted murderers got short shrift. Witness *MacAvoy, Sundahl, Iron Bear, Grandsinger,* and *Starkweather.* Others might show sympathy for or leniency to first-degree murderers. This court would not. It could be surprisingly sympathetic, though, as was the case in *State ex rel. Nebraska State Bar Assn. v. Fisher,* (1960), a decision that seems quite unjustified by today's standards.

The court's caseload was quite moderate, and there was no real backlog of cases dragging on for years. As a result, the general public seemed quite approving of the work of the court, if indeed it was even aware of how the judges worked. All the judges on the Simmons court were voted in by the populace, and gubernatorial appointment and retention elections awaited them in the future. In only one election was the result at all close, when Adolph Wenke was first elected having only 50.33 percent of the vote in 1942.

Neither personal nor philosophical differences led any of the members of the Simmons court to dissent with any degree of frequency. Simmons himself was the most active dissenter, and he dissented in less than 2 percent of the cases heard by his court. The Simmons court presented a united front to the public and the bar in virtually all instances, except during the brief period of intramural scrapping, as table 2 demonstrates. Messmore, who was on the court for Simmons's entire tenure, averaged one dissent per year, and Carter, also aboard for the entire time, averaged two dissents per year. During 1955–58, Carter wrote six dissents, and Wenke wrote six.

The type of case did not seem to influence the number of dissents. There was no greater outpouring of dissent in criminal cases than in civil cases. Rather, it was when court procedures, as in *Ruehle,* or court precedents, as in *Capitol Bridge* or *Gillespie,* were being challenged or changed that the judges felt compelled to dissent.

In volume 167 of *Nebraska Reports,* covering the years 1958 and 1959, the court decided ninety-three cases. Simmons dissented twice and Yeager once. No one else dissented. But even more importantly, in that volume the court reversed more cases than it affirmed—the only volume between 1938 and 1995 with this reversal rate. There were forty-seven reversals, equal to 50.53 percent of the cases, while the court affirmed only thirty-five cases, or 37.63 percent of the cases. Perhaps Simmons's complaints that the court was changing the law to the detriment of district judges were well founded. Perhaps once the court realized that the district judges were in trouble, they decided that they had to end their quarrels and go back to presenting a united front.

Table 2. Dissents by members of the Simmons court, 1938–63

JUDGE	DISSENTS	% OF TOTAL CASES	RANK
Simmons[a]	75	1.84	1
Carter[a]	59	1.45	2
Yeager	56	1.37	3
Paine	47	1.15	4
Chappell	34	0.83	5
Wenke	27	0.66	6
Messmore[a]	26	0.63	7
Rose	22	0.54	8
Johnsen	15	0.36	9
P. Boslaugh	13	0.31	10
Eberly	10	0.24	11
Spencer	9	0.22	12
L. Boslaugh	8	0.19	13
Brower	2	0.04	14

Note:

Total cases decided by Simmons court	4,065
No. of total cases in which there was a dissent	265
% of total cases in which one or more judges dissented	6.51

[a]On court for entire period of Simmons's incumbency.

Judges dissent for many reasons. Scholars feel that partisanship, either political or philosophical, is the major factor leading to dissent. Ohio's supreme court had dissent rates of 34.9 percent in 1966, 38.7 percent in 1968, 34.9 percent in 1977, and 41.4 percent in 1981.[75] But most judges on state supreme courts, and especially Nebraska's, dissent far less than the judges of the U.S. Supreme Court.

As indicated previously, the dissent rate on the Simmons court was negligible, and Simmons can scarcely be said to be failing in leadership when his own dissent rate was 1.84 percent. However, he was the most frequent dissenter. One can hardly say that he was not encouraging collegial deliberation or the development of common perspectives concerning the law. Nonetheless, it is unusual for the chief justice, the nominal leader of the court, to be its most divisive voice.

Jaros and Canon theorize that dissent in state supreme courts is more common in states with greater socioeconomic and political diversity and with supreme courts that are insulated from trial courts by an intermediate ap-

Table 3. Decisions of the Simmons court, 1938–63

Total cases	4,065
Civil cases	3,687
Criminal cases	378
% of civil cases	90.7
% of criminal cases	9.2
Total cases, no. of affirmances	2,264
Total cases, % of affirmances	55.69
Criminal cases, no. of affirmances	250
Criminal cases, % of affirmances	66.13
Total cases, no. of reversals	1360
Total cases, % of reversals	33.45
Criminal cases, no. of reversals	98
Criminal cases, % of reversals	25.92

pellate court.[76] They believe that dissent is not as strongly associated with economic and political factors in states where there is no intermediate appellate court and where the supreme court hears appeals directly from the trial courts.[77]

In a state such as Nebraska, which seems relatively homogenous, the judges are likely, as on the Simmons court, to come from similar backgrounds and to share similar attitudes and beliefs. But unlike their predecessors during Simmons's time, judges from Lincoln and Omaha now might have a tendency to heed the wishes of an urban constituency. Urbanization and industrialization are associated with a more diverse economy and thus with greater specialization. Urbanization produces a basis for a large number of relatively specific interests, and judges might want to see the interests of such constituencies reflected in their opinions.

The Simmons court decided 4,065 cases over a twenty-five year span, for an average of 162.6 cases per year. The great bulk of the cases were civil cases, as is shown in the tabulations in table 3. Only 9.2 percent of the total cases were criminal cases. The court had an eleven point higher affirmance rate—at 66.13 percent to 55.69 percent—for criminal cases than it did for all cases as a whole. The court reversed 33.45 percent of all cases it heard but reversed only 25.92 percent of criminal cases.

Carter was the most prodigious writer of all the Simmons judges, contributing approximately 15 percent of all the opinions of the court. Simmons ranked third in output. Both Carter and Messmore, the only two judges to have served every day of the Simmons incumbency, wrote more opinions than Simmons,

Table 4. Simmons court opinions, 1938–63

JUDGE	NO. CONTRIBUTED[a]	% OF 4,065	RANK
Carter[b]	608	14.95%	1
Messmore[b]	581	14.29%	2
Simmons[b]	529	13.01%	3
Yeager	503	12.37%	4
Wenke	411	10.11%	5
Chappell	392	9.64%	6
P. Boslaugh	279	6.86%	7
Paine	232	5.70%	8
Rose	97	2.38%	9–10
Eberly	97	2.38%	9–10
L. Boslaugh	53	1.30%	11–12
Spencer	53	1.30%	11–12
Johnsen	49	1.20%	13
Brower	40	0.98%	14
Per curiam	7	0.017%	
Retired and district judges	126	3.09%	
Total	**4,057[c]**		

[a]Does not include dissents or concurrences.
[b]On court for entire period of Simmons's incumbency.
[c]Eight decisions did not involve a formal signed written opinion.

though when Simmons's dissents are added to his output, and Messmore's dissents are added to his, their output is virtually identical: 607 for Messmore and 604 for Simmons (see table 4).

Prior to the tenure of Simmons as chief justice, the Nebraska court had utilized the unsigned *per curiam* opinion a great deal. Between 1930 and 1940 the court used *per curiam* opinions on about one-fourth of its cases.[78] Because Simmons's court had only seven *per curiam* opinions from 1938 to 1962, there must have been a substantial volume of such opinions early in the thirties. *Per curiam* opinions appear to have been brief memorandum orders that appeared at the end of the volumes of *Nebraska Reports*. When a full *per curiam* opinion was written, it was often because the writer had personal reasons for keeping his identity unknown. The court also submitted *per curiam* opinions for other reasons: the court wishes to briefly state why it is disposing of the case as it is; the case does not deserve much judicial attention; the judge assigned to write the opinion, as in Nebraska, disagrees either with the majority's conclusion or the majority's reasoning; or the court is anxious to present a united front on the issue, without dissent or concurrence.

Per curiam opinions do not meet with much approbation from the practicing bar. Lawyers believe that judges use the *per curiam* opinion, which preserves the anonymity of its author, for a wide variety of reasons. Simmons was obviously aware of the bar's discontent, as he saw fit to state, in his dissent in *Ruehle*, that "as the bar well knows, it has been several years since *per curiam* opinions were used."[79] The great frequency of *per curiam* opinions by courts subsequent to Simmons's were a major source of discontent among lawyers.

Simmons Legacy

The Simmons court was protective, not innovative. It first and foremost protected the power of the judiciary as an integral part of the three branches of government, as in *Ralston v. Turner* and *Reller v. Ankeny*. It protected the rights of the states as integral units of America's federal governmental system, as in *Johnson v. wow* and *Hawk v. Olson*. "Don't tread on me" might well have been its motto.

It protected the right of the citizenry to be safe in their homes and workplaces and found little reason to deny death penalties to killers. The court had even affirmed two death sentences, in *Griffith* and *Grandsinger*, that the executive branch of government later commuted.

The Nebraska Supreme Court protected the right of the legislature to legislate in *Ritchie*, and it protected the financial well-being of a wronged wife in *Kroger*. It protected the business community and the insurance industry from new and potentially expensive causes of action, as in *Drabbels v. Skelly Oil*. And it protected the occasional wandering spouse from Victorian notions of criminal wrongdoing, as in *Armstead v. State*.

After World War II, most states, including Nebraska, experienced a pronounced shift in appellate law from matters of civil concern to the criminal law, although the change occurred more slowly in Nebraska. On the civil side, courts heard fewer cases involving the economic market place and more family, tort, and public law cases. Some state courts, not including those in Nebraska, began to discover whole bundles of rights in state constitutions, rights that state courts could grant without regard to how federal courts construed the U.S. Constitution.[80]

The Nebraska milieu in which the Simmons court functioned did not demand a great deal of innovation. The court coped with the changes wrought in the state by World War II and the Korean conflict and with a slow but gradual escalation of criminal activity, all the while projecting an image of dignity and probity, keeping its docket current, adhering to its established precedents, and meeting only a few new challenges. Judges faced the voters and either ran unopposed or, with one exception, were returned to office with very substantial margins. If, as Lawrence M. Friedman claims, "law is a product of society," law did not need to show much change during the Simmons years, because society in Nebraska was itself slow to change.[81]

The Simmons judges were formalists. They could rely on established precedent, and if they were conscious of the societal implications of their decisions, the language of their opinions did not reveal any such awareness. And the public, as reflected in their votes, seemed to approve of the court's approach. Nebraska was still a quiet, agricultural backwater during the Simmons court. Scores of now-vanished small towns still hummed with activity. Rural interests dominated the legislature. Lincoln and Omaha were still very large "small" towns. But clouds were beginning to appear on the judicial horizon. Both America and Nebraska would soon be caught up in change, and the court would be caught up with them.

As Simmons' final term as chief justice neared its close, things seemed to be going well at the court. The public appeared to be satisfied with the court members, as demonstrated by election results. There was little or no backlog of cases awaiting argument or decision. The court's decisions had not received any significant criticism from the press.

At the end of his tenure, Simmons was replaced by a new chief—Paul White of Lincoln, a sitting district court judge. Wenke died and was replaced by Robert Brower of Fullerton. Chappell and Paul Boslaugh were succeeded by Spencer and Leslie Boslaugh. Messmore was in his final term, as was Yeager. New faces, new issues, and many new cases were about to plunge the court into an unprecedented backlog and into a period when public confidence in courts and judges declined not only in Nebraska but across the land.

3. "A Real Physician of Applied Liberty"
The White Court, 1963–78

Paul W. White took office as chief justice of the Nebraska Supreme Court in January 1963, succeeding the retiring Robert G. Simmons. White won the final Nebraska Supreme Court judicial election on November 6, 1962. He defeated district judge and former attorney general Clarence Beck of North Platte by 225,073 to 175,551 votes, or 56 percent of the vote to 44 percent.[1] Both White's victory and the margin by which he won came as a surprise to political observers because Beck was a well-known Republican state office holder for many years and had won the primary rather handily.

White led the court from January 1963 until the summer of 1978, and over that fifteen-year span the output of opinions of the court increased substantially, even though the court took longer to decide cases—an anomaly not entirely of the court's making, as we shall subsequently see. Furthermore, a curtain of anonymity no longer protected the court as new and more combative judges replaced the superannuated colleagues who had served with Robert Simmons. And White, by dint of his own idiosyncrasies, contributed significantly to a decline in the court's prestige, especially in the eyes of the bar; leading a court that at times seemed ludicrous, internally quarrelsome, and anything but punctual, White and his fellows let the court slide to a state of disrepute in the eyes of both lawyers and litigants. Justice delayed really was justice denied during White's tenure.

Who Was White?

White, born in 1911, graduated from the University of Nebraska College of Law in 1932 and began his practice in Lincoln. He served in the army for fifty months during World War II and was an active member of the American Legion upon his return from the war. He was never a member of a large firm, instead engaging in several office-sharing relationships. For a time he served as a deputy county attorney during the administration of Max Towle. He ran for district judge in 1952, and after conducting a door-to-door campaign, he defeated Bob

Devoe, Republican county chairman and a regent of the University of Nebraska, for the job. A Methodist, White was also a member of Veterans of Foreign Wars and various Masonic bodies.[2]

During his primary campaign for chief justice in 1962, White barely defeated fellow Lancaster County district judge Herbert Ronin for second place. Clarence Beck won the primary with 90,270 votes. White garnered 69,483 votes, while Ronin had 69,231, leaving White a margin of just 252 votes. During the general election, White flew around the state in an airplane owned by Lincoln lawyer Thomas Gorham. He campaigned enthusiastically, shaking hands in taverns and grocery stores, and he confounded the political pundits who expected the same candidate they saw in the primary. White's efforts bore fruit, and he easily won the general election.

White served as chief justice until September 17, 1978, when he retired in a move that caught virtually everyone by surprise, including state court administrator James Dunlevey.[3] During the fifteen-plus years of White's incumbency, the court decided more cases annually than the court of White's immediate predecessor, Robert Simmons. Despite the markedly increased output, the White court, by the time of White's retirement, was bogged down in a huge backlog of cases that would take twenty years to alleviate and necessitate the creation of an intermediate court of appeals to reduce the case load to manageable proportions.

White and His Court

When White assumed the reins at the Nebraska Supreme Court, he inherited the entire Simmons court except Simmons: Edward Carter, Frederick W. Messmore, John W. Yeager, Harry A. Spencer, Leslie Boslaugh, and Robert C. Brower all stayed on the court. The court maintained that configuration until early 1965, when Messmore and Yeager retired in January at the expiration of their terms. Governor Frank Morrison, a Democrat, made the first two merit plan appointments to the supreme court, using the constitutional amendment passed by Nebraska's voters in 1962 that ended judicial elections and called for gubernatorial appointments.[4] Under the Missouri, or "merit," plan, panels of lawyers and laymen submit a list of approved names to the governor, who must make the appointment from the list submitted to him. In Nebraska, if the governor fails to act on the list, the chief justice makes the appointment in his or her stead.

Hale McCown of Beatrice was Morrison's first appointment. He replaced Messmore. Robert L. Smith of Omaha, Morrison's second appointment, replaced Yeager. Smith suffered from some physical ailment—perhaps narcolepsy—that made it very difficult for him to function during daylight hours. He did most of his work at his chambers in the early hours of the morning, and if the court was not sitting, Smith would leave for home before any of his colleagues arrived at the statehouse. A capitol security guard once apprehended Smith and had to be convinced that a supreme court judge might actually be wandering the capitol halls at three o'clock in the morning.[5]

Smith believed that one could find an exact word for every shade of meaning and that if a judge used the appropriate language, judicial opinions could be kept very short.[6] His opinions were known to the bar as "Smithograms," and his method was subject to considerable dispute because his opinions were, for the most part, so terse and epigrammatical as to be almost unintelligible. A classic example of a "Smithogram" is found in *United Mineral Products Co. v. Nebraska Railroads* (1965).[7] A rate discrimination case, it fell far short of explaining railroad rate discrimination, or, for that matter, anything else. Smith did, however, set a standard for his colleagues to follow, and while he was on the court—Smith resigned in 1973—opinions from all members grew demonstrably shorter. Smith's example was reversed when his successor, Donald Brodkey, also of Omaha, took office. Brodkey won the prize for judicial prolixity hands down.

Governor Norbert T. "Nobby" Tiemann made only one appointment to the supreme court, placing John E. Newton of Ponca on the high bench in 1967, when Robert Brower retired. Newton was not Tiemann's first choice, but Vance Leininger of Columbus, who was, refused to allow his name to be submitted to the nominating commission.

Democratic governor J. James Exon made three supreme court appointments. He first appointed Lawrence M. Clinton of Sidney to replace Carter, who retired in January 1971 upon the expiration of his term. Clinton later died in office in December 1982, during the incumbency of Norman Krivosha as chief justice. Exon appointed Donald Brodkey, a district judge from Omaha, to replace Robert Smith when Smith resigned in 1973. Finally, when Newton retired in 1977, the governor appointed District Judge C. Thomas White of Columbus. Thomas White became chief justice when William Hastings retired in 1995 and retired himself in 1998.

Constitutional and Administrative Changes

Paul White's accession to the center seat on the supreme court bench coincided with two far-reaching changes in Nebraska's judiciary. The first was the adoption of the Missouri Plan for appointing judges in 1962. And in 1970, the voters changed the constitution to make the chief justice the administrative head of the courts.

At the same election in which White was selected as chief justice, the voters of Nebraska adopted a constitutional amendment calling for a Missouri, or merit, plan for selecting judges. The amendment, after being heavily promoted and lobbied for by the Nebraska State Bar Association, passed by 220,181 to 150,212 votes, a winning margin of 59.44 percent.[8] Judicial selection in Nebraska would never be the same again. Flavel A. Wright, president of the Nebraska State Bar Association during the campaign, recalled that the judiciary, including the supreme court, took a strictly "hands-off" attitude on the issue.[9]

Under the new plan, the state bar elected three commissioners, with no more than two from each political party, and the governor appointed another three commissioners, also with no more than two from each party. The six commissioners, whose commission was chaired by a non-voting judge of the supreme court, heard applicants for a judicial vacancy and recommended at least two applicants to the governor, who would then make the appointment to the court. If the governor failed to make the appointment within sixty days, the chief justice would make the appointment from the same approved list. Separate commissions were established for the chief justice and for each supreme court and district seat.[10] The law has since been amended to increase the size of each commission to four lawyers and four lay people.

After an appointment was made, the newly appointed judge faced the voters in his or her district at the next general election after serving three years, and then every six years thereafter. The voters voted "yes" or "no" on the question, "Should Judge X be retained in office?" The chief justice faced the entire state in his or her retention election. Running against no opponent is a pleasant electoral circumstance. In 4,588 retention elections nationwide between 1964 and 1999, only fifty-two judges lost.[11]

White was therefore the last of a dying breed of judges who were forced to campaign to get into office. Subsequent judges ran as incumbents, standing on their records. Aspiring jurists no longer had to buttonhole voters in hair salons, restaurants, and grocery stores. White proved an indefatigable campaigner, and he applied that same energy to the work of the court, but being chief justice was a very different job when White retired than when he entered the corner chambers of the chief justice for the first time.

Supreme court judges had been elected in Nebraska from judicial districts on a nonpartisan basis since the voters adopted the constitutional amendments proposed by the 1919–20 constitutional convention.[12] The new Missouri Plan removed the electoral process from the equation and set the stage for additional constitutional tinkering with the operation of Nebraska's court system.

Just four years after the passage of the Missouri Plan, Nebraska's voters considered more judicial changes. In November 1966, they passed a constitutional amendment creating the Judicial Qualifications Commission and establishing new methods for the removal and retirement of judges by 323,244 to 77,877 votes, with 80.5 percent of voters approving the amendment.[13] In 1968, following President Lyndon Johnson's message on the criminal justice system and justice of the peace courts, the Nebraska Unicameral Legislature began an intensive study of how to overhaul Nebraska's county court system. In 1969 the legislature proposed a constitutional amendment that would give the supreme court administrative authority over all Nebraska courts, an authority that would be exercised by the chief justice. The proposed amendment also permitted the creation of a single-level trial court, removed the constitutional restrictions on trial jurisdiction, and eliminated justice of the peace courts. The amendment passed in 1970 by a vote of 198,450 to 165,087, a narrow 54.5 percent winning margin.[14]

The legislature then introduced LB1032, which would have implemented the constitutional amendment in 1971, but the body carried the amendment over until 1972 to provide more time to study the various methods of implementation. The legislature eventually passed LB1032 in April 1972, and on May 24, 1972, Chief Justice White announced the appointment of James E. Dunlevey as the first state court administrator. The administrator's office opened July 1, 1972, with three people on staff. White and Dunlevey then embarked upon a tedious and time-consuming process of remaking the court system, a job that White had not bargained for when he first sought the approval of voters in 1962.[15]

In its final form, LB1032 did not create a one-tier trial court. Instead, it significantly revamped the county courts, whose principal function had always been probate, guardianship, and the trial of inconsequential cases. The new bill organized the county court system into districts, just as the district, or

Table 5. Nebraska Supreme Court cases, 1965–75

YEAR	NO. DOCKETED	OPINIONS WRITTEN	NO. FALLEN BEHIND
1965–66	279	227	52
1966–67	320	231	89
1967–68	321	223	98
1968–69	322	243	79
1969–70	362	238	124
1970–71	474	279	195
1971–72	446	337	109
1972–73	546	324	222
1973–74	484	340	144
1974–75	571	368	203
Total	**4,125**	**2,810**	**1,315**

trial, courts were organized. County judges were required for the first time to be lawyers. Many appeals from county court to district court would be on the record, and each county court proceeding would henceforth be taped. Civil and probate appeals from county court, but not traffic and misdemeanor appeals, would be heard *de novo*, or anew, in the district court.

The administrator's office had to explain all of the proposed changes to county officials, bar groups, judicial candidates, and court employees, develop salary and personnel programs for court employees, and purchase and install tape recording equipment. It also offered a training institute for all new judges and court personnel in December 1972.

A Very Busy Supreme Court

The new amendments, legislation, and court system, however, did little to alleviate the backlog of undecided cases that began to build up shortly after White assumed office. Table 5 shows the increase in cases docketed in the supreme court from 1965 to 1975, the number of opinions issued, and the backlog. It is quite apparent that the court was falling behind and that calling up district judges to sit with the supreme court in two divisions of five judges each did little to ameliorate the problem.

The supreme court would have preferred to try to reduce the backlog by increasing its membership to nine judges, thus allowing the court to sit in two five-judge panels by only calling up one district judge to sit with them. The court was quite discerning when it came to which district judges it utilized as temporary members of the high bench, calling up those whom it knew well and who were among the more talented district judges. The court frequently used Judge William Colwell of Pawnee City and often extended invitations to judges Merritt Warren of Creighton, John Kuns of Kimball, Robert Flory of Fremont, and Robert Moran of Alliance to join the more august assemblage. However, busy district court judges did not always view being invited to come to Lincoln and spending a week hearing cases and then writing several opinions as a significant honor.

Increasing the size of the court, though, required the consent of the legislature, a consent that was not forthcoming. The major sticking point was the super-majority required by Article V, Section 2 of the Nebraska Constitution, which mandates that no legislative act may be declared unconstitutional except by a vote of five judges.[16] Commentators have argued that the super-majority rule makes little sense. It exists in only a few states, and it was adopted in Nebraska only after a speech by William Jennings Bryan at the 1920 Constitutional Convention, in which he said that the rule was necessary to prevent nullification of the will of the people.[17] The constitution also fixes the number of supreme court judges at seven. Five out of seven translates to 71.42 percent. If there were nine members of the court, the same percentage majority would require the vote of 6.42 judges, which could be either dropped to six or increased to seven. Also, if a five-judge panel were to hear a constitutional issue, an unlikely occurrence, the panel would need unanimity to declare a statute unconstitutional. No one seemed able to agree upon the necessary number of votes, and the legislature refused to give the extra two judges its imprimatur.

Moreover, the court did not enjoy good relations with all the legislators. Dunlevey tells of a meeting between the court and the legislature's judiciary committee to discuss the proposed increase to nine justices. The meeting was held in the court's conference room, and White stood at the door, greeting legislators as they arrived. State Senator Ernie Chambers of Omaha, Nebraska's sole African American solon, refused to shake White's hand as he entered. Neither White nor Dunlevey knew why. The slight apparently affected White greatly, as Dunlevey learned when White loudly discussed the incident with him in a Denver hotel bar populated mainly by blacks.[18]

Why the Backlog?
The court workload increased largely because of decisions of the U.S. Supreme Court, many of which dealt with court-mandated changes in criminal law and

procedure. In the first four volumes of Nebraska Supreme Court *Reports* issued after White became chief justice, the Nebraska court wrote opinions in thirty-six criminal cases. In the last four volumes of White's fifteen-year tenure, the court issued 167 criminal opinions.[19]

The U.S. Supreme Court, under Chief Justice Earl Warren, issued two very significant criminal procedure opinions that impacted the states: *Gideon v. Wainwright* and *Miranda v. Arizona*.[20] The Court decided *Gideon* in 1963 and *Miranda* in 1966. Gideon was charged with breaking and entering in Florida. He asked for court appointed counsel but was denied. He represented himself, and lost both at trial and on appeal to the Florida Supreme Court. He then appealed to the U.S. Supreme Court. Gideon prevailed. The supreme court held that the Sixth Amendment gave all persons the right to counsel and that it required that felony defendants be furnished with state-appointed and state-paid lawyers, because the Fourteenth Amendment made the Sixth Amendment applicable to the states.[21] As a result of *Gideon*, many more criminal defendants were represented by counsel at every stage of the legal process, and briefs and arguments in the Nebraska Supreme Court became more involved and intricate, and cases took more time to decide. The feeble efforts of untutored prisoners could no longer be brushed aside by a busy court.

In *Miranda v. Arizona* a detainee was accused of rape. After interrogation he confessed and was subsequently convicted. He alleged that he had been coerced into confessing. Although police denied beating or entrapping Miranda, the supreme court reversed and established a new test: that a defendant being questioned had to be advised of his right to remain silent and of his right to have a lawyer.[22] In case after case the court subsequently litigated the parameters of the doctrine: How and when did the warning have to be given? What about the defendant who did not understand English? These and a myriad of other issues occupied courts all over America for years until they were resolved.

During the 1960s and 1970s, drug use increased sharply and criminal prosecutions for the use and possession of controlled substances began to show up on the court's docket fairly regularly. In addition, violent crimes increased substantially. The Nebraska Crime Commission began keeping crime statistics in the 1970s, and many of the cases cited often found their way to the Nebraska Supreme Court. For example, in 1971 there were 2,330 violent crimes in Nebraska. By 1991, twenty years later, the number of violent crimes had increased to 5,330, an increase of 3,000 crimes.[23]

The Simmons court decided 378 criminal cases out of its 4,065 decisions, equal to about 10 percent of all cases. The Simmons court affirmance rate for all cases was 55.69 percent, while for criminal cases alone it was 66.13 percent, some 10.44 percent higher. The White court decided 1,237 criminal cases out of 4,148 total cases. Thus, 29.82 percent of the total case load for the White court involved criminal cases, and although the White court heard only eighty-three more cases than the Simmons court, it heard 859 more criminal cases, a rather startling increase.[24]

The White court had an affirmance rate for all cases of 73.11 percent, an increase of 17.42 percent over the total affirmance rate of the Simmons Court. Part of this increase may be attributable to a higher caliber of lower court judges after the inception of the Missouri Plan. The White court affirmance rate in criminal cases exclusively was an astonishing 87.39 percent, 14 percent higher than its total affirmance rate, and 21 percent higher than the Simmons court's affirmance rate in criminal cases.[25]

In twenty-five years the Simmons court heard an average of 163 cases per year. At the end of its fifteen-year span, the White court was hearing 276.5 cases per year, 114 more cases per year than the Simmons court heard on average. This large increase placed tremendous pressure on the White court. It seems more charitable, and hopefully also more accurate, to assume that the overwhelmed judges gave brief or slipshod affirmances not because they had somehow acquired a callous disregard for the rights of criminal defendants but because they simply wanted to move cases along. Courts with large caseloads are often forced to limit the amount of time they can spend on a case or the kind of effort or research they can devote to it. And though Nebraska went from employing law students as part-time clerks to hiring full-time clerks for supreme court judges as a result of a federal grant in the early 1970s, these full-time clerks did not solve the backlog problem.

Death Penalty Decisions

Six years before Chief Justice White retired, another U.S. Supreme Court decision significantly impacted Nebraska Supreme Court business. In *Furman v. Georgia* (1972), the U.S. High Court, in one fell swoop, invalidated all existing state death penalty statutes.[26] For the first time, the U.S. Supreme Court, in a 5–4 decision, held that the death penalty was unconstitutional for violating the cruel and unusual punishment clause of the Eighth Amendment.

Nebraska had not had an execution since Charles Starkweather sat in the electric chair in 1959. It now appeared that it could not have another. Then, in 1976, the U.S. Supreme Court decided *Gregg v. Georgia* (1976), which upheld a Georgia statute that provided for special procedures in death penalty cases and allowed the penalty only if certain circumstances were present.[27] The Nebraska Legislature adopted new death penalty statutes in 1973, after *Furman*, and again in 1978, after *Gregg*. The new procedures made judges and juries establish guidelines for imposing the death penalty, and most states, including Nebraska, settled on listing aggravating and mitigating circumstances.

White and his court labored valiantly to solve the death penalty problem. On February 2, 1977, near the end of White's service as chief, the court handed down opinions in four death penalty cases: *State v. Stewart, State v. Rust, State v. Holtan,* and *State v. Simants*.[28] The four opinions, written by four different judges, spelled out in some detail the standards the court would apply and affirmed the imposition of the death penalty in three of the four cases.

State v. Stewart came from Douglas County. Rodney Stewart, a sixteen-year old high school student, developed a penchant for marijuana. His suppliers, Thomas Ehlers and Daniel Evans, agreed to sell him marijuana for a specified price. He could sell the marijuana he didn't consume for a profit. They sold him twelve bags to sell for ten dollars per bag at retail. Their wholesale price was one hundred dollars. Stewart sold seven bags and gave Evans and Ehlers seventy dollars but kept the remaining five bags for himself. He told the suppliers that he had been arrested and that the police had confiscated the five bags. Evans and Ehlers learned this was a lie and threatened Stewart, but they continued to sell to him. He owed them at least fifty dollars.

On January 19, 1975, Stewart telephoned Evans and told him that he had a buyer for two pounds of marijuana and that the profit from the sale would make up for what he owed the suppliers. Evans and Ehlers agreed to sell the defendant the marijuana for six hundred dollars, and they agreed to drive Stewart to a place near the buyer's house. Stewart was to go and collect the money from the buyer and then deliver the marijuana. In fact, Stewart had no buyer, and he intended to cheat his suppliers out of the marijuana.

Evans and Ehlers met Stewart on the evening of January 25, 1975. Unknown to the suppliers, Stewart had a concealed gun, and he was also carrying a can of gasoline to cover up any shooting that might occur. Stewart told Evans and Ehlers that he was going to deliver the gasoline to a friend after the sale took place, and he directed them to a certain address. On the way he told them to stop the van that Ehlers was driving.

When the van stopped, Stewart fired two shots, killing Ehlers instantaneously and wounding Evans. He then poured gas on the floor of the van and ignited it. Evans jumped out of the van and rolled in the snow to put out the fire on his clothes. Stewart fled on foot. When Evans was discovered and taken to the hospital, he told the police that Stewart had shot him. Stewart was arrested and confessed to the crime. He was tried and found guilty of first-degree murder.

In an opinion written by Judge Donald Brodkey, the court reviewed the Nebraska death penalty statutes enacted in 1973 after *Furman v. Georgia*. It assessed each of the eight aggravating circumstances and the seven mitigating circumstances set out as statutory standards.[29] The trial judge had found that subsection (1)(d) of Sec. 29-2523 R.R.S. 1943 was applicable to this case, and that the murder was especially heinous, atrocious, cruel, and manifested exceptional depravity by ordinary standards of morality and intelligence, thereby justifying the death sentence.

The statute cited the following aggravating and mitigating circumstances from sections 29-2521 and 29-2522:

(1) Aggravating Circumstances:

(a) The offender was previously convicted of another murder or a crime involving the use or threat of violence to the person, or has a substantial prior history of serious assaultive or terrorizing criminal activity;

(b) The murder was committed in an effort to conceal the commission of a crime, or to conceal the identity of the perpetrator of such crime;

(c) The murder was committed for hire, or for pecuniary gain, or the defendant hired another to commit the murder for the defendant;

(d) The murder was especially heinous, atrocious, cruel, or manifested exceptional depravity by ordinary standards of morality and intelligence;

(e) At the time the murder was committed, the offender also committed another murder;

(f) The offender knowingly created a great risk of death to at least several persons;

(g) The victim was a public servant having lawful custody of the offender or another in the lawful performance of his or her official duties and the offender knew or should have known that the victim was a public servant performing his or her official duties;

(h) The murder was committed knowingly to disrupt or hinder the lawful exercise of any governmental function or the enforcement of the laws; or

(i) The victim was a law enforcement officer engaged in the lawful performance of his or her official duties as a law enforcement officer and the offender knew or reasonably should have known that the victim was a law enforcement officer.

The facts upon which the applicability of an aggravating circumstance depends must be proved beyond a reasonable doubt.

(2) Mitigating Circumstances:

(a) The offender has no significant history of prior criminal activity;

(b) The offender acted under unusual pressures or influences or under the domination of another person;

(c) The crime was committed while the offender was under the influence of extreme mental or emotional disturbance;

(d) The age of the defendant at the time of the crime;

(e) The offender was an accomplice in the crime committed by another person and his or her participation was relatively minor;

(f) The victim was a participant in the defendant's conduct or consented to the act; or

(g) At the time of the crime, the capacity of the defendant to appreciate the wrongfulness of his or her conduct or to conform his or her conduct to the requirements of law was impaired as a result of mental illness, mental defect, or intoxication.

The supreme court said that it had to decide whether the murder of Ehlers was a conscienceless or pitiless crime that was unnecessarily tortuous to the victim. Medical testimony established that Ehler's death was instantaneous. He was not tortured. Stewart testified that he set fire to the van to conceal the crimes and his identity and that he did not do it to cause further harm to Ehlers. The supreme court held that (1)(d) had not been proved beyond a reasonable doubt, the applicable burden of proof.

The court concluded that only one, or at the most two, of the aggravating circumstances were present, and it also found at least two mitigating circumstances. Brodkey said, "Under our statute, a sentencing judge may properly impose a sentence of life imprisonment, rather than a sentence of death, where the mitigating factors only approach or equal the weight given to the aggravating circumstances. They need not 'outweigh' the aggravating circumstances." The court proceeded to modify Stewart's death penalty to life imprisonment and affirmed the conviction. There were no dissents.

In *State v. Rust*, Judge Lawrence Clinton wrote for the court. In another case from Douglas County, Rust was tried and convicted of killing Michael Kellogg in the course of a robbery. He was found guilty and sentenced to death. Rust and two accomplices had robbed a grocery store at gunpoint. They fled in an automobile. Police began to chase them and blocked a street, trapping the robber's car. Rust began to fire at the police cruisers and hit two cruisers. He and one accomplice left the car and ran. Police killed the third robber. Rust shot and seriously wounded one policeman and shot and killed Kellogg, a civilian who had come to the aid of the police. He shot Kellogg four times, including in the body after Kellogg had fallen from another shot by Rust.

The supreme court reviewed all the mitigating and aggravating circumstances and agreed with the trial court sentencing panel, which had found that aggravating circumstances did exist. Clinton said that aggravating circumstance (1)(d) exists where the murder is so coldly calculated as to indicate a state of mind totally and senselessly bereft of regard for human life. The court, after its review, affirmed the death sentence, saying, "We fully agree with the sentencing panel that the existing aggravating factors in this case clearly outweigh any mitigating factor. We further conclude that the death penalty under the facts in this case is not excessive and is not disproportionate to that imposed in the other cases before us." The decision appeared to be unanimous.[30]

State v. Holtan, another Douglas County case, was a Judge John Newton opinion. Holtan entered the Dugout Bar in Omaha, robbed the cash register, herded the bartender and his girlfriend, together with the only patron, into a restroom, and ordered the bartender to tie the other two up. He then shot and killed the bartender, wounded the girlfriend, and fired at and missed the patron. After firing four shots, he fled. He was apprehended, tried, convicted, and sentenced to death.

The court again reviewed all the mitigating and aggravating circumstances. The sentencing court had found (1)(d) to be applicable, and the supreme court agreed with the lower court, explaining, "[A]lthough torture was not involved, it is clear that this element was applicable. The defendant killed, and attempted to kill unresisting victims of the robbery. The act was totally and senselessly bereft of any regard for human life. It was wanton, deliberate, cruel and inexcusable." Having set this standard, the court would find itself struggling with its own precedent when, several years later, it faced the horrifying facts in State v. Hunt. In Holtan the court found that the aggravating circumstances outweighed the mitigating factors and affirmed the death sentence.

The last of the four death penalty cases was State v. Simants. Judge Spencer wrote the opinion for a unanimous court. Simants was convicted on six counts of first-degree murder and sentenced to death. The supreme court affirmed. Simants had been drinking in a bar in Sutherland, in Lincoln County, for some time. At approximately 8:00 p.m., he asked his sister to take him to her house, where he was staying. She did and then returned to the bar. He went into her house, talked to his nephew, and then went into his brother-in-law's bedroom, got a .22 rifle, loaded it, and went next door to the residence of Henry Kellie. About forty-five minutes later he returned to his sister's house, left a note expressing remorse for his crime on the kitchen table, and then told the nephew that he had killed the entire Kellie family. He left the house, went to his parent's home, and told them that he had killed the Kellies. After the visit to his parents' home, Simants went to two downtown bars and drank some more, before finally returning to his sister's home, where he slept in a field until the next morning. He tried to enter his sister's house, but she called the police, who apprehended him. He gave a statement outlining the crimes.

When he entered the Kellie house, he attempted to have sexual relations with Florance Kellie, a ten-year-old girl. When she resisted, he shot her in the forehead with the .22 rifle, killing her. Her grandfather, Henry Kellie, came to investigate, and Simants shot him. Shortly thereafter, Audrey Kellie, Henry's wife, entered the house, and Simants shot her. The evidence indicated that Simants had sexually molested Mrs. Kellie. David Kellie, Henry Kellie's son, and his two children—Daniel, aged five, and Deanna, aged seven—then came to the house, and Simants shot and killed all three of them. There was also evidence that Simants had sexually molested Deanna.

On appeal, Simants questioned the constitutionality of the death penalty, and the court concluded that the U.S. Supreme Court's ruling in *Gregg v. Georgia* allowed it. The court further found that it did not need to use jury sentencing in a capital case.[31] The court said that Simants's position—that Nebraska's death penalty procedures were constitutionally invalid because they were silent as to what burden must be met before an aggravating circumstance is proven to exist—was without merit. Simants argued that aggravating circumstances must be proved to exist beyond a reasonable doubt, and the court agreed, but it concluded that the aggravating circumstances clearly existed beyond a reasonable doubt in this case. Spencer added, "We believe it is the intent of the act to require the facts upon which the aggravating circumstances referred to in Sec. 29-2523, R.R.S. 1943, are based be proved beyond a reasonable doubt, and so construe it."

Spencer also explained the role of the court in reviewing aggravating and mitigating circumstances: "In other words, we will compare each capital case under review with those previous cases in which the death penalty has or has not been imposed under the new statute. By this means review by this court guarantees that the reasons present in one case will reach a similar result to that reached under similar circumstances in another case."

The trial court found that (1)(d) was applicable to the deaths of Florance, Audrey, and Deanna Kellie. The supreme court affirmed, mentioning the attack on Audrey Kellie's body after her death. The court stated, "[T]he use of the word 'exceptional,' however, confines it only to those situations where depravity is apparent to such an extent as to obviously offend all standards of morality and intelligence. We find such depravity was present in the murder of the three females."

The supreme court ruled that the aggravating circumstances far outweighed the mitigating circumstances and announced the rule, "In the balancing of the aggravating and mitigating circumstances, we emphasize the death penalty will not be imposed simply because the aggravating circumstances may outnumber the mitigating circumstances. Rather, the test is whether the aggravating circumstances in comparison outweigh the mitigating circumstances."

Thus, the court as an institution attempted to find its way through the labyrinth created by *Furman v. Georgia* and *Gregg v. Georgia*. Judicial construction rectified the legislature's failure to define the requisite burden of proof. White's role in finding a solution was not clear. He wrote none of the four opinions, but because the court had no dissents in any of the four, he almost certainly acquiesced in attempting to articulate the standards that would be applied in the future.

Problems of Administration

Prior to 1970 and the constitutional amendment handing the administration of Nebraska's court system to the chief justice, each tier of the Nebraska court system operated on its own. The supreme court exercised no control over district or county courts, other than to review their decisions on appeal. Each set of courts was similar to a medieval fiefdom, operating independently but subject ultimately to review by the Nebraska Supreme Court. Many county judges, who held important probate powers and responsibilities, were not even lawyers.

During the White administration, the Omaha Bar Association tried to repeal the constitutional provision requiring all supreme court judges to live in Lincoln. The court opposed the effort, fearing that it would destroy the court's collegiality.[32] Judge Lawrence Clinton served as the court's spokesman on the issue and testified before the legislature. He received fire from an unexpected quarter when some of the legislature's constitutional "experts" questioned his residence, because he lived in an unincorporated subdivision south of the Lincoln city limits.

During White's incumbency, the supreme court and the bar association combined to appoint a study committee, chaired by Thomas W. Tye of Kearney, to investigate whether Nebraska should go to a one-tier court system, in which the county court, essentially a probate and guardianship court, simply became a division of the district court, similar to the district court in Iowa, for example. The court, somewhat dissatisfied with the bar association's penchant for always appointing the same association nabobs as representatives of larger firms, made sure that the membership of the committee was more diverse than usual. The idea met with fierce opposition from district judges, who had always considered themselves vastly superior to county judges, especially before LB1032 imposed the requirement that county judges had to be lawyers and before the merit system began moving some county judges through the ranks to district courts.

White and Dunlevey found district judges to be a rather unruly lot. Fiercely independent, they opposed any effort by the court administrator's office to exercise any administrative authority over them. White told Dunlevey that they tolerated his own attendance at their meetings only because he had been both a district judge and a past president of the district judges association, but they did not like to have Judge Boslaugh attend their meetings, as he always did, because Boslaugh had never been a district judge.[33] According to White, the district judges felt that a centralized administration was the first step toward the supreme court telling them how to decide cases.

The court administrator's office made the first tentative move toward exercising administrative authority over the district courts by enacting rules for certifying the district court reporters. Consequently, the reporters kept the administrator's office aware of district court cases from all over the state. The effectiveness of the reporters was in full display when newly appointed district judge Francis Kneifl of Dakota City held his first criminal sentencing. Kneifl, a lackluster law student and inept practitioner, was the only willing applicant for a district court appointment in Nebraska's rural northeastern corner. His accession to the bench did little to bolster faith in the appointive process of the Missouri Plan.

The following sentencing colloquy flashed across Nebraska through the court reporters' network:

> *Kneifl*: Do you have anything to say before I pronounce sentence?
> *Defendant*: Fuck you.
> *Kneifl*: Fuck you, too.[34]

Kneifl was suspended without pay for three months in 1984 for other transgressions, and he was ultimately removed from the bench by the electorate the same year, after having received a favorable retention rate of only 25 percent in the 1984 bar poll.

As an administrator, White left something to be desired. Judge Hale McCown, upon whom White relied most for administrative help, believed that White had some ability in administrative matters but little interest in them.[35] When administrative chores started accumulating, White frequently told Dunlevey, "This is not the job I ran for." John Newton, White's closest friend on the court, seemed to be a thorn in White's side on most administrative matters, especially if the administrative action appeared to move the court in a "liberal" direction.

One of the more intriguing administrative issues during White's incumbency emanated from White himself. During construction of the new Lancaster

County city building in the 1960s, the Lancaster County district judges showed the supreme court judges their new courtroom facilities. White walked into the courtroom of then district judge William C. Hastings while smoking a large and pungent cigar. Hastings, virtually apoplectic, chastised White, who replied that he would smoke a cigar in any courtroom in the state if he felt like it. Hastings, who would himself later become chief justice of the supreme court, did not appreciate White's response. White must have changed his somewhat arrogant stance when he subsequently appeared in Lancaster County Court as a defendant in a drunk-driving case.[36]

Before assuming the position of chief justice, White was used to functioning entirely on his own, as all district judges do. As a district judge White had been directly elected by the people and was not subordinate to anyone. He no doubt found it difficult to realize that as chief justice he now had to oversee groups who were used to functioning as they saw fit, a job somewhat like trying to herd cats.

White's Personal Side

Some of the problems White encountered came from the bench, while others were of his own making. His personal idiosyncrasies provoked concern in his colleagues on the supreme court and tended to weaken his authority in the eyes of both judges of inferior courts and the bar. Members of the general public who were aware of his activities must have questioned his behavior when they contrasted it with the glacial dignity of Simmons, his predecessor.

White displayed a penchant for strong drink. With his ever-present cigar and his booming voice, he was a figure to be avoided at cocktail parties if at all possible, and pity the young lawyer who was not sufficiently imaginative to extricate himself from the chief's clutches at a gathering. White had a large trove of stories that he told well, no doubt because he told them often.

One of White's judicial colleagues (who wished to remain anonymous) recounts an incident that took place when White and several members of the court left the Cornhusker Hotel after lunch and walked back toward the state capitol. As the entourage passed Mitch Tavlin's liquor store, Tavlin, spotting White, raced out of the store and buttonholed the chief justice. Apparently White, while buying supplies from Tavlin, had paid for his purchases by endorsing a dividend check over to Tavlin. But White had temporarily misplaced the check and had had it cancelled by the issuing corporation. The corporation stopped payment on the check and issued White a replacement. In the interim, White found the missing instrument and passed it off to Tavlin. Tavlin was understandably irate about being stiffed by the chief justice. White placated him by issuing a new, personal check, but the entire vignette apparently proved highly informative to White's colleagues on the bench.[37]

While White was chief justice, he was arrested for driving under the influence. He entered a plea of guilty and spent the night of his arrest in jail. The supreme court was sitting the following day. When he was preparing to go to municipal court for arraignment with the other prisoners, White, in an apocryphal story, reportedly said, "I've got to be in court at nine o'clock," to which one of the rummy denizens replied, "Don't worry, buddy, we all do." White was released on the order of City Attorney Dick Wood and was taken home by Merlin Reibolt, bailiff of the supreme court. As he was leaving the courthouse, he met a Lincoln lawyer whom he knew well who said to him, "Over visiting the inferior courts, I presume." Chastened, White replied, "Believe me, in Nebraska there are no inferior courts."[38] White returned to the supreme court after the morning's cases and discussed the matter with his colleagues. The incident did not seem to affect his relationship with other members of the court, though it earned him many jibes and much surreptitious whispering from lawyers.

White's drinking continued after the arrest. Another former judge recalls that while White was attending a conference of chief justices in Seattle, he got drunk and fell into a swimming pool. The action diminished the Nebraska court in the eyes of those who were present.[39] On another occasion, White had problems with his somewhat ill-fitting toupee. Dunlevey recalls an animated conversation with White in Dunlevey's office during which White, while gesticulating, knocked his own toupee off onto the floor. Dunlevey sat transfixed as White picked the toupee up and reinstalled it.[40]

White and Judge John Newton were quite close. After Newton's death, White, by then retired, paid eloquent tribute to his old friend at the memorial service the court holds to honor every judge of the court who has died. His words were a far cry from the eulogies he delivered for other deceased brethren when he was serving as chief justice. He gave virtually the same eulogy at the memorial services for John Yeager, on January 8, 1968; Elwood B. "Jimmy" Chappell, on May 26, 1969; Frederick Messmore, on April 6, 1970; and Robert G. Simmons, on May 4, 1970. The services for Messmore and Simmons were less than a month apart. One would think that someone would have recognized the familiar ring of White's words during each ceremony. White apparently believed that you cannot get too much of a good thing. One of his favorite eulogy phrases was to recognize the decedent as "a real physician of applied liberty." Other than its orotund sound, the phrase seems to have virtually no meaning, especially in a legal context. (See White's memorial speeches in appendix 3).

Despite his personal quirks, White managed to lead Nebraska's high court intelligently, and the jurisprudential output of his court was quite satisfactory. Judges occasionally ventured into hitherto unknown territory in the designation of opinions, and there were several epigrammatic "Smithograms," but on the whole the work product reflected favorably on the court and on the state.

White's Jurisprudential Legacy

Almost from the outset of White's term, the mix of cases considered by his court began to shift from the kinds of cases heard by the Simmons court. The White court considered more criminal cases, due process issues, public law questions, and new tort theories. Thankfully, White had both the intellect and the energy to try to cope with the demands of the new jurisprudence. He also had a new supporting cast to assist him once the "settled seven" who had served together for so many years on Simmons's court left the bench.

Gideon v. Wainwright (1963) galvanized the Nebraska Legislature into action, and in its 1965 session it passed a law providing for the appointment of counsel in felony cases. In *State v. King* (1965) the supreme court wrestled with the impact of the Nebraska statute. King asked the district court to appoint appellate counsel for him, and it never acted on the motion. King handled his own defense before the supreme court, briefing and arguing the matter. During the oral argument he told the court that he had asked for counsel. The court, by a 4–3 majority, vacated the submission of the case (cases are deemed submitted upon the conclusion of oral argument before the court), ordered the district court to appoint appellate counsel, and extended the brief date for new counsel. White, Carter, and Brower dissented, arguing that the new statute had not yet gone into effect when King's case was heard by the supreme court and that it did not have retroactive effect. The dissenters contended that King had not been denied counsel and that the court was under no duty on its own motion to appoint counsel for him, conveniently overlooking King's motion for the appointment of appellate counsel and the failure of the district court to rule upon it.[41]

In a related case, *State v. Miller* (1965), Miller filed a motion in the supreme court for the appointment of appellate counsel. In a *per curiam* decision, the court observed that such a motion should have been filed in the district court under the new statute. The court therefore denied the motion directed to it, giving Miller sixty days to make application to the district court for counsel and also extending Miller's brief date.[42] The dissent in *King* bears overtones of Carter's lingering resentment over the intrusion of the U.S. Supreme Court into matters of state procedure—a sentiment he had expressed, for example, in *Johnson v. Radio Station wow*, and an opinion that Simmons had indirectly articulated in *Hawk v. Olson*.[43]

In addition to recognizing and dealing with issues emanating from decisions of the U.S. Supreme Court, the White court also had to deal with homegrown criminals whose crimes would have been considered heinous without any guidance from the nation's highest tribunal. In *State v. Alvarez* (1967), Alvarez, a transient, raped and murdered a Lincoln socialite while working as a laborer in her yard. The murder and assault took place before several preschool-aged children. Alvarez was apprehended when he attempted to flee from the city. He entered a plea of guilty and was sentenced to death. The supreme court upheld the conviction and sentence, but Alvarez was never executed because his post-trial maneuvering kept him alive until *Furman v. Georgia* saved all prisoners who had been sentenced to death.[44]

State v. Nokes (1975), one of Nebraska's most bizarre murder cases, involved an employee of the Nebraska Game and Parks Commission named Harold D. Nokes, who lived in McCook. Nokes and his wife were engaged in a ménage à trois with a younger woman who lived in the area. As the relationship began to sour, the parents of the younger woman accosted Nokes. He shot and killed them both and then butchered their bodies, wrapping the parts in butcher paper and placing them in his freezer. He went to work the next day, and after work, he took the frozen parts out of the freezer, put them in his boat, and dumped them in Harry Strunk Lake, near McCook. He burned the wrapping paper that had contained the body parts on the shore of the lake. Several days later he returned to the lake and discovered that some of the parts had washed ashore. He hid them under a rock, left the lake, and never returned. After months went by, other parts were discovered, and Nokes was finally arrested. After pleading guilty, he was sentenced to two consecutive life sentences.[45]

A man destined to live in infamy in Nebraska legal and journalistic circles—

Erwin Charles Simants—first surfaced during White's term as chief justice. Simants, who (as discussed above) later became a depraved mass murderer, took his first trip to the supreme court because he and several companions had been convicted of contributing to the delinquency of a fourteen-year-old girl. Simants appealed his conviction in county court to the district court on the grounds that the statute was unconstitutionally vague. The district court agreed and dismissed the case. The Lincoln County attorney appealed, and in 1968 the supreme court reversed the district court decision, holding that the statute fell within acceptable parameters. McCown dissented, arguing that the statute should have spelled out specific acts but did not. McCown appeared to have the better of the argument because delinquency is a rather nebulous concept. Did it entail smoking? Drinking? Staying out late? Talking back to one's mother? Perhaps the court realized, in pragmatic fashion, that Simants was a dangerous individual who needed to be reprimanded in some way. The court could have had a stronger case against Simants, however, if the record had set forth what he and his buddies did to or with the girl.[46]

A majority of the court, but not a super-majority, showed constitutional concerns for other juveniles in *DeBacker v. Brainard* (1968), a case in which a teenager asserted the unconstitutionality of the Juvenile Court Act of 1967, arguing that he had been deprived of the right to a trial by jury and that the standard of proof was, unfairly, the civil "preponderance of evidence" standard rather than the criminal "beyond a reasonable doubt" standard. Four judges—McCown, Boslaugh, Spencer, and Smith—held that the act was unconstitutional. Three judges—Carter, White, and Newton—held that it was not. Because the constitution required that the court needed at least five votes to hold an act unconstitutional, the Juvenile Court Act passed muster. The unsuccessful majority issued a *per curiam* opinion, holding that In re Gault, a 1967 U.S. Supreme Court opinion, governed the case.[47] *Gault* established the rule that a juvenile has a constitutional right to trial by jury if the offense was one that would give rise to a jury trial if it was committed by an adult and could be tried in adult criminal court.[48] McCown added a separate opinion along the same lines, while Carter wrote the controlling opinion for the three dissenters, contending that *Gault* did not apply.

In *McMullen v. Geiger* (1969), the same factions reached a similar result in another juvenile proceeding. The four-man group of McCown, Boslaugh, Spencer, and Smith held that the Juvenile Act was unconstitutional because it did not grant a jury trial. The controlling three-judge majority established the rule that juvenile proceedings were to be tried *de novo* on the record below when they reached the supreme court.[49] The super-majority rule still secured the preference of the constitutional drafters of yesteryear for legislative, rather than judicial, solutions to state problems. It leaves legislative efforts inviolate unless there is virtually no doubt about the errancy of the legislative remedy.

The White court, though it generally behaved in a very gentlemanly fashion, occasionally revealed philosophical differences among the judges. Such differences almost always exist, but more than any other court in recent Nebraska history, the White court was not loath to air its internal disagreements. For example, in *Pedersen v. Schultz* (1975), a *per curiam* opinion, the court was very succinct and to the point in stating the judges' votes. In its entirety, the opinion read: "Plaintiff appeals after return of a jury verdict for him, filing of an alternative motion by defendant for judgment not withstanding the verdict or a new trial, and rendition of judgment not withstanding the verdict. The judgment is affirmed. For affirmance: White, C.J. and Carter and Newton, J.J. For reversal and remand for a new trial: Spencer and Boslaugh, J.J. For reversal and remand with directions to render judgment on the jury verdict: Smith and McCown, J.J."[50]

In *State v. Walker* (1972) Smith introduced a new form of opinion. The defendant was charged with escape. He did not want a lawyer and spit at the judge after being sentenced. He appealed *pro se*, challenging the excessiveness of the sentence. The court, in a *per curiam* opinion, had no problem with the sentence, except for Smith. Smith wrote an opinion entitled "dubitante," the first time such an appellation had appeared in Nebraska jurisprudence at least since 1938.[51] Smith concluded, "The proposition that the State has not violated Walker's right to counsel on appeal may ring true, or dissonance may linger. I am in doubt." The legal import of such a confession would appear to be nil, but the opinion may have assuaged Smith's conscience. Nonetheless, acknowledging such fractionalizations adds nothing to the potency of the majority opinion or to Smith's position. If he didn't like the majority opinion, he could have dissented. The fact that he was confused was interesting but irrelevant to the case.

In *State v. Little Art Corp.* (1973) an Omaha theater was convicted of showing pornographic films. The supreme court affirmed the conviction. Newton wrote the court's opinion, in which he criticized the "permissiveness" of the

U.S. Supreme Court. McCown concurred but stated: "I emphatically do not join in the assertions that the federal courts have gone to great lengths to protect malefactors at the expense of public need for protection, and that public obscenity has been sanctioned and permissiveness engendered in our society by the United States Supreme Court. Such statements, whether dicta or not, lend support to unjustified and misinformed public criticism of all courts and magnify misunderstanding between state and federal courts."[52]

Stung by McCown's statement, Newton replied in an *accentatus*, writing, "No court or judicial decision is sacrosanct. Sycophantic agreement, or blind obeisance, restraining constructive criticism, can only perpetuate errors."[53] McCown's criticism of Newton spelled out exactly why state courts should refrain from attacking the U.S. Supreme Court, even if they don't like what it is saying, and Newton's riposte is redolent with insulting implications that McCown's position was simply toadyism. It came as quite a surprise to McCown, though he knew that Newton regarded him as a "nutty liberal."[54] For Newton to so criticize either McCown or the U.S. Supreme Court appears rather arrogant when one compares Newton's own lackluster judicial output to the relative worth of McCown's work or that of the U.S. Supreme Court.

In *State v. Micek* (1975) McCown apparently voted with the court—it is not clear whether he dissented or concurred—but he added a brief "caveat," saying that the majority had extended the principle of probable cause into auto searches to the ultimate limit: "There should be no discouragement or unreasonable detention of citizens beyond the time necessary for reasonable verification of critical information."[55]

Orleans Education Assn. v. School District of Orleans (1975) was a Clinton opinion in which the court held that the legislative act creating the Court (now Commission) of Industrial Relations was constitutional. Newton dissented, arguing that this court, for policy reasons, had assumed a legislative function. Clinton, in a *respondente*, spent some time attacking Newton's dissent, on logical, as opposed to *ad hominem*, grounds.[56]

Halligan v. Cotton (1975) concerned a medical malpractice action against a doctor. The trial court directed a verdict for the doctor, and the supreme court affirmed the verdict. Clinton wrote the opinion for the court. Although there were no dissents or concurrences in this case, Clinton contributed a "personal addendum," obviously because he sympathized with the plaintiff: "I am not unmindful of the fact that a meritorious case may sometimes fail for lack of expert testimony or opinion, and that likewise non-meritorious cases are sometimes unnecessarily brought for the same reason. The remedy for the problem must necessarily be a legislative one involving cooperation of the medical and legal professions."[57] Clinton, undoubtedly sincere in his belief, seemed not to appreciate the fact that such personal comments had not appeared before in Nebraska Supreme Court opinions.

In *Kimball County Grain Coop. v. Yung* (1978), Brodkey wrote the majority opinion and then wrote a concurrence to his own opinion: "Although authoring the majority opinion in this case, I do not believe it goes far enough, and I believe that this court should squarely face and resolve the question of whether the defendant was a 'merchant' as defined in section 2-104, U.C.C."[58] Spencer also wrote a concurrence in which he disagreed with Brodkey and agreed with the majority opinion. Perhaps frustrated judges would like to have another chance to argue their case if their ideas do not find acceptance by the majority, but very few indulge their frustration by writing two opinions in the same case.

Spiker v. John Day Co. (1978), a worker's compensation case, involved the issue of whether an injured worker who was totally disabled, and who would need nursing care for the rest of his life, could recover the cost of that nursing care even if it would not cure or lessen his disability. The court, in an opinion written by Boslaugh, agreed that the worker could recover. Brodkey concurred, and Boslaugh joined in Brodkey's concurrence, along with McCown and C. Thomas White. Paul White concurred in part and dissented in part, and Spencer and Clinton joined him. Thus every member of the court, including the author of the majority opinion, either wrote or joined in an opinion other than the majority opinion, a somewhat confusing circumstance to those seeking to ascertain what the court really said.[59]

The relationship of the White court to other branches of government gave rise to several opinions that are difficult to reconcile logically. One of the more far-reaching pronouncements of the White court came in *Board of Regents v. Exon* (1977), in which the court refused to defer to the legislative branch. The issue in *Exon* was the extent to which the legislature might control or interfere with the discretion of the Regents in the general governance of the university. Holding generally for the Regents, the court depended on the Nebraska Constitution to conclude that the legislature could not play a role in fixing university salaries. Ever since *Exon*, the general governing of the university has been clearly vested in the Board of Regents. The legislature's control over the university ends when it appropriates money in the state budget for the benefit of the university. Once the appropriation is made, how it is specifically spent is beyond the ambit of the senators.[60]

In 1968 certain tax opponents attempted to kill the Nebraska income tax that had been enacted at the 1967 legislative session. They mounted an initiative campaign to eliminate the income tax, which would have left the sales tax as the only source of state government revenue, the state property tax having been thrown out by the voters in 1966. The secretary of state then held that the groups opposed to the income tax had obtained an insufficient number of valid signatures because many petitions were turned in on July 5 and therefore had not been filed more than four months before the general election on November 5. The initiative organizers sued for mandamus in the Lancaster County District Court, and Judge William C. Hastings granted mandamus in September 1968. The case was appealed to the supreme court and was advanced for hearing so that a decision could be reached before the November 5 election.

On October 21, 1968, the court entered a *per curiam* judgment that affirmed the district court, with a written opinion to follow. In the later opinion, which was authored by McCown and filed November 8, 1968, three days after the election, five members of the court approved the mandamus, with Spencer and Newton dissenting. McCown's opinion provided: "As this court said in *State ex rel. Ayers v. Amsberry, supra*: 'the amendment under consideration reserves to the people the right to act in the capacity of legislators. The presumption should be in favor of the validity and legality of their act. The law should be construed, if possible, so as to prevent absurdity and hardship and so as to favor public convenience.'"[61]

McCown went on to say that Nebraska's prior decisions almost universally held that the power of initiative must be liberally construed to promote the democratic process and that the right of initiative that was granted by Nebraska's constitution should not be circumscribed by restrictive legislation or narrow and strict judicial interpretation of the statutes. But the court also said in dicta, "The power to tax is essential to the continued existence of a state. A constitutional amendment which would destroy or completely emasculate that power might well be itself unconstitutional. That issue is not presently here."[62] Thus the majority recognized that in some circumstances there might be a legitimate brake upon the power of initiative.

Spencer's dissent took the opposite tack: "First, I do not believe that the initiative process may be used to limit the power of the legislative branch of government to provide for the proper financing of the state government."[63] Newton's dissent was even more fundamental: "The truth of the statement that 'the power to tax is the power to destroy' is unquestioned. Conversely, the power to prevent taxation is just as surely the power to destroy government. No government be it federal, state or local, can exist without revenue; and governmental revenue is synonymous with taxation." Newton went on to add that the enabling act creating Nebraska as a state required that Nebraska have a republican form of government, and that without the revenue derived from taxation, the state government would be brought to a standstill and rendered inoperative.[64]

The majority obviously took the position assuming that the voters might vote to keep the income tax, which they did, and make the issue moot. The court did not issue its opinion until after the election. If the tax had been voted out, in all likelihood the court would have adopted the position advanced by Spencer and Newton in their dissents. The court's position allowed it to issue pious pronouncements concerning the people's right to legislate by initiative and still gave it another "bite at the apple" if the measure passed and the taxing power of the state was constrained. The court offered fairly wise political judgment, while paying homage to the Populists and Progressives.

Hanna v. State Board of Equalization and Assessment (1967) was the first in a series of ten cases challenging the State Board's increased land valuations in various counties across the state. The Board action generated legal challenges both by various counties and individual taxpayers. The supreme court ruled against the State Board in every instance, primarily on the basis of deficient procedural records. The legislature had been insisting that the Board equalize valuations among the various counties, but when the Board tried to do so, the court prevented it from taking action, and rightfully so. Due process, in the court's eyes, was not simply an empty phrase.[65]

Another example of close judicial scrutiny of legislative and administrative action is found in *State ex rel. Meyer v. Steen* (1965). This case, an original action in the supreme court to test the validity of the Game and Parks Headquarters Construction Act of 1967, challenged whether the headquarters building could be financed by bonds backed by a pledge of state game fund receipts derived from hunting, fishing, and trapping license sales. The court found the act to be in violation of Article XIII, Section 1 of the Nebraska Constitution, which forbade the state from incurring indebtedness in excess of $100,000. The Game and Parks Commission argued that the debt was payable only from a special fund and not from general revenue. The court reasoned that the legislature had the power to determine how the game fund was to be spent, so it was not a special fund. The court also found that such an appropriation of funds would constitute a continuing appropriation, which is banned by Article III, Section 22, thus temporarily ending construction of the Game and Parks headquarters.[66]

The court would willingly have struck down another legislative act, this time a scheme to sell school trust lands, but for the fact that declaring a legislative act unconstitutional requires a super-majority of five judges, and those judges opposed to the sale could only muster four votes. *State ex rel. Belker v. Board of Educational Lands and Funds* (1969) involved a statute that forced the Board of Educational Lands and Funds to sell school lands if a prospective buyer offered the price at which the lands had previously been appraised, even if the Board could sell at an even higher price.[67] The act, essentially a cattleman's relief act crammed through the legislature by Senators Elvin Adamson, Chet Paxton, Ramey Whitney, and Bill Wylie—all ranchers—let the cattlemen buy land that had been leased, giving them more deeded land and precluding anyone from leasing the land out from under the historical lessee. The act refused to allow the Board of Educational Lands and Funds to reject bids. A four-judge majority consisting of Spencer, White, Newton, and William Colwell, a district judge sitting with the court, held that the act unconstitutionally invaded the prerogatives of the Board, much as a valid majority decided in *Exon* several years later. Boslaugh, Smith, and McCown all voted that the act was constitutional, and their opinion was controlling, though it seemed to miss the point that the school lands are held in trust for the common schools and that a trustee's fiduciary duty is to secure the best price he can for the beneficiary of the trust.

Belker came back to the court the following year on a motion for rehearing. This time Carter, who previously had been ill, sat with the court. Now that he had regained the bench, Carter showed flashes of his old self but tempered his remarks at the end. He said, in a long dissent,

> This case has been twice argued. In each argument four judges were of the opinion that the statutes were unconstitutional. In the first argument, Colwell, District Judge, sat as a member of the court. In the second, I resumed my place on the court and Colwell,

District Judge, did not participate. The result is that five judges sat
on the two arguments who firmly believe that the act before us is
unconstitutional. On the other hand, the same three members of
the court have stood in the shadow of Article V, Section 2, of the
Constitution, and insisted that the act is constitutional. I do not
intend to infer any irregularity in constituting the court in either
instance. There was none.

Carter removed any hint of *Ruehle* discord over the way the court was constituted with the district judge, though he should have said that he was not "implying," rather than not "inferring." Both Spencer and Paul White filed dissents, but the controlling three judges remained adamant, and the court was
forced to adhere to its former opinion. Even though more judges disagreed
than agreed with the solons, there were not enough judges to discard the act
decreeing sales of school lands.[68]

Both the majority and the dissenters showed great reverence for school trust
lands in *Banks v. State* (1966), which antedated *Belker* by several years. The legislature, in 1965, had directed the Board of Educational Lands and Funds to sell
school lands at the expiration of then-current leases. The legislature's act did
not describe what should happen to improvements that had been made on the
school lands by the lessees. Banks was a lessee who had made many improvements on his tract, and he had purchased other existing improvements from
the prior lessee. At the expiration of the lease, the Board advertised the sale of
all improvements made without the approval of the Board. Existing statutes
required Board approval before the construction of improvements, and the
tenant had failed to secure such approval, except for one irrigation well.

After reviewing the legislative scheme, the majority, in an opinion written
by Smith, held that tenants had to be compensated for improvements they had
made, whether or not they had first obtained approval, and held that the school
land could not be sold until the value of the tenant improvements had been determined. Carter, McCown, and Boslaugh concurred, while Brower, Spencer,
and Colwell dissented. Spencer wrote a separate dissent, criticizing the concurring opinion for its lack of precedental authority. It thus became clear that
school lands enjoyed elevated status in the eyes of the court but that legislative enactments did not.[69]

The court again cast serious doubt on a legislative effort in *State v. Cavitt*,

(1968), a case in which a retarded woman had been committed to the Beatrice State Home because of a mental deficiency. The superintendent of the Home filed a petition with the Board of Examiners of Mentally Deficient, asking if the woman should be sterilized as a condition for being released from the Home. The Board ordered that she be sterilized. The woman's guardian appealed to the district court, which held that the evidence justifying sterilization was insufficient and that the statutory scheme justifying sterilization was unconstitutional. The state appealed.

Reversing the district court, the supreme court held that the statute was constitutional, but in a 3–4 decision. The controlling three-judge opinion written by Carter provided, in part: "Acting for the public good, the state, in the exercise of its police power, may impose reasonable restrictions upon the natural and constitutional rights of its citizens. Measured by its injurious effect upon society, the state may limit a class of citizens in its right to bear or beget children with an inherited tendency to mental deficiency, including feeblemindedness, idiocy or imbecility." Smith dissented from the controlling opinion, raising the issue of substantive due process. McCown joined him in dissent. In a separate opinion, Newton, joined by Boslaugh, also asserted unconstitutionality. But again, the need for a super-majority of five votes kept the legislative pronouncement from being jettisoned by the court.[70]

However, Cavitt's guardian, Vince Dowding, appealed the supreme court's decision to the U.S. Supreme Court, which granted certiorari. Seeing the handwriting on the wall, the legislature amended the law at once to eliminate involuntary sterilization, restoring at least some measure of civil rights to the retarded. Between 1924 and 1966 1,523 people appeared before the Mentally Deficient Evaluation Board. Of those, 716 people, or 47 percent, were sterilized by board order.[71]

The court wrestled with questions of constitutionality in Prendergast v. Nelson (1977), a declaratory judgment action seeking a determination of the constitutionality of the Nebraska Hospital–Medical Liability Act. The act capped tort liability judgments, and the director of insurance refused to implement it. The district court found the act to be constitutional and ordered the director to implement its provisions. The supreme court affirmed and stated that the act was constitutional after reviewing all questions of constitutionality raised by the answer, even though some of those issues were not applicable to the case before the court.[72]

Clinton dissented, arguing that *Prendergast* was the court's first advisory opinion. He believed that there was no case or controversy—that no party was before the court whose rights were affected by the act. C. Thomas White also dissented but on different grounds. He argued that two sections of the act were clearly unconstitutional. Clinton joined in White's dissent but refrained from calling the act unconstitutional because he did not believe that its constitutionality was an issue before the court.

McCown and Boslaugh each dissented in part but only with regard to the issue of standing. Boslaugh answered Clinton's advisory opinion attack, saying, "The issues raised in this case were of great public interest. This court would have been guilty of a disservice to the public if it had refused to decide the issues presented.[73] Here one sees shades of Mr. Dooley. Perhaps courts *do* follow the election returns.

The court appeared to act in lieu of legislative action in *Stadler v. Curtis Gas, Inc.* (1967). Stadler leased his home in Curtis from the Board of Regents of the University of Nebraska. The water heater in the home had a defective valve, and when it exploded the home burned. Stadler suffered serious burns and ultimately died from his injuries. Curtis Gas had serviced the heater and had learned that the valve was defective. It told the Board of the problem, but neither the Board nor Curtis Gas took any action to fix the valve. Stadler's administrator sued, and the Board appealed. The Board contended that it was an agency of the state and that as such, it was immune from tort liability. The supreme court reversed, holding that the administrator had the right to present evidence of the Board's negligence and stating that the Board could be liable when acting solely in a proprietary capacity.[74]

Newton dissented, and Paul White and Carter joined in a separate dissent, with Carter writing his own separate dissent as well. In all the dissents the judges argued that such a change in tort liability was really the role of the legislature, not the court. White explained, "What we are doing today is responding to the 'felt necessities of the time,' under the guise of judicial power. The end does not justify the means and an objective born of judicial impotence should not be accomplished by judicial usurpation." McCown and Spencer concurred, saying that the majority opinion did not constitute an immediate and complete abrogation of the entire doctrine of governmental immunity in Nebraska.[75]

The White court showed a strong penchant for self-protection in two cases involving Lydia Haug, an Omaha resident who delighted in suing members of

Table 6. Decisions of the White court, 1963–78

Total cases	4,148
Civil cases	2,911
Criminal cases	1,237
% of civil cases	70.18
% of criminal cases	29.82
Total cases, no. of affirmances	3,033
Total cases, % of affirmances	73.11
Criminal cases, no. of affirmances	1,081
Criminal cases, % of affirmances	87.39
Total cases, no. of reversals	797
Total cases, % of reversals	19.21
Criminal cases, no. of reversals	104
Criminal cases, % of reversals	8.40

the court and bar at the slightest provocation. Both cases, each entitled *Scudder v. Haug*, involved litigation between Charles Scudder, an Omaha lawyer who had previously represented Haug, and Haug herself. In both cases the trial court ruled against Haug and in favor of Scudder, and the supreme court affirmed in each case. The two supreme court opinions were *per curiam*, a device the White court utilized only fifty-seven times in fifteen years. Haug therefore could not easily identify her primary adversary on the bench.[76]

The White court wrestled with many thorny problems, the most difficult being those involving the death penalty. But it also displayed a willingness, at least on the part of some of the judges, to scrutinize the work of the legislature more closely, often falling only one vote short of invalidating legislative enactments. The court also displayed a modern attitude in setting out new guidelines for university governance and in prescribing new standards for the tort liability of governmental agencies. But it also adhered to traditional beliefs about the sanctity of land ownership, even if the owner was the state.

The court, expending its energies in the realm of criminal law primarily on death penalty issues, affirmed virtually all the other criminal cases it heard. It gave more thought and discussion to civil cases. Crime did not pay under the White court.

The Work of the Court

Table 6 reflects the work product of the White court. It was a busy court, hearing more cases in fifteen years than the Simmons court did in twenty-five. Spencer was its most prolific member in terms of opinions written, with

Table 7. White court opinions, 1963–78

JUDGE	NO. CONTRIBUTED[a]	% OF 4,148	RANK
P. White[b]	545	13.13	3
Carter	266	6.41	8
Messmore	45	1.08	12
Yeager	43	1.03	13
Spencer[b]	603	14.53	1
Boslaugh[b]	552	13.30	2
Brower	91	2.19	10
Smith	295	7.11	7
McCown	478	11.52	4
Newton	382	9.20	5
Clinton	310	7.47	6
Brodkey	155	3.73	9
C. T. White	52	1.25	11
Per curiam	57	0.13	
Retired and district judges	281	6.77	
Total	**4,155[c]**		

[a]Does not include dissents or concurrences.

[b]On court for entire period of White's incumbency.

[c]The court wrote seven opinions on matters not involving an actual case decision.

Boslaugh second and White third. McCown, Newton, and Clinton, who were all on the court for much of White's leadership, followed in that order in number of opinions authored. Retired and district judges called up to sit with the court authored 281 opinions, nearly 7 percent of the White court's opinion output.

In contrast, retired and district judges produced only 126 opinions under Simmons, a mere 3 percent of that court's decisions. The sharp increase in the number of cases decided with district judges reflects the worsening backlog of the court, but it pales in comparison to the number of decisions cranked out by retired and district judges during the subsequent terms of Norman Krivosha and William Hastings, when the court often sat in two five-judge panels. Table 7 reflects the opinion efforts of all judges during White's term.

Neither Simmons nor White led his court in the number of opinions written, though there is more of an apparent excuse for this smaller output for White, who became enmeshed in administrative duties midway through his term. But Simmons also led his court in dissents, while White was fourth in dissents

Table 8. Chief Justice White dissents, 1963–78

Total White dissents	97
Dissents as % of total cases heard by the court	2.33
No. of dissents in which White wrote an opinion	39
% of dissents in which White wrote an opinion	40.20
Total White sole dissents	2
Sole dissents as % of total White dissents	2.06

on his court. In absolute numbers, White dissented ninety-seven times, while Simmons dissented seventy-five times, but the White court dissented almost twice as often as the Simmons court, the most of all the four courts studied.

The White court dissented in 11.33 percent of all the cases it heard. Such a dissent rate seems laughably low when compared to the dissent rates of recent, more contentious courts, in which dissent rates have run as high as 40 percent. In Nebraska, however, where two of the four modern courts have dissent rates below 10 percent, the White court's rate indicates a real absence of unanimity.

The judges may have even disagreed more often than the dissent rate implies. As Hale McCown stated, in many cases that are less than unanimous, the judges in the minority either did not have the time or sense the necessity to write a dissent. The opinion appears to reflect a unanimous count, when in fact the decision could have been 4–3, 5–2, or 6–1.

McCown, with 173 dissents, was the clear leader of dissent on the White court, and he did not come to the court until 1965. Still, he averaged only 13.30 dissents a year. As one might expect, the three judges who served together for White's entire incumbency—Spencer, Boslaugh, and White—ranked next. Spencer authored 155 dissents, Boslaugh wrote 129, and White submitted 97. As judges came to the White court, they seemed quite willing to dissent from the inception. Only Newton, Brodkey, and C. Thomas White did not dissent in the first volume of Nebraska Reports issued after they joined the court, and Brodkey never dissented much at all, writing only seven dissents during White's term. Table 9 shows the dissents of all members of the White court.

McCown, the most enthusiastic dissenter, was easily the best lawyer of the members of the White court. A man of wide-ranging intelligence and, for Nebraska, a liberal social philosophy, his dissents often alerted the other members that they were venturing into the realm of error. For example, in a case that was decided by a six to one margin, McCown dissented from the notion

Table 9. Dissents by members of the White court, 1963–78

JUDGE	DISSENTS	% OF TOTAL CASES	RANK
P. White[a]	97	2.33	4
Carter	65	1.56	7
Messmore	3	0.07	13
Yeager	4	0.09	12
Spencer[a]	155	3.73	2
Boslaugh[a]	129	3.10	3
Brower	23	0.55	9
Smith	53	1.27	8
McCown	173	4.17	1
Newton	82	1.97	5
Clinton	81	1.95	6
Brodkey	7	0.16	11
C. T. White	18	0.43	10

Note:

Total cases decided by White court	4,148
No. of total cases in which there was a dissent	470
% of total cases in which one or more judges dissented	11.33

[a]On court for entire period of White's incumbency.

that a policeman could stop a car to check the driver's registration and license simply because the driver did not look as if he belonged in the car. The case ultimately wound up in federal district court, which upheld McCown's dissenting position. The Eighth Circuit reversed, and the case ultimately made it to the U.S. Supreme Court, which reversed the Eighth Circuit and upheld the validity of McCown's dissent and the ruling of the federal trial judge.

White's ninety-seven dissents constituted 2.33 percent of the cases decided by his court, but he frequently abjured writing an opinion when he was dissatisfied with the majority. He wrote a dissenting opinion in thirty-nine cases, or 40.2 percent of the cases in which he dissented. Usually he was content to join in another's dissent, a sign that he did not consider the dissent a tool with which to instruct his unenlightened brethren. He gave further, more emphatic evidence of this mindset with the fact that he was the sole dissenter on only two of the ninety-seven dissents he crafted. By contrast, Robert Simmons was the sole dissenter in 44 percent of the cases in which he dissented, or thirty-three out of seventy-five dissents.

White's use of the dissent could not have contrasted more with the tactics of Robert Simmons, his predecessor, who was far and away the most active dissenter on his court. If personal dissent rates are, as some scholars posit, evidence of a lack of leadership, then White was clearly a more effective leader than Simmons. But subjective criteria suggest that the opposite was true.

White's court dissented far more than Simmons's court, and White may well have been too busy with administrative matters to dissent. In 60 percent of his dissents, he eschewed writing an opinion and simply joined in the work of another judge. Although he was dealing with a much smaller and less diverse bar, Simmons appeared to be well accepted by lawyers, although there is a paucity of evidence in this regard. White's brush with the law, as well as his drinking, smoking, and personal style, all made him the butt of lawyers' often cruel humor.

What Did White Achieve?

The results of the White court would, in the parlance of Wall Street, best be described as mixed. The judges avoided the messy infighting of the Simmons battle period, but they submitted enough *accentatus*, *respondente*, and *caveat* statements to signal to the bar that all might not be well. The increased number of dissents might be construed to indicate "trouble in paradise." Election results, however, would indicate that the general public remained satisfied with the work of the court. A 78 percent rating in retention elections amounted to the lowest total of "yes" votes received by any judge during the White regime. Two judges—White and Clinton—received that rating at the polls. Bar polls, which indicated lawyer evaluations of the judges, were a few years away.

The court began to accumulate a substantial backlog of cases, but not because it was lazy. District judges came to the statehouse to sit with the court, but the court selected them carefully, and as a result, the district judges were unable to hear enough cases to impact the backlog significantly.[77] U.S. Supreme Court decisions and congressional enactments added to the workload by creating new causes of action. The public grew more litigation-conscious, and the court received many more appeals each year than it could readily accommodate. Clogged dockets are not unique to Nebraska. A flood of appeals is inundating appellate courts all over the country, even those courts that have discretion to accept or reject an appeal.

The court, in spite of White's peccadilloes, did not attract either a great deal of public attention or criticism. But a great deal of both awaited the court, with Norman Krivosha, Governor Exon's political jack-of-all-trades, waiting in the wings, ready to assume command when White retired to look after his family business. Krivosha's personality, management style, and attitude toward publicity and openness could not have been more different from White's and immediately promised a culture shock for both the court and the bar.

1. The Nebraska Supreme Court in 1939 after Simmons took office. Back row, *left to right*: Frederick W. Messmore, Bayard H. Paine, Edward F. Carter, Harvey M. Johnsen. Front row, *left to right*: William B. Rose, Robert G. Simmons, George A. Eberly. Photo courtesy of the Nebraska State Historical Society Photograph Collections.

2. The Simmons court, 1950. *Left to right*: Adolph E. Wenke, John W. Yeager, Edward F. Carter, Robert G. Simmons, Frederick W. Messmore, Elwood B. "Jimmy" Chappell, Paul E. Boslaugh. Photo courtesy of the Nebraska State Historical Society Photograph Collections.

3. William B. Rose.
Photo courtesy of the
Nebraska State Historical
Society Photograph
Collections.

4. Edward F. Carter.
Photo courtesy of the
Nebraska State Historical
Society Photograph
Collections.

5. Paul Boslaugh administering the oath of office to his son and successor, Leslie Boslaugh, January 1961. Photo courtesy of the Estate of Leslie Boslaugh.

6. Paul W. White. Photo courtesy of the Nebraska State Historical Society Photograph Collections.

7. Hale McCown.
Photo courtesy of the
Nebraska State Historical
Society Photograph
Collections.

8. Harry Spencer.
Photo courtesy of the
Nebraska State Historical
Society Photograph
Collections.

9. Norman Krivosha.
Photo courtesy of the
Nebraska Supreme Court.

10. The Krivosha court, 1984. Back row, *left to right*: Thomas M. Shanahan, William C. Hastings, D. Nick Caporale, John T. Grant. Front row, *left to right*: Leslie Boslaugh, Norman Krivosha, C. Thomas White. Photo courtesy of the Nebraska Supreme Court.

11. William C. Hastings.
Photo courtesy of the
Nebraska Supreme Court.

12. The Hastings court, 1990. Back row, *left to right*: John T. Grant, D. Nick Caporale,
Thomas M. Shanahan, Dale E. Fahrnbruch. Front row, *left to right*: Leslie Boslaugh,
William C. Hastings, C. Thomas White. Photo courtesy of the Nebraska Supreme Court.

4. The Norman Conquest
The Krivosha Court, 1978–87

By retiring in September 1978, Paul White allowed a new chief justice to take his place at the beginning of the September term of the supreme court. Terms of court in today's society are anachronistic. The Nebraska Supreme Court works year-round. The judges are busy enough that they cannot afford to take the summer off, as was their wont earlier in the twentieth century during the tenure of Chief Justice Robert Simmons. They do not hear cases during two summer months, but they are still in their offices, grinding out opinions.

Had White been more "modern" or politically attuned, he might have delayed his resignation until after the general election in November 1978. J. James Exon, a Democrat, was governor in 1978. In November Charles Thone, a Republican, won the gubernatorial seat rather easily, defeating Lieutenant Governor Gerald Whelan by a vote of 275,473 to 216,754.[1] Thone's victory was reasonably expected, and if White had wanted Thone to have the appointment, he could have timed his resignation for January 1979. Had he done so, no one knows whom Thone would have appointed as his successor, but it is virtually certain that it would not have been avid Democrat Norman Krivosha, unpaid counsel and trusted advisor to Democratic governor Exon. If Krivosha had not become chief justice, the course of the supreme court during the latter years of the twentieth century would have been much different, and much of the controversy that raged about the court might have never occurred. White's timing was critical.

According to former court administrator James Dunlevey, White resigned to devote more time to his family's business. Dunlevey was unsure what the business entailed, but he thought that it included ownership of a Holiday Inn near Chicago as well as a company that manufactured signs for Holiday Inns. Dunlevey did not know of any immediate need for White to rescue the enterprise.[2]

White's timing gave Exon the opportunity to put his choice in the chief jus-

tice's seat, and when Krivosha applied to the nominating commission, sage political observers felt that the result was virtually decided. Bill Hoppner, Exon's
chief of staff, asked Krivosha if he wanted the job. Krivosha replied that he
might consider it but only if Exon would not be embarrassed by his application.
Hoppner checked with Exon, and word came back to Krivosha that Exon had
no problem with Krivosha seeking the post. Krivosha maintains that he never
talked to Exon about the job prior to his appointment, other than through the
obligatory interview given to all successful candidates whose names were forwarded by the commission.[3]

Krivosha's chief rivals for the position were Judge Leslie Boslaugh, by then
a seventeen-year veteran of the court, and Omaha district judge John Burke.
Lancaster County district judge Dale Fahrnbruch was another applicant, and
the entire assemblage at the nominating commission hearing was startled
when a disgruntled litigant in Fahrnbruch's court appeared to voice strong,
if illogical, opposition to his appointment. He characterized Fahrnbruch as
a peevish, arrogant, ideological martinet—a description that some observers
felt came fairly close to the mark.

The Omaha bar pushed hard for Burke, feeling it was entitled to chose a chief
justice, and Omaha lawyers had a great deal of hard feeling toward Krivosha
when he was appointed. Burke, however, graciously accepted Krivosha's nomination and appeared to bear him no ill will.[4]

Krivosha was appointed on December 22, 1978. He had been Exon's point
man on political issues during virtually all of Exon's two gubernatorial terms,
starting in January 1971. He had incurred the wrath of the Lincoln Journal by
questioning the accuracy of its reporting on matters detrimental to Exon. He
and Exon were extremely close. Visiting Old Bailey while on a trip to London,
Dick Herman remembers sitting in the gallery watching the legal maneuvering unfold and being startled to see Exon and Krivosha enter, apparently on the
same sort of sight-seeing trip. It was his understanding that they were either
going to, or returning from, Israel, where Exon had been Krivosha's guest.[5]

Krivosha was a native of Detroit but lived in Lincoln for many years and attended the University of Nebraska for both his undergraduate and law school
education. After graduation and admission to the bar, Krivosha joined the
Lincoln firm of Ginsburg, Rosenberg, and Ginsburg.

In the late 1950s, when Krivosha joined the bar, Lincoln had no black or hispanic firms (it still does not), and the Ginsburg firm was the only Jewish firm of

consequence. Brothers Herman and Joe Ginsburg and Hyman Rosenberg were all excellent lawyers, well liked and respected by the bar. Krivosha—young, self-confident, and energetic—could not have had better mentors, and as he matured in the practice, he began to assume the major courtroom load for the firm. He became an excellent and indefatigable trial lawyer. Herman Ginsburg served as president of the Nebraska State Bar Association in 1966. The other members of the firm eschewed much activity in the organized bar, a fact that would prove somewhat difficult for Krivosha when he became chief justice.

Krivosha served as city attorney for Lincoln on an unpaid basis during the mayoral incumbency of Sam Schwartzkopf in the late 1960s, before Exon was elected governor. Krivosha was selected by a majority of the Lincoln City Council because the city attorney's office was in a chaotic state.[6] The incumbent city attorney had been moved laterally to another position by Schwartzkopf. Bill Davidson and Helen Boosalis, ardent Democrats and members of the council, led the charge for Krivosha. He worked at city hall all day Monday, the day of the council meeting, and mornings during the rest of the week. He trained his successor, Dick Wood, currently general counsel of the University of Nebraska, and added the services of Charles Humble and Jack Wolfe, now both successful Lincoln practitioners.

Krivosha's Impact

Unlike his predecessors Robert Simmons and Paul White, Norman Krivosha relished administrative detail and came to the court determined to function as leader of his colleagues, much in the same manner that the chief justice of the U.S. Supreme Court operates. He wanted to show his colleagues the way and to reshape legal doctrines that he believed were outmoded. He wanted to let the bright light of publicity shine upon the court, so the public would know who the judges were and how they operate.

All his goals were laudable. But he attained none of them. During Krivosha's incumbency, and despite Herculean labor on his part, the court continued to be bogged down in a morass of undecided cases. His colleagues, all older and more conservative than he was, resented his application of whip and spurs and preferred to work in anonymity, unknown to disgruntled litigants and potential assassins. Moreover, so many district judges were called up to sit with the court in order to alleviate the backlog of cases that the spate of new faces around the court's conference table sometimes stymied efforts of the court to sit down and formulate new and coherent legal doctrine.

Krivosha was a political figure when he came to the court. He was very well known in Lincoln, and his work in the Exon administration had brought him state-wide name recognition. His efforts to take control of the court ran afoul of the conservatism of his brethren and perhaps provoked jealousy on their part. Especially in the area of the death penalty, a particularly thorny issue for the Krivosha court, Krivosha was at odds with all his colleagues virtually all the time.

Despite the many obstacles, the Krivosha court achieved a great deal. It struggled valiantly to reduce the backlog of cases. It clarified death penalty law and offered innovative solutions to some issues in the law of torts. But Krivosha's well-publicized battles with Chicago columnist Mike Royko and the scathing personal criticism of Krivosha by Charles "Mike" Harper, the grandest nabob in Omaha society, gave the court public notoriety of a kind far different than Krivosha had hoped for. Instead of lauding the hard work and intellectual probity of the judges, the media opened the court to a barrage of public criticism, some of it well-founded.

Krivosha tried hard to establish cordial relationships between the bar and the court. But his penchant for taking charge led many of the state's lawyers to fear that he wanted to run the bar association as well as the court. His efforts ultimately worsened bar-court relationships and widened the divide between the court and its officers. Bar leaders understood and appreciated what Krivosha was trying to do, but the great bulk of Nebraska's lawyers viewed him as a liberal meddler.

Marching along Together—Krivosha's Court

When Krivosha took office, the other six members of the court, all White veterans, included Harry Spencer, Leslie Boslaugh, Hale McCown, Lawrence Clinton, C. Thomas White, and Donald Brodkey. However, that configuration changed quickly, as Spencer retired and was succeeded by Lancaster County district judge William C. Hastings in late January 1979. Brodkey retired in 1982 and was succeeded by Omaha district judge D. Nick Caporale. Clinton died in office in December 1982, and Ogallala attorney Thomas M. Shanahan replaced him in March 1983.

Hastings, a native of Newman Grove, Nebraska, got his law degree from the University of Nebraska in 1948, following service in World War II. He began his practice with the Lincoln firm of Chambers, Holland, and Dudgeon in 1948.

Both Guy Chambers and Lyle Holland were among Lincoln's top trial lawyers, and the firm did a vast amount of insurance defense work. Hastings quickly established himself as a competent trial lawyer and tried innumerable defense cases until he was appointed to the district court in 1965, after Chambers was no longer with the firm, and when Lyle Holland was waging a losing battle against substance abuse. Hastings served on the district bench as a very popular trial judge until his appointment to the supreme court.

Hastings had one interesting idiosyncrasy as a trial judge. His years of insurance defense work led him to question immediately the first lawyer to advance an argument on a motion or other pleading. The defense files many motions in district court, and so the plaintiff could enjoy the opportunity of seeing a defense-oriented judge in Hastings arguing with a defense lawyer. Lawyers on both sides would exercise all their ingenuity in an effort to avoid being the first to give their argument in Hastings's court. Hastings subsequently became chief justice when Krivosha resigned in 1987.

The final member of the Krivosha court was John T. Grant, a district judge from Omaha, who succeeded McCown when he retired in 1983. Judicial district gerrymandering allowed an Omaha judge to replace a jurist from Beatrice, thus giving Omaha, the state's largest city, two seats on the supreme court.

Taking the Court Public

Krivosha was a great believer in the public's right to know, including the right to know how the court worked and what type of work it did. He spoke at luncheon clubs, high school commencements, and almost anywhere else he could find an audience. He estimated that he made approximately two hundred public addresses per year, explaining the work of the court to the public. He "had the view that the public needed to respect the court and they wouldn't do it by being awed."[7] He also acknowledged that his colleagues were unhappy with his public tour. Some critics of his policy felt that he was removing the mystery from the court by speaking publicly so often, and that this mystery was what made the court almost sanctified. Others felt that he was improperly discussing sensitive judicial decisions, which Krivosha vehemently denied.

He instituted the practice of having the court sit at both the University of Nebraska and Creighton University law schools, so students could see firsthand how the court operated and dealt with issues. The court did not entirely support him on this measure either, with some judges preferring not to go to

Creighton because it meant an overnight stay in Omaha.[8] Krivosha wanted to take the court to small towns around the state, host a covered dish supper the night of the court's visit, and then have the court sit on the stage of the high school auditorium the next day. His colleagues would have none of it. Perhaps Krivosha's efforts to educate the public went for naught. The percentage of "yes" votes in judicial retention elections declined during his term and during the term of William Hastings, his successor as chief justice.

Enterprises of Great Pith and Moment, Their Currents Turn Awry

Krivosha's efforts at change and innovation cost him the support of his colleagues on many administrative matters, and that lack of support carried over to the juridical work of the court as well. If Krivosha took a position, the majority of the court opposed it. If he spelled out a rule in a majority opinion, there was sure to be a dissent criticizing the rule. And nowhere was this reaction more apparent than in cases involving the death penalty.

Krivosha came to the supreme court with a strong predilection against the death penalty. The court, having considered four significant first-degree murder cases during White's term, was not initially disposed to follow Krivosha's lead. Krivosha was not absolutely opposed to the penalty in every instance, but he was troubled when he compared cases in which the death penalty was imposed with cases in which it was not imposed: "Once the facts establish the totally unnecessary, meaningless and wasteful but deliberate killing of another, I have difficulty significantly distinguishing the circumstances under which the crime was committed."[9] He remained constant with that view.

Nebraska's death penalty sentencing statute, Sec. 29-2523, defines what constitutes aggravating and mitigating circumstances, for the consideration of the sentencing judge or panel. Paragraph (1)(d) of 29-2523 outlines as an aggravating circumstance that "the murder was especially heinous, atrocious, cruel, or manifested exceptional depravity by ordinary standards of morality and intelligence." The requirements are disjunctive, not conjunctive. Any one of them should be sufficient to establish proof of the existence of an aggravating circumstance. The Nebraska court said as much in State v. Palmer (1986).[10] Palmer robbed Grand Island coin merchant Eugene Zimmerman of coins, money, and jewelry. He tied Zimmerman hand and foot and placed him on an upstairs bed while he ransacked Zimmerman's store. Zimmerman's body was discovered by police. He had many bruises about his head and face, which preceded his death, his windpipe and voice box were broken, and police found an electrical cord wrapped around his neck. It was apparent that Palmer had beaten Zimmerman after he tied him up and before Zimmerman died.

Palmer was convicted of first-degree murder and sentenced to death. The sentencing panel found that the murder manifested exceptional depravity under Sec. 29-2523(1)(d). The Nebraska Supreme Court agreed. Palmer had questioned how (1)(d) was to be interpreted.[11] In response to Palmer, the court laid out the following rule:

> Thus, aggravating circumstance (1)(d) of Sec. 29-2523 describes in the disjunctive at least two distinct components of an aggravating circumstance which may relate to a murder and which "may operate in conjunction with or independent of one another". The presence of any of the components will sustain a finding that aggravating circumstance (1)(d) exists. . . . [R]egarding "heinous, cruel or depraved", such statutory expression is in the disjunctive, so either all or one could constitute an aggravating circumstance.
>
> As a meaning for the words "especially heinous, atrocious, cruel" found in circumstance (1)(d) of Sec. 29-2523, this court in State v. Simants, (citation omitted), has adopted the definition utilized by the Florida court in State v. Dixon, supra, that is, "especially heinous, atrocious, cruel" is directed to the conscienceless or pitiless crime which is unnecessarily torturous to the victim.
>
> In applying the "exceptional depravity" component of Sec. 19-2523(1)(d), we have interpreted and construed that phrase to mean "totally and senselessly bereft of any regard for human life."
>
> Therefore, for the purpose of Sec. 20-2523(1)(d) as an aggravating circumstance in determining whether the death penalty may be imposed, we hold that "exceptional depravity" in a murder exists when it is shown, beyond a reasonable doubt, that the following circumstances, either separately or collectively, exist in reference to a first degree murder: (1) apparent relishing of the murder by the killer; (2) infliction of gratuitous violence on the victim; (3) needless mutilation of the victim; (4) senselessness of the crime; or (5) helplessness of the victim.

We emphasize that we do not state, nor do we imply, that "exceptional depravity" may not exist independent of "especially heinous, atrocious, cruel", although existence of a murder which is "especially heinous, atrocious, cruel" may well establish "exceptional depravity" such as a murderer's relishing the victim's murder or infliction of gratuitous violence.

Manifesting Exceptional Depravity

The Palmer case was decided in 1986, over a year after the court's decision in *State v. Hunt* (1985).[12] In *Hunt* the supreme court based its arguments on the first part of (1)(d) rather than the "exceptional depravity" clause, much to its later chagrin. Hunt, the defendant, selected Beverly Ramspott as his victim after viewing her engagement photograph in the *Norfolk Daily News*. He shoplifted women's panties and nylons along with a BB gun and some nylon rope, and he then went to her mobile home and knocked on the door. When she opened the door, he pointed the BB gun at her and walked in. He demanded that she lie down on her kitchen floor. He tied her arms and legs with the stolen nylon rope, stuffed a pair of panties into her mouth, and dragged her into the living room. He took a nylon stocking and placed it around her neck, tightening it until he rendered her unconscious. He then untied the rope, took off her robe, and carried her nude into her bedroom where he masturbated, ejaculating onto her stomach. She still had a pulse. He then carried her into her bathroom, filled her bathtub with about a foot of water, and placed her in the tub, putting her head under water. Although unconscious, she was shaking and twitching while he placed her in the tub. He subsequently admitted that before putting her in the tub, he had performed oral sex on her, but "it didn't give me the kick that I thought it would." He stated that his intent was to kill Ms. Ramspott and to have sex with her body.[13]

Hunt was tried and convicted of first-degree murder and sentenced to death. The sentencing panel found that aggravating circumstances (1)(b) and (1)(d) were present in his actions. Aggravating circumstance (1)(b) is a murder committed to conceal the commission of a crime. The supreme court rightfully found that (1)(b) was not applicable in this case because the killing was obviously not done to conceal the commission of a crime. However, the court also found, in a 4–3 decision authored by D. Nick Caporale, that (1)(d) did not exist and reversed the death sentence, remanding the case for resentencing.[14]

Caporale did not distinguish between the first and second parts of (1)(d), as the court did a year later in Palmer. He instead used the first clause and held that because Ms. Ramspott was killed shortly after Hunt forced his way into her home, there was no evidence that the acts were performed for the satisfaction of inflicting either mental or physical pain or that the pain existed for any prolonged period of time. He stated, "In order for aggravating circumstance (1)(d) to be present, the method of killing must entail something more than the ordinary circumstances which attend any death-dealing violence."[15] Caporale cited State v. Reeves (1984)[16] but did not cite State v. Holtan (1977), a case in which the victims were herded into a bar's restroom, ordered to lie down, and then immediately shot.[17] The court found (1)(d) applicable in Holtan, a case in which the victims obviously were not apprehensive for their well-being for as long a period as Ms. Ramspott was in Hunt. Holtan killed on the spur of the moment. Hunt went to Ms. Ramspott's home with a well-designed plan for murder clearly in mind and with a coldly calculating purpose. Caporale also said, in concluding the opinion, that "although the method by which defendant achieved sexual gratification may be accurately described as exceptionally heinous and atrocious, and as manifesting exceptional depravity by ordinary standards of morality and intelligence, the murder itself, given the inherent nature of a killing, cannot."[18] Hunt's action was part of a carefully planned scheme of murder for sexual release, and Caporale confused the method of killing and the treatment of the victim. The court might also have added another factor, the mistreatment of, or heaping indignity on, the body of the victim.

Boslaugh, Shanahan, and Grant dissented, arguing that the second part of (1)(d) was applicable. Boslaugh, the author of the dissent, replied, "If this murder did not manifest exceptional depravity by ordinary standards of morality and intelligence, I am at a loss to imagine what type of a killing would conform to the statutory description." Clearly, under the rule announced in Palmer just a year later, Boslaugh would have been absolutely right. The per curiam opinion in Palmer did not cite Hunt. One can only assume that the clarification was the court's belated penance for what was a serious mistake, a mistake that brought down a firestorm of criticism in very short order.

Hunt was decided on August 9, 1985. Before the end of the month, the nationally syndicated columnist Mike Royko had beaten the court about the head and shoulders for its illogical confusion of act and scheme. In a column appearing in the Omaha World-Herald on August 30, 1985, Royko stated, in graphic language, his belief that Hunt's scheme was very heinous and that it clearly violated the statutory guidelines.[19] He then speculated that the judges in the majority would find it heinous if their robes were stuffed down their throats.

The court did not formally respond to Royko's column, but in a speech to a journalism class at the University of Nebraska–Lincoln shortly after the column appeared, Krivosha said that Royko apparently had not read the opinion, that he had the facts wrong, and that he did not understand what the court was saying.[20]

It did not take Royko long to return to the keyboard and lay into the court again. In a column appearing on September 22, 1985, Royko acknowledged that he had not read the opinion before he wrote the initial column and that he had received his information from news reports. He had read the opinion twice since Krivosha's criticism appeared, however, and in his new column he proceeded to call out Krivosha's criticism as nit-picking pettifoggery. He implied that the citizens of Nebraska should vote against retaining Krivosha in office when he next faced a retention election.[21]

Royko's call for Krivosha's job led the *Omaha World-Herald* to editorialize in favor of the Hunt majority. On October 2, the paper discussed Royko's column and the efforts of the four-judge majority to correctly apply the statute. The *World-Herald* wrote, "We think the four were wrong. But their decision was not capricious. They analyzed the meaning of the law, and tried to divine legislative intent. They studied the facts, and they reached their conclusion with what appeared to be painstaking care."

The four judges in the majority were Caporale, author of the opinion; Krivosha; C. Thomas White; and Hastings. The paper concluded: "The vote on whether to retain Judge White comes up next year. Judging by the intensity of the debate in recent weeks, the *Hunt* case may still be fairly fresh in many voters' minds. It would be unfortunate if one faulty decision should make the difference in the votes that determine whether White and the other three judges are retained."[22]

The journalistic angst of the *Lincoln Journal* and the *Norfolk Daily News* outweighed the *World-Herald*'s cautious approach. In editorials written shortly after the *Hunt* decision, both papers expressed the view that the court was in error and questioned whether opposition to the death penalty had guided the court in its deliberations.[23] Letters to the editors in the three papers expressed outrage at the *Hunt* decision and urged voters to bear the case in mind at the next judicial retention elections.[24]

Hunt has become the standard by which heinous murders are measured in Nebraska. Omaha defense attorney J. William Gallup, one of the premier criminal lawyers in Nebraska, says that he points to Hunt when he argues whether a killing is especially heinous. "You simply say, whatever your client did, it wasn't as heinous as what Hunt did—and he didn't get the death penalty."[25]

Krivosha, who was appointed in 1978, faced the voters only once before Hunt, in 1982. He received a "yes" vote of 77.48 percent at the time. He resigned in 1987 before his next examination by the electorate, which was scheduled for 1988.[26] C. Thomas White, the judge whose district encompassed Norfolk, the site of Hunt's murderous activity, had faced his first retention election in 1980. At the time his "yes" percentage was 77.24 percent. In 1986, a year after the Hunt decision, his percentage fell to 59.30 percent, clearly the result of citizen outrage against the court. When he faced the voters again in 1992, White's percentage had risen to 70.04 percent.[27]

Caporale, the author of the Hunt opinion, apparently suffered little or no fallout from Hunt. In 1986, just a year after the decision, his "yes" percentage in a retention election was 71.49 percent. In 1992, the only other time Caporale faced the voters, his "yes" percentage dropped to 69.11 percent.[28] Hastings had his first retention election as an associate judge of the court. In 1982 he garnered a "yes" percentage of 82.04 percent. He would have been scheduled for another election in 1988, but because he assumed the seat of chief justice after Krivosha's retirement in 1987, his next retention election was in 1990, when his approval percentage was 75.70 percent.[29]

All in all, with the exception of White, none of the judges who were in the majority in Hunt appeared to bear the brunt of the public's wrath. Why Caporale did not remains a puzzle, but because Krivosha was the object of Royko's scorn, in all likelihood the Omaha electorate that voted on Caporale may not have realized that he was the author of the unfortunate opinion.

Black Letter Law

Hunt was not the only death penalty case to occupy the Krivosha court, although it was by far the most controversial. A number of other murders, many with bizarre factual situations, came to the court for resolution.

Erwin Simants, whose death sentence had been affirmed by Paul White's court, made two appearances before the Krivosha court. In his first appearance, he filed a writ of error *coram nobis* some two years after his death sen-

tence had been affirmed. The basis for his writ was that Lincoln County sheriff Gordon Gilster, a prosecution witness, had visited the North Platte motel
where the Simants jury was sequestered during trial and had talked and played
cards with some of the jurors. The sheriff had testified at the trial, claiming
that Simants had been in jail before and that he seemed mentally alert when he
was arrested for the Kellie murders. Gilster had talked and played cards with
jurors, but the district court held that it was not prejudicial error and that the
testimony of the sheriff was cumulative and not critical.[30]

The supreme court reversed the district court's decision, and it vacated
Simants's convictions and death sentence. It held, in a McCown opinion, that
the sheriff was an important witness on the issue of Simants's sanity, the only
real issue in the trial. McCown said in his opinion, "We believe the better view
to be that when an improper communication with a juror or jurors is shown
to have taken place in a criminal case, a rebuttable presumption of prejudice
arises and the burden is on the state to prove that the communication was not
prejudicial."[31]

Simants came back to the court after he had been retried. In the second trial,
he was found not guilty by reason of insanity.[32] The district court thereafter,
acting as required by the verdict, found him to be mentally ill and dangerous to
others and committed him to the Lincoln Regional Center. Simants argued to
the supreme court that he was treated differently under the law because he had
been acquitted by reason of insanity, contending that at the Lincoln Regional
Center he was kept under much stricter surveillance and was given far fewer
privileges as an acquitted murderer than he would receive if he had simply been
mentally ill. The supreme court denied him any relief, and Simants remains
confined to the Lincoln center.

State v. Holtan was reprised twice, after first being disposed of by the White
court. Holtan's first appearance was from a denial of post-conviction relief.
As a procedure, post-conviction relief is different than either appeal or habeas
corpus and is utilized primarily to litigate issues not involved in the actual trial,
like newly discovered evidence or constitutional issues. The supreme court
affirmed in perfunctory fashion.[33] Holtan then went to the U.S. District Court
on a writ of habeas corpus, which was denied. He appealed the denial to the
Eighth Circuit, which reversed the district court and remanded the matter for
further proceedings. The Nebraska court now considered the very narrow question of whether it was an abuse of discretion for the Nebraska district court

to deny him the right to withdraw a plea of *nolo contendere*, or no contest. The supreme court held that it was not an abuse of discretion.[34]

Wesley Peery, who first surfaced during the Simmons court, was convicted of first-degree murder by the White court and sentenced to death. He made three appearances before Krivosha's court. He first visited the court on a motion for new trial, claiming that the prosecution had suppressed certain exculpatory evidence. Neither the trial court nor the supreme court found any validity to his claim.[35]

His next effort was a claim for post-conviction relief on the grounds that the death penalty was unconstitutional. In an opinion written by McCown, the supreme court found the argument to be both specious and *res judicata*.[36] His third appearance was on another claim for post-conviction relief, in which he alleged that jurors opposing the death penalty were eliminated from his jury panel and that his trial counsel was not effective. The supreme court held against him on both grounds.[37]

While brushing aside the reiterative appearances of Simants, Holtan, and Peery, the court gave careful attention to other cases. In *State v. Williams* (1979), the court considered the appeal of a frequent felon who raped a woman vaginally and anally, shot her in the head twice, and then shot her roommate three times. The same day he raped yet another woman in Lincoln, and the next day he raped and killed a woman in Iowa. He was tried and convicted of two counts of first-degree murder.[38]

The sentencing panel found that the aggravating factors outweighed the mitigating factors and sentenced Williams to death. The supreme court agreed with the sentence. It reviewed thirty-two first-degree murder cases. In an opinion authored by McCown, the court stated, "Analysis of all these cases indicates that a callous, cold-blooded and cruel disregard for human life, coupled with convictions for previous crimes involving violence to the person has tended to be given great balancing weight as aggravating circumstances, and that extreme youth, coupled with the absence of any substantial record of previous criminal conduct, has tended to be given great balancing weight as mitigating circumstances."[39] Williams was thus doomed by his age and past criminal record of violent sexual assaults.

Krivosha concurred in part and dissented in part. He stressed the comparison issue: "Once the facts establish the totally unnecessary, meaningless and wasteful but deliberate killing of another, I have difficulty significantly distinguishing the circumstances under which the crime was committed."⁴⁰ After many court appearances and almost two decades on death row, Williams was executed in Nebraska's electric chair on December 2, 1997.

Harold "Willie" Otey came before the Supreme Court twice before he, like Williams, met his fate in the electric chair on September 2, 1994. Otey, a groom at the Ak-Sar-Ben race track in Omaha, raped and robbed a young Omaha woman, cut her in the head with a knife, told her he was going to kill her, stabbed her, hit her in the head with a hammer, and strangled her with a belt. He was tried, convicted and sentenced to death. The three-judge panel found that aggravating circumstance (1)(d) was applicable, and the supreme court agreed.⁴¹ In an opinion by Judge Boslaugh, the court also found that the death sentence was not excessive or disproportionate when compared to other death penalty cases. Krivosha concurred in part and dissented in part on the issue of the death penalty.

Otey filed a motion for post-conviction relief. He was denied permission to attend the hearing but testified by deposition. He alleged that the denial of attending was error and also alleged ineffective assistance of counsel. The supreme court cited the statute that said the prisoner did not have to be in attendance at the hearing, and it held that there was no error in having Otey testify by deposition. As to the claim of ineffective assistance of counsel, the court pointed out that at trial the "defendant did not claim that he was innocent, gave counsel no facts which could be the basis for a defense, and was of little help in any of the preparations for trial. Against this background, defendant's claims made now that he did not have adequate assistance of counsel are not persuasive."⁴²

Krivosha departed from his usual stance of opposition to the death penalty in *State v. Anderson and Hochstein* (1980), an opinion he wrote.⁴³ Anderson, an employee of Ron Abboud, employed Hochstein to shoot Abboud, and Hochstein did so for a fee of fifteen hundred dollars. The duo were tried, convicted and sentenced to death. On appeal, they argued that the sentencing panel had misapplied aggravating and mitigating circumstances. Krivosha countered,

> To the contrary, when this case is compared to the other 32 cases
> noted by this court in *State v. Williams*, supra, and examined in light
> of Neb. Rev. Stat. Sec 29-2523 (Reissue 1979), it clearly speaks in
> favor of imposing the death penalty. While the author of this opin-

ion has heretofore disagreed with imposing the death penalty in certain of the cases reviewed by this court, finding that they were not sufficiently different from those cases in which the death penalty had not been imposed, the author has no such difficulty in this case. The appellant's absolute and total disregard for the value of human life as displayed by the evidence in this case makes it separate and different from any other case previously considered by this court. . . . Hochstein's willingness to kill another for $1,500 displays how little he valued another's life. The evidence in this case of the careful, deliberate premeditation and malice aforethought make this type of crime exactly the type contemplated by the "aggravating and mitigating circumstances" standards of our statutes.[44]

Krivosha's analysis seemed to rely on the second prong of (1)(d)—the exceptional depravity of the killer—rather than on the first prong—the especially heinous acts against the victim. Abboud was shot and from all accounts died instantly. He was not tortured or abused prior to death. If the murder in *Hunt* was not especially heinous, neither was the murder in *Anderson and Hochstein*. One could logically question why killing for money outraged Krivosha so, in contrast to his position in *Hunt*, where Hunt killed in cold blood in furtherance of a deliberate scheme to obtain perverted sexual satisfaction. Be that as it may, in at least one death penalty case, Krivosha came down on the side of electrocution.

State v. Harper (1981) was another first-degree murder case with rather bizarre facts.[45] Steven Harper had been in a romantic relationship with Sandra Johnson. She terminated it and married Duane Johnson. Harper went to the house of Sandra's mother and wounded her mother and brother with a shotgun blast. He was tried, convicted, and incarcerated. When he got out of prison, he took a job caring for research animals at the Eppley Research Institute in Omaha. He had access to carcinogens, stole some, gained access to Sandra's home, and poisoned milk and lemonade in her refrigerator. Several of her family became ill, and her husband and nephew died lingering, painful deaths. Harper was tried, convicted, and sentenced to death. The supreme court affirmed the death sentence, finding that there were clearly aggravating circumstances. Krivosha dissented, saying, "I find no other alternative but to conclude that the Constitution of the United States and the Constitution of the State of Nebraska preclude the imposition of the death penalty except in but a few extremely isolated cases."[46]

Harper's scheme was carefully planned, but it was not at all victim-specific. Sandra Johnson, her children, her husband, or any visitors could have been victims of Harper's plan. Such action would seem to indicate that he was totally bereft of any regard for human life. Krivosha did not discuss the details of Harper's plan in his dissent, nor did he assail the second prong of "exceptional depravity."

State v. Reeves (1984), a *per curiam* opinion, was the next major death case to come before the Krivosha court.[47] Reeves, drunk and under the influence of peyote, raped and stabbed Janet Mesner and also killed Victoria Lamm, who apparently died instantly. Mesner lived long enough to reach a phone, call police, and identify Reeves. She was in great pain until her death. Reeves was found guilty on two first-degree murder counts, and the sentencing panel gave him the death penalty. He appealed.

The supreme court found that (1)(d) applied because Janet Mesner had tried to defend herself and had engaged in a violent struggle with Reeves. She did not die at once. She lived for hours and suffered greatly. The court found that two aggravating circumstances outweighed one mitigating circumstance. The court reviewed fifty-eight cases to see if the death penalty was disproportionate and said, "Our analysis is not confined to a mere counting process of aggravating and mitigating circumstances, but, rather, to a reasoned judgment as to what factual situations require the imposition of death and which of those can be satisfied by life imprisonment in light of the totality of the circumstances present." Krivosha dissented as to the death penalty. Reeves's case was heard again by the Nebraska court in 2000. His sentence of death was vacated, and the case was remanded for sentencing.[48] In September 2001 Lancaster County attorney Gary Lacey decided not to ask for the death penalty for Reeves, who instead received a life sentence for the murders.[49]

Krivosha's oft-repeated dissents on first-degree murder death sentences make it quite clear that he evolved to believe that no one person or group could make a rational judgment as to when the death penalty was merited. He seems to suggest that in the absence of some foolproof and mechanical fact-finder, the penalty could not, and should not, be imposed. But if one recognizes that human fallibility always exists, what group could more safely and properly be assigned the responsibility for determining when the circumstances of a killing were sufficient to invoke the death penalty than a state supreme court, especially one charged with the statutory responsibility of reviewing prior cases to determine whether circumstances in one case equated with those in another. Of course, the supreme court's review would be at the appellate level because the U.S. Supreme Court has held that if a trial judge or judges determine the presence or absence of aggravating factors contained in a death penalty sentencing statute, they violate the defendant's Sixth Amendment right to a jury trial in capital cases.[50]

State v. Joubert, decided in 1986, was a first-degree murder case in which Krivosha maintained the position that there was only one prong to (1)(d): the first, or "exceptionally heinous," prong. In a per curiam opinion, the majority held otherwise.[51] John Joubert, an airman at Offut Air Force Base near Bellevue, abducted, tortured, and killed two young boys in separate incidents. Each boy was stabbed to death, each knew he was going to die, and each suffered both physically and emotionally, according to expert testimony. When Joubert was arrested on an unrelated matter, he confessed to the two murders. He pleaded guilty to two counts of first-degree murder. A three-judge panel sentenced him to death. He appealed, claiming he had been promised benefits for pleading guilty and that the panel was wrong in finding that (1)(d) applied. The supreme court affirmed and upheld the death sentence.[52] The sentencing panel had found that (1)(d) was applicable to the second murder, because Joubert by then had a history of serious, assaultive criminal activity as a result of the first murder. The supreme court agreed. The sentencing panel also found that (1)(b) applied to both murders, as both boys were killed in part because Joubert wished to conceal his identity. The supreme court agreed.

The sentencing panel discussed (1)(d) at length. It came up with a legal analysis that was subsequently adopted by the Nebraska Supreme Court as its own. In speaking of (1)(d), the panel concluded, "This aggravating circumstance describes in the disjunctive two separate situations which may operate in conjunction with, or independently of, one another. The first is where the murder is especially heinous, atrocious or cruel. In short, the first situation must be looked upon through the eyes of the victim. With respect to the second clause of this aggravating circumstance, the crime must be viewed to determine the defendant's state of mind as manifested by his conduct." The supreme court approved the findings of the sentencing panel and also determined that proportionality had been satisfied: "We have determined that the purpose of that statute is to insure that no sentence imposed shall be greater than those imposed in other cases with the same or similar circumstances and that the review should include only those cases in which the death penalty was imposed."[53]

Krivosha concurred in the result and said that Joubert deserved to die, but he reiterated his view that there was only one prong, the "especially heinous" clause. He also argued with the court's position that the proportionality review could be used only with cases in which first-degree murder had been charged and the death penalty imposed.[54] Joubert was executed on July 17, 1996. Following Krivosha's concurrence in *Joubert*, in *Moore v. Kinney* (2002) a panel of the Court of Appeals for the Eighth Circuit threw out the "exceptional depravity" clause of (1)(d), holding that a sentencing panel could not rely on Nebraska Supreme Court decisions narrowing and construing the "exceptional depravity" language because the language from the decisions offered only "subjective and unilluminative fragments." Carey Dean Moore had shot and killed two Omaha cabdrivers, robbing them in the process. He loitered about a cabstand and engaged older drivers, whom he thought he could overpower, to take him on fictitious errands. While riding with them, he shot and killed two. He was tried, convicted, and sentenced to death for his depraved scheme of coldly selecting older drivers.[55] *Moore* held that the language of the second prong, even as defined and limited by case law, was unconstitutionally vague and provided "insufficient guidance to a sentencing body."[56] The decision was challenged and was heard *en banc* by the entire bench of the Eighth Circuit late in the fall of 2002. The full court reversed the panel and upheld the second prong.[57] The first, or "especially heinous," prong, has thus far passed muster with the federal court.

Non–Death Penalty Murders

The Krivosha court found any number of complicated criminal cases that stretched the law and engaged a concerned public. For example, the Krivosha court wrestled with a hot potato in the manslaughter case of *State v. Ellis* (1981). Deborah Forycki, a University of Nebraska–Lincoln student, disappeared without warning, and over a year later her remains were found in an antique water wagon on a Cass County farm near Elmwood. John R. Ellis was tried in Lancaster County and convicted of manslaughter. In a 4–3 *per curiam* opinion, the court upheld the conviction, with Krivosha, McCown, and Brodkey dissenting.[58]

Many questions surrounded the conviction. The body was found in Cass County, but the trial was in Lancaster County. Where did the killing take place? What was the proper venue for the trial? There was no proof as to the cause of death nor proof that Ellis and Forycki knew each other. There was no proof Forycki was killed as the result of a sudden quarrel or in the commission of a crime, necessary elements of a manslaughter charge.

The case was a sensational one, and the Lincoln papers were full of news reporting the discovery of the body, the investigation, and the trial. The prosecution presented evidence showing that Ellis had assaulted two other women, one on the same farm, some one hundred and fifty feet from where Forycki's body was found. Virtually all of the prosecution's case was circumstantial, and on appeal the prosecution struggled to prove beyond a reasonable doubt that Ellis was guilty.[59]

In another sensational criminal case, convicted murderer Harold D. Nokes came back to the court with a request for post-conviction relief. His request was quickly dispatched in an opinion by Boslaugh, who set out the rule, "A motion to vacate a judgment and sentence under the Post Conviction Act cannot be used as a substitute for an appeal or to secure a further review of issues already litigated.[60]

One of the worst monsters in Nebraska legal history made his first appearance before the court in *State v. Ryan*.[61] Michael Ryan, head of a bizarre religious sect and a right-wing antigovernment fanatic, operated a camp on a farm near Rulo. He was arrested and pled guilty to possessing a machine gun. Stolen merchandise worth $125,000 was found at the farm, including thirty-five weapons, some of which were automatic, and ninety-seven thousand rounds of ammunition. Ryan was sentenced to five years in prison. He appealed, claiming that the trial court, in fixing his sentence, relied on material not contained in the presentence report, and that the sentence was excessive.

The trial judge stated at the sentencing that he was taking into consideration public statements made by Ryan. Ryan's counsel did not move for a specification of those comments, and the supreme court, in affirming, felt that such a failure obviated any harmless error which might have resulted from the judge's action.[62] Subsequently, Ryan was arrested, tried, and found guilty of two counts of first-degree murder in the slayings of one of his adherents and a young child. His conviction was affirmed, and he is still on death row.

In the *Ellis*, *Nokes*, and *Ryan* cases, the Krivosha court showed that it could be very firm in dealing with criminals when the death penalty was not involved. Even Krivosha, often castigated for his "bleeding-heart" attitude in death penalty cases, had no difficulty giving short shrift to malefactors if the electric chair was not looming in the background.

"Our Chief Justice Speaks With an Eastern Accent"

Criminal law was not the only area where the Krivosha court became embroiled in controversy. Corporate law, especially in the area of corporate takeovers—not something one would usually associate with Nebraska's economy—provoked a great controversy between the court and the bar association on one hand and one of Nebraska's well-known business titans on the other.

Charles M. "Mike" Harper, a former King of Ak-Sar-Ben, Omaha's grandest social organization, was the man who turned Nebraska Consolidated Mills, once a sleepy grain-dealing enterprise, into one of America's largest and most powerful diversified agricultural colossi, ConAgra. Harper decided that ConAgra ought to buy MBPXL, a meatpacking operation doing business primarily at Rockport, Missouri. After protracted negotiations, ConAgra and the MBPXL board agreed upon a purchase price for MBPXL to be paid by ConAgra and signed a contract for the sale. Before the agreement was submitted to the MBPXL shareholders for their approval, Cargill, Inc., a very large, privately owned company in Minneapolis, came forward with a more attractive offer than the ConAgra offer, and the MBPXL board recommended to its stockholders that they accept the Cargill offer, which they did. ConAgra thereupon sued Cargill for tortious interference with a business relationship in district court in Omaha. The district court gave ConAgra a judgment for $15,996,000. Cargill appealed the decision, and the Nebraska Supreme Court reversed, denying ConAgra its huge judgment.[63]

The supreme court determined that the major issue in the case was to determine what obligation a corporate board of directors had, pursuant to a merger agreement, prior to the approval of the merger by the respective stockholders. The court said, "The appellants [Cargill] assert that ConAgra has no claim to the 'benefits' of the bargain because consummation of the merger agreement was dependent upon and subject to the approval of the shareholders of MBPXL and ConAgra. . . . [W]e cannot imagine a greater duty owed to shareholders than advising them of the existence of a higher offer for their stock before asking them to approve a lower offer."[64]

The court rendered a *per curiam* opinion in the ConAgra case. On the majority side were Krivosha, Boslaugh, District Judge William Rist of Beatrice, and retired district judge William Colwell of Pawnee City. White, Grant, and Shanahan dissented in an opinion authored by White.

Rist and Colwell had been appointed to hear the ConAgra case because Hastings and Caporale had disqualified themselves. Colwell had for years been the court's top replacement whenever a judge could not sit, and Rist was only forty miles away from Lincoln. Both of them were from the same supreme court district as Hastings, a fact that was to become significant later on.

Cargill was represented on appeal by the Lincoln law firm of Cline, Williams, the largest firm in the capitol city. Frederic Kauffman, who argued the appeal, was the firm's leading litigator. Kauffman had represented Krivosha in the past, successfully defending a legal malpractice case brought when Krivosha was a member of the Ginsburg firm in private practice.

The supreme court handed down its decision on Friday, March 7, 1986. The following day, in the *Omaha World-Herald*, Harper had a ballistic response. As reported by the newspaper,

> Harper was especially critical of Chief Justice Norman Krivosha and indicated that the company put primary blame on Krivosha for the decision. "I hope we stay here (in Omaha) forever," Harper said. But he said the company must consider whether it is being harmed by "the quality of justice" in Nebraska. Harper continued, "A lot of Eastern investment bankers and lawyers have been following this case, hoping the law of the jungle prevails, so they can make a ton of money."
>
> Of Krivosha, Harper said: "our chief justice speaks with an Eastern accent." Harper called the Supreme Court decision "a miscarriage of justice."[65]

The Nebraska State Bar Association had a "Committee to Support the Legal System" at the time. It was chaired by retired district judge John C. Burke of Omaha, president of the Omaha Bar Association and general counsel of Boys Town. Burke had been one of Krivosha's most significant rivals for the position of chief justice. The purpose of the committee was to come to the defense of judges who, according to the committee, had been inappropriately attacked in public and who were not in a position, because of judicial ethics and con-

straints, to come to their own defense. The committee contacted me because at
the time I was the state bar president, and it asked if a response to Harper's out-
burst could be formulated on behalf of the bar association. In Burke's words,
"If we are to be an effective committee in the future, we are going to have to
develop a system of early response; otherwise, falsehoods will be criss-cross-
ing the state while truth is putting on her boots."[66]

On March 14 I responded to Harper by letter, coming to the defense both
of Krivosha and the court. (The full text of the letter is given in appendix 2.) I
questioned what evidentiary basis Harper had for any of his conclusions about
Krivosha's aid to financial interests. I also told Harper that while legislators
might try to aid Nebraska citizens, courts looked to the facts and to the law, not
to the identity or citizenship of the parties, when they decided cases.[67]

On Saturday, March 15, Harper responded to my letter in an interview with
Robert Dorr of the World-Herald. Harper retorted, "I find it curious that [Hewitt]
goes on for 2 ¼ pages on a case that he knows absolutely nothing about."
Editorial comment was divided, with the McCook Gazette and the Lincoln Journal
weighing in on the side of Krivosha and the court and the Omaha World-Herald
thundering to the side of Harper.[68] Law journals and teachers came down on
the side of the court. Roland J. Santoni of Creighton Law School approved the
court's decision in an article in the Creighton Law Review,[69] and Professor Stephen
E. Kalish of the University of Nebraska–Lincoln College of Law wrote in the
Lincoln Journal that the ConAgra case clarified a corporate director's responsibilities and would become an important decision in corporate law.[70]

As charges, counter-charges, and insults were exchanged, ConAgra filed a
motion with the supreme court, invoking Ruehle and asking the court to throw
out the decision because it felt that the panel that heard ConAgra was improperly constituted. In Ruehle, the case that started the warfare on the Simmons
court, Judge Edward R. Carter contended that the court had called a district
judge to sit with it without statutory authority to do so. ConAgra contended
that in their case it was not necessary to replace Hastings and Caporale, because five supreme court judges were enough to hear the case; that if replace-
ments were necessary, they should have been selected from the three retired
supreme court judges (Paul White, Spencer, and McCown) rather than by appointing district judges; that there was absolutely no basis for appointing
Rist; and that both Rist and Colwell came from the same supreme court judicial district. The motion criticized Krivosha's appointment of the two district

judges, Krivosha's relationship with Frederic Kauffman—terming it "hardly distant"—and Krivosha conducting some prehearing proceedings before the case was heard by the supreme court.

The ConAgra motion was overruled in its entirety by a court consisting of Krivosha, Boslaugh, White, Shanahan, and Grant. Citing *Ruehle*, the court retraced the extensive Simmons concurrence in that case and held that both Rist and Colwell were de facto judges and that a litigant could not challenge de facto authority. The court also said, in its best response, that ConAgra had not raised the issue about Rist and Colwell until after the opinion had been issued, even though ConAgra had actual notice at oral argument, before the case was submitted or decided, that Rist and Colwell were sitting, and that it should have raised the issue at that time.[71]

After the court's decision the case closed, and whether or not the decision seriously harmed ConAgra is a matter of opinion. This much is certain. ConAgra is still in Omaha, with an extensive campus almost on the banks of the Missouri. Bruce Rohde, one of ConAgra's attorneys, was until 2005 head of ConAgra after Harper retired in 1992. ConAgra's stock price is less than it was in Harper's halcyon days. How much of the decline is attributable to Cargill's victory cannot be ascertained, yet ConAgra earnings are up, and Rohde earned several million dollars in 2001.

Harper's diatribe was obviously the result of his disappointment over losing a substantial judgment. But based on both fact and the current state of the law, his loss was deserved, and the court's attempt to protect shareholders was quite correct. It is not possible to determine what ConAgra's future litigation strategies will be, but the company should know that assailing the supreme court and its leader in the popular press is risky business.

Civil Wrongs Are Righted

Beginning law students generally find that the definition of a tort—a "civil wrong"—is less than helpful. They struggle to grasp nebulous concepts such as negligence, duty, and foreseeability. Once they master these concepts, however, law students and lawyers tend to separate themselves into two clearly delineated groups: those who favor expanded tort liability, and those who do not. The exact definition of tort liability remains in flux, expanding or contracting depending on the factual pattern in any given case.

The Krivosha court considered four significant tort cases, and in these cases it defined itself neither as a liberal plaintiff's court nor as a conservative defendant's court. At least one of its decisions was quite progressive, breaking new ground in allowing recovery, while another paid at least lip service to the moral posture of an earlier era.

James v. Lieb (1985) was an opinion authored by C. Thomas White, who is generally acknowledged to be a strong advocate for plaintiff's rights. It was a groundbreaking decision with regard to the right to recover for the negligent infliction of emotional distress.[72] Gregory James and his sister were riding their bicycles. Gregory saw a garbage truck back into and over his sister and her bike, killing her, and he was too far away to try to help her. He was not hurt or even touched by the truck, but he became physically ill, and according to the medical evidence, would continue to suffer mental anguish and emotional distress as a result of seeing his sister killed.

White extensively reviewed the law in Nebraska and elsewhere in the United States and stated Nebraska's new rule: "We hold that a plaintiff bystander has a cause of action for negligently inflicted foreseeable emotional distress upon a showing of marital or intimate familial relationship with a victim who was seriously injured or killed as a result of the proven negligence of a defendant."[73] The new rule liberalized Nebraska's law and brought it into accord with prevailing American jurisprudence. Krivosha concurred, adding, lest there be any doubt, "[F]rom this point forward one in Nebraska may recover for emotional distress proximately caused by the defendant's negligence even if no physical injury is sustained."[74] Boslaugh, Caporale, and Hastings, who had previously worked primarily on the defense side, dissented.

In Kreifels v. Wurtele (1980), a suit involving the constitutionality of Nebraska's guest statute, White again sided with the majority but did not establish a new rule. The guest statute denied recovery to a passenger in an automobile accident unless the driver has been guilty of gross negligence. The purpose of the act was to prevent collusive actions against insurance companies, but it had long been an obstacle for plaintiff's lawyers.

Jimmy Kreifels, aged thirteen, was a passenger on a motorcycle driven by fourteen-year-old Randy Wurtele. Randy negligently entered an intersection and hit a car, injuring Jimmy. Jimmy's father sued on his behalf. The trial court dismissed the petition based on the guest statute. The supreme court reversed.[75] Jimmy asked the court to reconsider its previous decision in Botsch v. Reisdorff,[76] a 1975 decision of the White court that had upheld the constitutionality of the guest statute. The court declined to do so because five judges could not be found to overturn the guest statute, but the court did find that Randy was guilty of gross negligence, thus giving Jimmy a chance at recovery even though the guest statute remained intact.

Krivosha sent a clear message to the bar in *Kreifels*. Concurring in part and dissenting in part, he said,

> While the majority has correctly noted that there are, as yet, insufficient votes on this court to reconsider our decision in *Botsch v. Reisdorff*, 193 Neb. 165, 226 N.W. 2d 121 (1975), I would not wish to leave the impression that that holding is so firmly supported that it should not continue to be considered. I, for one, would join with the as yet less than constitutional majority who would reconsider our decision in the *Botsch* case and would hold that our guest statute is unconstitutional on the basis of the 14th Amendment to the United States constitution. It seems clear to me that our guest statute does, indeed, deny to certain persons within our jurisdiction equal protection of the laws.[77]

In an intriguing development, White, who wrote the majority opinion, joined with McCown in adopting Krivosha's dissent and appeared to be on both sides of the case.

A more conservative view of the law, which also included a deferential nod to legislative authority, prevailed in *Smith v. Columbus Community Hospital* (1986).[78] Barbara Smith delivered a stillborn male child, and she sued on his behalf for wrongful death, alleging negligence on the part of the hospital. The hospital's demurrer was sustained, and when Smith declined to plead further, the suit was dismissed. She appealed.

The court defined the case as follows: "The sole question raised in this appeal is whether or not the personal representative of the estate of an unborn child, as a viable fetus which dies prior to birth as a result of another's negligence, has a cause of action for damage recoverable under the Nebraska wrongful death statute." The court answered the question in the negative, reaffirming its decision in *Drabbels v. Skelly Oil Co.* (1951). In *Drabbels*, which was decided by the White court, the supreme court had refused to consider a child born dead as a person for purposes of maintaining a wrongful death action. Deferring to the legislature, the court said, "[I]f a viable fetus is to be included within the scope of the Nebraska wrongful death statute, Sec. 30-809, the right to recover under the wrongful death statute is still a matter for legislative enactment so expressing and not a matter for this court to include in the wrongful death statute a cause of action of a child born dead."[79] The legislature later accepted the court's invitation to change the law with the passage of LB294 in the 2003 session.[80]

Finally, in *Vacek v. Ames* (1985), the supreme court rendered a decision more in keeping with the jurisprudential notions of 1915.[81] Donald Vacek sued G. Ronald Ames for alienation of affections and criminal conversation. Cherie Vacek, Donald's wife, was Ames's secretary. Their relationship grew to be quite warm. They traveled together and admittedly engaged in illicit sexual intercourse. A jury gave Vacek a verdict for $100,000. The trial court found the damages to be excessive and granted a new trial on the issue. The trial judge set aside the verdict of criminal conversation, stating that such actions should not be considered criminal in modern day Nebraska.

The supreme court reversed, holding that the $100,000 in damages for alienation were not excessive. The court also reinstated the verdict for criminal conversation, a cause of action pertaining to a spouse's right to the exclusive privilege of sexual intercourse.[82] Since January 9, 1986, Nebraska law has provided that no action for alienation of affections or criminal conversation can be brought.[83]

Krivosha, White, and Boslaugh dissented in the case, arguing that the $100,000 award of damages was in reality punitive damages, which are not allowed in Nebraska. They also maintained that actions for criminal conversation, a common law as opposed to a statutory cause of action, should not exist in Nebraska. The defense had all the better of it, and the case appeared to be a sport, just like Mrs. Vacek and Mr. Ames.

The Krivosha court showed real movement toward a more liberal position concerning tort matters in *James v. Lieb*, allowing recovery for emotional distress. And though it did not overturn the guest statute in *Kreifels v. Wurtele*, it allowed recovery and suggested that the guest statute might be thrown out if the right case came along. It maintained Nebraska's prior conservative position in *Smith v. Columbus Community Hospital*, leaving it up to the legislature to give unborn children rights under the wrongful death statute. Krivosha's efforts, along with those of C. T. White, bore some fruit, but some social change takes years to ripen.

Business Law and the Krivosha Court

The Krivosha court felt obligated to intervene in the economy to protect competition and to modernize business law. Several cases illustrate this dual concern. The court adopted an equal protection constitutional argument in *Casey's General Stores v. Nebraska Liquor Control Commission* (1985).[84] Casey's, a chain of convenience stores, had beer licenses at its stores in Albion and Beatrice. Sec. 53-124.01 of Nebraska's statutes prohibited any person or business from having an interest in more than two beverage licenses, unless the applicant was a hotel chain with at least twenty-five rooms per hotel, a bowling alley, a city, or a restaurant. Casey's applied for a beer license for its store in Stanton. The Liquor Control Commission denied the application. Casey's appealed to the district court, which dismissed the appeal. Casey's then went to the supreme court, which reversed and remanded the case to the liquor commission.

In an opinion written by Judge William Hastings, the court accepted the equal protection argument and said that the classifications set out in the statute were unjust and discriminatory. The court held that the original purpose for keeping chain stores out of the liquor business no longer obtained: "[T]he original policy of favoring local businesses to avoid chain store monopoly of the liquor industry flies in the face of recent case law denouncing legislative attempts to destroy lawful competition."[85] The court proceeded to declare Sec. 53-124.01 unconstitutional.

The Law Merchant

ConAgra was the biggest business law decision rendered by the Krivosha court, both in import and in dollar amount, but at least two other cases were of considerable significance.

Doyle v. Union Ins. Co. (1979) was a class action on behalf of the policyholders of a mutual casualty insurance company.[86] The policyholders alleged that the directors had sold the assets of the insurer to a newly formed stock company for much less than their actual value. The state director of insurance had approved the plan in which the mutual company ceded all its business to the new stock insurer, and the majority of policyholders had approved the transaction. But the district court still found for the plaintiffs in the amount of $2,567,500.

On appeal, the supreme court affirmed the district court's decision, holding that approval by the director did not relieve the company's directors of their fiduciary duty and that the vote of the policyholders was not controlling because the scheme had not been fully disclosed to them. The court also announced the rule that a lawyer's communications to his client are not privileged if the lawyer's services are instrumental in planning a fraud.[87]

One opinion that Krivosha thought would have considerable nation-wide significance but that ultimately proved noteworthy only to sellers of real estate was *Occidental Sav. & Loan Assn. v. Jenco Partnership* (1980).[88] In his lengthy opinion, Krivosha held that the "due on sale" clause in a real estate mortgage, a clause that precluded the purchaser of mortgaged property from simply assuming an existing, low-interest mortgage, was valid, enforceable, and not a restraint on alienation. The clause required the existing mortgage to be satisfied, if the mortgagee so desired, and the purchaser of the property had to take out a new mortgage, usually at a higher interest rate. Judge Clinton concurred but offered a verbal jab at his chief: "The opinion contains considerable dicta and arguments from analogy, concerning the full import of which I am uncertain. I, therefore, limit my concurrence." Clinton and Krivosha seldom saw eye-to-eye on legal matters.[89]

Water, Water Everywhere

Nebraska is privileged to contain a major part of the extensive Ogallala aquifer, a huge underground sea of freshwater that furnishes drinking and irrigation water to the length and breadth of the state. But even in the midst of such plenty, questions about the use of water and its portability have become pressingly important in the Cornhusker state. The Krivosha court faced two water law issues of great significance and reached apparently divergent results, which were subsequently rectified by the U.S. Supreme Court.

In *Little Blue N.R.D. v. Lower Platte North N.R.D.* (1980), the supreme court reversed a precedent of some fifty years standing.[90] The Little Blue Natural Resources District went to the director of the Nebraska State Department of Water Resources to apply for permission to divert water from the Platte River basin to the Blue River basin. The director denied the application. The Little Blue N.R.D. appealed, and the supreme court reversed the director's decision, holding that trans-basin diversion is not barred either by the Nebraska Constitution or by statute. The director had found that there was enough unappropriated water in the Platte basin to meet the needs of Little Blue's proposed project, but he felt that *Osterman v. Central Nebraska P.P & I.D.* (1936) was controlling.

Osterman had severely limited the scope of the Tri-County Project, a vast irrigation scheme from the 1930s involving Phelps, Kearney, and Adams Counties. *Osterman* said that water could not be moved from the Platte basin to the Blue basin, thus effectively removing Adams County, which was in the Blue basin, from the Tri-County Project. The *Osterman* decision was widely criticized, both on legal and economic grounds, but it stood for many years.

Krivosha wrote the *Little Blue* opinion, but one wonders about the behind-the-scenes influence of Boslaugh, a resident of Adams County and an observer of the detrimental impact of *Osterman* since his youth. The court specifically overruled *Osterman* and determined that Article XV, Section 6 of the Nebraska Constitution was controlling. Senator Richard Marvel of Hastings had proposed a trans-basin statute in the early 1950s, but a huge assemblage of agricultural interests had cowed the legislature into taking no action. Krivosha and his cohorts achieved the same result in one fell swoop, with no congregation of embattled farmers even in sight.

Even more meaningful to Nebraska water law than *Little Blue* was *State ex rel. Douglas v. Sporhase* (1983).[91] Jay Sporhase owned land on the western Nebraska border and adjoining land across the border in Colorado. He had a well on his Nebraska land that brought water to his Colorado land. Nebraska had a statute requiring anyone who moved water across the state line to have a permit. Sporhase did not seek such a permit, and Nebraska brought an action to enjoin him from transporting ground water across the border. The trial court in Nebraska entered an injunction and specifically found that water was not an article of commerce, so Nebraska could require such a permit without violating the commerce clause of the U.S. Constitution. The trial court also said that even if water were an article of commerce, the permit requirement did not impose an unreasonable burden on interstate commerce.

Sporhase appealed, and the supreme court affirmed. Krivosha dissented, arguing that prohibiting the director of Nebraska Water Resources from issuing a permit on the basis that Colorado did not grant reciprocity in such cases was an unconstitutional and unreasonable classification and that it violated equal protection notions. He argued that a statute attempting to prohibit a transfer of water based solely on the acts of another state was a violation of the Fourteenth Amendment.[92]

Sporhase was not finished. He appealed to the U.S. Supreme Court, which in *Sporhase v. Nebraska* (1982), accepted Krivosha's view and held that water was an article of commerce and that the reciprocity clause imposed an impermissible burden on interstate commerce. The High Court reversed and remanded the case to Nebraska to determine if the reciprocity clause was severable. On remand, the Nebraska court, in an opinion written by White, decided that the reciprocity provision was severable and said that it was still legitimate to require a permit to transfer water across state lines. Sporhase agreed, and after receiving the permit, he moved water into Colorado and lived happily ever after.[93]

The implications of *Little Blue* and *Sporhase* are tremendous. Water is of great importance to Nebraska's agricultural economy, and the opportunity to move water from one river basin to another allows more of the state's farmers to benefit from the wise use of the precious resource. If water is plentiful in the Platte basin but not in the Blue basin, it can now be shifted to where it will do the most good, so long as the move does not detrimentally impact users in the Platte basin.

Sporhase, as the U.S. Supreme Court determined, means that Nebraska water is an article of commerce that can be purchased, sold, or leased, both within and outside of the state's boundaries. Water-grabbing cities on the front range of the Rockies, like Denver and Fort Collins, may well cast greedy eyes on the huge Ogallala aquifer lying beneath the Nebraska Sandhills. When and if a pipeline to Colorado proves economically feasible, struggling ranchers in northwest Nebraska may decide to pump some of their valuable underground water to irrigate lawns in the arid West.

Impeachment

Yet another controversy dropped into the lap of the Krivosha court when, in 1984, the Nebraska Legislature brought articles of impeachment against Attorney General Paul Douglas, pursuant to Article III, Section 17 of the constitution. Douglas was accused of a variety of offenses stemming from the collapse of Commonwealth Savings Company of Lincoln, a loss that wreaked havoc on the financial position of thousands of depositors. The legislature accused Douglas of having failed to investigate rumors of Commonwealth's impending doom because of his personal business relationship with Marvin Copple, the son of the head of Commonwealth, S. E. Copple, and an officer of Commonwealth in his own right. Douglas was also accused of having lied to both the special counsel investigating the matter and a legislative committee and of having violated provisions of the attorney's Code of Professional Responsibility.

Krivosha, Caporale, and White disqualified themselves from the proceed-ings, and district judges Robert Moran and Keith Howard, along with the ubiq-uitous William Colwell, were appointed to give the court the required seven members. Boslaugh, as senior associate justice, presided. The constitution requires a two-thirds majority in any vote of conviction in an impeachment pro-ceeding, which meant that at least five of the seven sitting judges needed to vote in favor of conviction on any single count for Douglas to be impeached.

Douglas was tried on six specifications. Four judges—Hastings, Shanahan, Grant, and Moran—voted guilty on the first specification. Hastings voted not guilty on the second specification, leaving only Shanahan, Grant, and Moran voting to convict Douglas. All seven judges voted not guilty on specifications 3, 4, 5, and 6.

In its *per curiam* opinion, the court stated that an impeachment proceed-ing was akin to a criminal prosecution and that the state had the burden of establishing the essential elements of the offense beyond a reasonable doubt. The court also made it quite clear that the act or omission for which an officer could be impeached must relate to the duties of the office, and thus general immoral conduct would not be grounds for impeachment. Four of the specifi-cations were based upon disciplinary rules of the lawyer's Code of Professional Responsibility, and the court made it clear that a violation of a disciplinary rule as such did not constitute an impeachable offense.[94]

The key specifications involved Douglas's duty not to misrepresent and not to lie. Specification 1 accused Douglas of misrepresenting to Special Assistant Attorney General David Domina the circumstance under which Douglas re-ceived $32,500 from developer Marvin Copple. Domina was investigating on behalf of the state because of Douglas's past legal work for, and close in-volvement with, Marvin Copple. As attorney general, even if he had personally recused himself, Douglas was duty bound to do all he could to further the suc-cessful completion of the investigation, but the court concluded that Douglas had disclosed receipt of payment from Copple and that he was under no obli-gation to go forward and volunteer information regarding issues that he had not been specifically asked about.

Specification 2 alleged that Douglas lied to Domina, the Counsel for Discipline of the Nebraska bar, and the special Commonwealth Committee of the Nebraska Legislature by saying that he had no idea that lots he sold to Judy Driscoll were being mortgaged by Mrs. Driscoll to Commonwealth in order to get the funds to pay Douglas for the lots. The court found that Douglas was not technically guilty of lying because he believed the statement he made to be true: "The essence of perjury is the belief of the witness concerning the veracity of his statement, not his knowledge of the interrogator's intent."[95] The court also approvingly cited a U.S. Supreme Court opinion holding that an unresponsive answer if literally true does not constitute perjury, even if it is intentionally misleading and by negative implication false.

The court concluded, "It is conceivable that if this allegation had been an element of conspiracy or of aiding and abetting a felony, and proven, there would be some substance to the charge. However, the only offense alleged here is that Douglas did not say what the state already knew and what it wanted him to admit. The state possessed the information sought from Douglas, and any of the answers given by Douglas on this subject neither hindered nor delayed any inquiry the state was making."[96]

Internecine Warfare

Matters of life and death, business law, and corruption occupied a good share of the time of the Krivosha court, but it also had to serve as an arbiter of disputes between various branches of state government. These matters involved the tenets of the civil law.

Having decided in Exon, a case of the White court, that the Board of Regents had general governance over the University of Nebraska, the court had to decide whether any governmental entity could hold sway over the Regents. In University Police Officers Union v. University of Nebraska (1979), the regents questioned whether the Commission of Industrial Relations (CIR) had any jurisdiction over the university.[97] The university argued that Exon meant that the legislature could not give the CIR any authority over university salaries and benefits. The court said that Article XV, Section 9 of the Nebraska Constitution did not exempt the university from dealing with the CIR but held that Section 9 came into play only if a dispute arose over university wages and benefits. Absent a dispute, the CIR did not have the necessary jurisdiction to find or declare what constituted an unfair labor practice by the university.[98]

In State ex rel. Douglas v. Thone (1979), the attorney general sued to enjoin the governor and the director of the Department of Economic Development from implementing LB571, which provided for the construction of ethanol alcohol plants.[99] The act authorized the state to contract with counties or cities to build ethanol plants and the municipalities and counties to sell bonds and pledge revenues of the plants to pay off the bonds.

The supreme court found that the act authorized the state to guarantee payment of municipal bonds and therefore violated Article XIII, Section 1 of the Nebraska Constitution, which prohibited the state from incurring debt in excess of $100,000. The court ruled that even though the state was not the primary obligee, and even though the obligation might be contingent, it was still a debt and was thus constitutionally proscribed.[100]

In *State ex rel. Douglas v. Beermann* (1984), a district court had judged a legislative scheme of reimbursing poorly paid legislators for their expenses during the legislative session to be unconstitutional. The supreme court—mindful, one supposes, of the fact that the legislature approves the budget of the supreme court and of all the lower courts—disagreed. The court held that the language of the constitution did not forbid the payment of expenses. The language provided that "members of the Legislature shall receive no pay nor perquisites other than said salary and expenses." The court concluded that "said" modified only "salary," thus opening the expense floodgates.[101]

State ex rel. Bryant v. Beermann (1984) involved a group that had filed a petition to use the initiative process. They wanted to pass an initiative stating that the people of Nebraska were in favor of a bilateral nuclear weapons freeze and that they opposed the deployment of MX missiles from Nebraska. The attorney general advised the secretary of state that there was no statutory authority for using the initiative process to gain an advisory vote on any question. The secretary of state therefore refused to file the petition but did stamp "Received" and the date on the petition. The petition filers sued for a writ of mandamus in the supreme court. The court denied the writ, responding, "Government should be spared the burdensome cost of election machinery as a straw vote on the electorate's opinions, sentiments or attitudes on public issues. This includes lawmaking through the Legislature or the initiative."[102] A dissent filed by Shanahan, Grant, and White appeared to miss the point entirely and can only be viewed as an attempt to pander to those filing the petition.

Jaksha v. State (1986) was an effort by Omaha tax opponent Ed Jaksha, who sued by leave of court, to determine the viability of an income tax increase passed by the legislature during a special session in October 1985.[103] Governor Bob Kerrey had called a special session of the legislature, and in the call he listed nine specific items that the legislature should consider. None of the items was an income tax increase. During the session, legislators introduced LB10, which called for an increase in income taxes. The attorney general opined that it was not within the ambit of the call. The governor then issued an amended call, adding the income tax increase as an item to be considered. Thereafter, the legislature scrapped LB10 and introduced and passed LB35, a new income tax increase, which was signed by the governor.

Jaksha argued that the call did not ask for an income tax increase and that the amended call could not cure the defect. The court disagreed, holding that the governor could amend the call and that LB35 was within the terms of the amended call. The court left little doubt as to what the governor could do, stating, "The subject matter restriction envisioned in Neb. Const. Art. IV, Sec. 8, empowers the governor to set the boundaries of legislative action permissible at a special session of the Nebraska Legislature. As a consequence of such authority under Neb. Const. Art. IV, Sec. 8, the governor may, during the legislature's special session convened pursuant to a gubernatorial proclamation, submit by an appropriate amended proclamation any additional subjects for valid legislation to be enacted at such special session of the Legislature."[104]

Thus the Krivosha court appeared to be both pragmatic and deferential when dealing with the other branches of government and their powers, placating the poverty-stricken legislators, denying ill-advised straw votes, and allowing the governor and the legislature sufficient wiggle room to deal with unforeseen budget shortfalls.

A Higher Standard for Lawyers and Judges

Krivosha's court showed little collegial sympathy for erring lawyers and judges. It did not adhere to the slap-on-the-wrist philosophy that had existed in the early days of the Simmons court. As the number of lawyers increased so too did the number of malefactors, and the court evinced a no-nonsense attitude when dealing with them.

State ex rel. Nebraska State Bar Assn. v. Michaelis (1982) involved an attorney in West Point named Michaelis who was running for the post of county attorney.[105] During the campaign Michaelis made several statements to local newspapers accusing other lawyers of perjury and unethical conduct. He gave a similar statement to radio station WJAG in Norfolk. Bar authorities charged him with unprofessional conduct and the violation of ethical rules. A referee concluded that Michaelis knew that the statements were false, deceptive, and misleading. Michaelis contended that he could not be disciplined for his statements because they constituted free speech and were protected by the First Amendment.

The supreme court made short shrift of his contentions, noting that he showed no remorse and that he had filed scurrilous documents with the court. It ordered Michaelis's disbarment, saying, "Although a lawyer may speak out and state his opinions on current campaign issues without fear of jeopardizing his license to practice law, his First Amendment rights are not absolute. The guarantee of free speech will not protect him from disciplinary action as a lawyer if he is guilty of known falsehood intentionally used and published for the purpose of misleading the voters and gaining personal advantage for himself or his candidate."[106]

In *State ex rel. Nebraska State Bar Assn. v. Duchek* (1987), the court considered the case of Douglas F. Duchek of Lincoln, who served in 1982 as chair of the House of Delegates of the state bar, one of its most prestigious positions.[107] Duchek was a member of the inner circle of bar leaders until he was charged in federal court with three counts of willful failure to file an income tax return. He agreed to plead guilty to one count, and the other two counts were dropped. The federal court sentenced him to two years of probation. The bar moved to discipline him, and the supreme court, noting that past willful failure cases had resulted in a one-year suspension of the miscreant's right to practice, gave the bar leader the same treatment and suspended him for one year.

State ex rel. Nebraska State Bar Association v. Green (1982) was an intriguing case in which the entire supreme court disqualified itself because Marvin Green, reporter of the court, had been convicted of soliciting a bribe and was subject to discipline by the bar association.[108] The supreme court appointed a special court of seven district judges consisting of Robert Moran, who served as chief justice; Donald Hamilton; Samuel Caniglia; Duane Wolf; George Stanley; Mark Fuhrman; and Bernard Sprague.

Green's problems grew out of his work as supreme court reporter. He told Elton Bowman, the owner of Gant Publishing Company, which published the bound volumes of the Nebraska Supreme Court *Reports*, that Gant would get the contract to publish the next three volumes of the *Reports* if Bowman would pay Green $7,500. Bowman declined. Green kept after him and finally tried to sell Bowman silver bars, which were worth much less than $2,500, for the $7,500. Bowman told his brother Donald, a Lincoln attorney, who went to the attorney general. Elton Bowman went to meet Green again, this time fitted with a body wire. Bowman paid Green $2,500 and got a silver bar from Green, who was immediately arrested by the State Patrol, then tried and convicted. The seven district judges simply set out the facts of Green's criminal activity in their opinion and summarily disbarred him.

Two judges also ran afoul of the Krivosha Court. *In re Complaint Against Kneifl* marked the beginning of the end of the judicial career of the infamous judge Francis Kneifl of Dakota City.[109] The Judicial Qualifications Commission heard four counts against Kneifl and found two to be proven. He was arrested in Iowa for driving under the influence, and he cursed and threatened the arresting officers. He also tried to get the Dakota County attorney to drop criminal charges against one of his friends.

The supreme court suspended Kneifl for three months without pay and ordered him to undergo alcohol evaluation. It spelled out the rules for misbehaving jurists in a *per curiam* opinion:

> The purpose of sanctions in cases of judicial discipline is to preserve the integrity and independence of the judiciary and to restore and reaffirm public confidence in the administration of justice. The discipline we impose must be designed to announce publicly our recognition that there has been misconduct; it must be sufficient to deter respondent from again engaging in such conduct; and it must discourage others from engaging in similar conduct in the future. Thus, we discipline a judge not for purposes of vengeance or retribution, but to instruct the public, and all judges, ourselves included, of the importance of the function performed by judges in a free society. We discipline a judge to reassure the public that judicial misconduct is neither permitted nor condoned.[110]

In re Complaint Against Kelly (1987) involved a county judge in Hall County who prevented a traffic ticket against his son from being prosecuted by taking the ticket and secreting it for several months. The supreme court found his action to be either in bad faith or willful misconduct, reviewed the facts at some length, cited its opinion in *Kneifl*, and ordered Kelly removed from office.[111] In six cases heard by the supreme court involving judicial misconduct between 1984 and 2001, the court removed three judges from office and suspended the other three without pay for periods ranging from three months to six months.[112]

The Sword of the Lord and of Gideon

Krivosha and his court heard two cases involving one of Nebraska's most mil-
itant right-wing Christians, Everett Sileven, the pastor of the Faith Baptist
Church in Louisville, Nebraska. In *State ex rel. Douglas v. Faith Baptist Church*
(1981), Attorney General Paul Douglas sued to enjoin the operation of a school
at Faith Baptist Church. The school was Bible-oriented, and the teachers were
not certified by the state. Sileven maintained that operation of the school was
simply an extension of the ministry of the church, and he argued that the
public schools only taught secular humanism. Sileven contended that the proposed injunction violated Ninth Amendment rights for parents to educate their
children as they saw fit and violated their First Amendment rights regarding
freedom of religion.

The court made short work of Sileven's arguments and affirmed the granting
of the injunction: "The refusal of the defendants to comply with the compul-
sory education laws of the State of Nebraska as applied in this case is an arbitrary and unreasonable attempt to thwart the legitimate, reasonable, and compelling interests of the state in carrying out its educational obligations under
a claim of religious freedom."[113]

Even though Sileven was enjoined from continuing to run the school, he bat-
tled on, operating it in defiance of the court's order. He appeared before the
trial court, and the court found him guilty of contempt. The trial court said
that he could purge himself of contempt by closing the school by a date certain
or by complying with state law. Sileven refused to do either. The court found
him in contempt and ordered him confined for four months. He served thirteen days and then filed an affidavit saying he had severed all connection with
the school. Accordingly, he was released from jail, but shortly thereafter he re-
opened the school. The court again found him guilty of contempt and ordered
him to serve the balance of the original four-month sentence for contempt.
After being jailed again he filed a petition for a writ of habeas corpus, which
the trial court denied, and which the supreme court affirmed on appeal. The
supreme court held that he was trying to attack the judgment of contempt col-
laterally by filing for a writ of habeas corpus and refused his writ. The court
said, "The extent to which the state must set aside its laws in order to accommodate religious beliefs is not to be determined, under our form of government, by the individual but, rather, by the court; and once this is determined
by the court, as it has been in this matter, it may not be ignored or rejected by

the individual without subjecting the individual to appropriate penalties."[114]
Somewhere, Pat Robertson frowned.

Summary Judgment

The Krivosha court wrestled with an increasing caseload, many more criminal cases, and the almost insurmountable problems surrounding the imposition of the death penalty. Some of its work concerning the death penalty was
subsequently overturned by the federal courts. But after weathering the Hunt
storm, the court began to carve out rules that withstood constitutional challenges, at least until the opinion of the U.S. Supreme Court in Ring v. Arizona,
the 2002 decision stating that only juries, not judges, could impose the death
penalty. The U.S. Supreme Court did not say whether the decision was retroactive. However, Nebraska has held that the decision in Ring is not, at least
regarding matters that were final before Ring was decided, because it set forth
a procedural, as opposed to a substantive, rule.[115] Apart from the death penalty, the Krivosha court made a major stride forward in the area of business law,
did what it could to restore public confidence in the judicial system through
its discipline of judges and lawyers, and attempted to maintain a tenuous relationship with other branches of government.

A curious trait of the Krivosha court was the significant number of unsigned
per curiam opinions. The Krivosha court wrote 3,513 opinions total, and of that
number, 621, or 17.67 percent, of the opinions were per curiam. When viewed
against the seven per curiam opinions in Simmons's twenty-five years at the
helm of the court, or against the fifty-seven such opinions in Paul White's sixteen years, the increase in such self-imposed anonymity is amazing and sends
a clear signal that something important had changed in how the court functioned. What changed, and why?

Krivosha himself professed to be distressed by the number of per curiam opinions. He suggested that the court used per curiam opinions so frequently to ensure
the safety of the court or because judges who tried to write majority opinions but
failed to get majorities could write what the majority wanted in a per curiam opinion, only without putting their names on the opinion.[116] Both points may have
some validity, but it is doubtful that there were 621 death threats or unsuccessful
tries at majority opinions. Some have speculated that law clerks wrote many of
the per curiam opinions, but Krivosha denied any knowledge of such practice. He
reiterated that he, and he alone, wrote all the opinions that bore his name.

Dick Herman, former editor of the Lincoln Journal, was highly critical of the

Table 10. Decisions of the Krivosha court, 1978–87

Total cases	3,513
Civil cases	2,602
Criminal cases	911
% of civil cases	74.07
% of criminal cases	25.93
Total cases, no. of affirmances	2,380
Total cases, % of affirmances	67.74
Criminal cases, no. of affirmances	694
Criminal cases, % of affirmances	76.18
Total cases, no. of reversals	753
Total cases, % of reversals	21.43
Criminal cases, no. of reversals	90
Criminal cases, % of reversals	9.87

court's intemperate use of the *per curiam* opinion, especially when it made public no valid reason for unsigned opinions.[117] The bar grew restive as well because signed opinions could often be rationalized as the work of a jurist whose biases and predilections were well known.

During his almost nine years as chief justice, Krivosha's court issued 3,513 opinions, or an average of 390.3 opinions per year, a startling increase from the White court's average of 259.2 opinions per year, and an even more impressive increase over the Simmons court's average of 162.6 opinions per year. How were Krivosha and his colleagues able to do it?

As has been discussed earlier, the Krivosha court issued 621 *per curiam* opinions, some of which may well have been written by law clerks. If none of them were, and the 621 opinions were divided among the seven judges of the court, then each judge would have written an average of 88.71 *per curiam* opinions over Krivosha's 8.7-year term, or 0.86 opinions per month.

Krivosha brought district judges to the court frequently to sit in panels of five judges. These judges wrote 417 opinions over Krivosha's term, or an average of 46.33 opinions per year. Krivosha was adamantly opposed to a court of appeals and said that if he were still the chief justice, there would be no such court.[118] He was also in favor of merging the district and county courts, an issue fraught with controversy, but one that would not have materially impacted the workload of the Nebraska Supreme Court. He felt that the court could work harder than it did, and that working harder, coupled with using district judges on panels, would alleviate the backlog. He was mistaken. Krivosha became chief justice at the end of December 1978. At the end of that month, 525 cases were

Table 11. Krivosha court opinions, 1978–87

JUDGE	NO. CONTRIBUTED[a]	% OF 3,513	RANK
Krivosha[b]	386	10.98	1
Boslaugh[b]	335	9.53	4
McCown	187	5.32	6
Clinton	127	3.61	9
Brodkey	98	2.78	10
C. T. White[b]	378	10.76	2
Hastings[b]	370	10.53	3
Caporale	263	7.48	5
Shanahan	165	4.69	8
Grant	167	4.75	7
Per curiam	621	17.67	
Retired and district judges	417	11.87	
Total	**3,514**[c]		

[a]Does not include dissents or concurrences.
[b]On court for entire period of Krivosha's incumbency.
[c]One case had two opinions.

on file in the supreme court. Krivosha left the court in July 1987. At the end of that year, there were 1,010 cases pending in the supreme court.[119]

Krivosha certainly did his part of the work. He led the court in number of opinions (386), dissents (139), and concurrences (177). He wrote 106 dissenting opinions and 87 concurring opinions in addition to the 386 majority opinions, a total of 579 written opinions, and an average of 5.62 opinions per month. The opinion writing was in addition to all his public appearances. He also read briefs in every case that came to the court, a technique he utilized to determine if a case should be assigned to a five-judge panel for hearing or, if it were significant enough, to a hearing by the full court.[120]

By the time Krivosha took over the reins of the court the criminal docket had grown substantially. His court wrote opinions in 911 criminal cases, or 25.93 percent of all the opinions it wrote. Criminals did not fare well before the high court: only 9.87 percent of criminal cases were reversed, as compared to a 21.42 percent reversal rate for all cases.

Of the three judges who were on the court for the entirety of Krivosha's incumbency, not including Krivosha, C. Thomas White produced the most opinions (378), followed closely by Hastings (370). Boslaugh, who turned out 335, trailed White and Hastings but was well ahead of any other judge.

Table 12. Chief Justice Krivosha dissents, 1978–87

Total Krivosha Dissents	139
Dissents as % of total cases heard by the court	3.95
No. of dissents in which Krivosha wrote an opinion	106
% of dissents in which Krivosha wrote an opinion	76.25
Total Krivosha sole dissents	63
Sole dissents as % of total Krivosha dissents	45.32

The Krivosha court ranks second in number of dissents when compared to the Simmons, White, and Hastings courts, trailing only the White court. Krivosha dissented in 10.78 percent of the cases heard by his court. In sixty-three of his 139 total dissents, or 45.32 percent of the time, he was the sole dissenter. He wrote 106 dissenting opinions and therefore was content to go along with a colleague's dissenting reasoning less than 25 percent of the time.

Somewhat surprisingly, C. Thomas White was no longer the next most active dissenter, Boslaugh having dissented 106 times to White's ninety-eight. Hastings dissented forty-nine times, or 1.39 percent of the time, a higher percentage of dissents than when he succeeded Krivosha as chief justice.

Krivosha did not believe that all opinions had to be unanimous. He thought that good, well-reasoned dissents were fine and that they often anticipated what the law would be fifteen years hence. His major concern with dissents was to make sure that they were not angry or personal.[121] He obviously viewed the dissent as a tool to try to educate his colleagues, a tactic he utilized, for example, in *Sporhase*. In *Sporhase* the U.S. Supreme Court followed his lead, holding that water was an article of commerce. Some of Krivosha's dissents had a bit of a pedagogical tone, as though he were leading the uninformed step-by-step to the logical conclusion. But the other six judges were not often swayed by his arguments. As Thomas Gray has said, "Where ignorance is bliss, 'tis folly to be wise."[122]

But for all the hard work that Krivosha and his brethren put in, they did not dent the ever-increasing backlog of cases that was building up on their docket. District judges and law clerks helped to alleviate the load. *Per curiam* opinions may have also helped, if they were in fact written by law clerks. However, the seven judges had to feel that they were slowly slipping into a maelstrom, and with a chief justice who did not want an intermediate appellate court, they must have wondered where it would all end.

Table 13. Dissents by members of the Krivosha court, 1978–87

JUDGE	DISSENTS	% OF TOTAL CASES	RANK
Krivosha[a]	139	3.95	1
Boslaugh[a]	106	3.01	2
McCown	44	1.25	8
Clinton	54	1.53	4
Brodkey	15	0.42	10
C. T. White[a]	98	2.78	3
Hastings[a]	49	1.39	6
Caporale	48	1.36	7
Shanahan	50	1.42	5
Grant	35	0.99	9
Retired and district judges	31	0.88	

Note:

Total cases decided by Krivosha court	3,513
No. of total cases in which there was a dissent	379
% of total cases in which one or more judges dissented	10.78

[a]On court for entire period of Krivosha's incumbency.

Krivosha in Retrospect

Krivosha's service as chief justice easily constituted the most visible and controversial tenure of any chief justice since statehood in 1867. The *Hunt* case and the *ConAgra* controversy placed the court in the press for days on end. The death penalty became a source of concern to the bar and the public alike, with the court gingerly stepping through the minefield of controversy surrounding the legislatively mandated aggravating and mitigating circumstances. Prior chiefs had hardly ever appeared in the newspapers, but Krivosha was mentioned in them almost daily.

Krivosha contributed to his own press coverage, being willing to speak at almost any gathering more numerous than an afternoon bridge club. Many more people than ever before knew the name and face of Nebraska's chief justice. They did not know the names and faces of the other members of the court, however, and Krivosha thought that his public recognition might have been a sore point with his colleagues, who perhaps resented and at the same time desired the public attention Krivosha received. But public knowledge of the judges did not lead to public approbation: the percentage of "yes" votes in retention elections during the Krivosha years was lower than the percentage of "yes" votes during the White court.

Krivosha felt that the court became more difficult to lead as time wore on. His attempt to install a new, modern telephone system, one that would allow direct dialing into a judge's office, conference calls, and other attributes considered mundane and commonplace by any self-respecting business organization, was quickly and decisively rebuffed by the other judges. Krivosha told his wife that he thought he had pushed the court about as far as it was possible to push it.[123]

Krivosha was forty-four when he became chief justice. He served almost ten years before becoming somewhat tired of the same routine, and he was not enthralled at the prospect of serving another ten or fifteen years. When he was offered an outstanding opportunity at Ameritas Life Insurance Company, he resigned from the court to become the company's general counsel.

Viewed in its totality, Krivosha's tenure was very successful. He was bright, hardworking, and certainly in tune with modern innovative management techniques. He brought the notion of administrative process to the court, worked well and extensively with the court administrator, and opened up a process of meeting frequently and privately with bar leaders over matters of common concern. He felt that in its dealings with the bar, the court acted legislatively rather than judicially, and that the bar was an arm of the court that need not be held at length.[124]

Unfortunately, Krivosha was the only member of his court who wanted the court to go public, who wanted to grant easy access to the bar, or who felt that in most instances the death penalty was an affront to civilized society. When he left for Ameritas's suburban campus in east Lincoln, it was not long before many of his innovations were junked by his former colleagues, who were obviously more comfortable with things as they used to be. William Hastings moved up to chief justice, succeeding Krivosha, and Dale Fahrnbruch came to the court from the district court in Lancaster County. Silence and mystique surrounded the court again, but not for long.

Hastings realized that the backlog had to be addressed, and he took up a political club to make it happen. Fahrnbruch learned that the court simply could not act without advising other political entities of the possible consequences of its actions. And the whole court learned that it should not distance itself from another arm of the court. The Hastings court was soon back in the press, in the "soup," and in the bad graces of the electorate.

5. "With Malice toward None"
The Hastings Court, 1987–95

When the tumult and shouting died after Norman Krivosha announced his resignation from the post of chief justice in 1987, newly elected (1986) Republican governor Kay Orr was given the opportunity to select Krivosha's replacement. Krivosha, an ardent Democrat, frequently responded to inquiries about whether he was a liberal or a conservative judge by saying, "I hope I am a judicious judge." Semantics aside, there could be little doubt that Krivosha did not aspire to the conservative, right-wing, rock-ribbed Republicanism dear to Orr's heart. In many a precinct meeting for several weeks, the GOP faithful speculated which conservative Republican would be plucked from the pack, anointed, and installed. But Orr had other plans in mind.

It's a Hell of a Way to Run a Railroad

The nominating commission for chief justice was required to submit the names of at least two qualified candidates for chief justice to the governor. The commission, chaired by supreme court judge John Grant of Omaha, included four lawyers who had been elected by their peers in a mail ballot. The four lawyers were Larry Welch of Omaha; William Quigley of Valentine; Robert Sullivan of Wahoo; and myself, from Lincoln.[1] The commission was also supposed to have two Republican and two Democratic non-lawyers, who were to be appointed by the governor. But as the hearing to select the new chief justice approached, it became apparent that former governor Bob Kerrey had left vacancies on the commission. The Democratic laymen serving were Kay Winchell of Gering and Bill Sweet of Omaha. At the last minute before the hearing, Governor Orr appointed Michael Walsh of Omaha, president of the Union Pacific Railroad, and Dee Juelfs of Kimball, the wife of Republican activist and candidate Stan Juelfs.[2]

On the day of the hearing the commissioners met for breakfast at Lincoln's Cornhusker Hotel, at which time Judge Grant outlined the applicable procedures and explained how the hearings would proceed. Walsh informed the commissioners that Governor Orr had appointed him to be an advocate for

Cynthia Milligan, a Lincoln lawyer and now dean of the College of Business Administration at the University of Nebraska–Lincoln. Milligan is the daughter of Clifford M. Hardin, former Chancellor of the University of Nebraska–Lincoln and Secretary of Agriculture in the first Nixon cabinet. An office lawyer specializing in banking law, she had never tried a lawsuit.

Governor Orr had not communicated her desire to appoint Nebraska's first woman chief justice to the attorney members of the commission, who were less than enthusiastic at the prospect of a chief justice undergoing on-the-job training on matters of trial practice, procedure, and evidence. After a lengthy and oftentimes bitter closed session following the public hearings, a session at which Walsh, a former U.S. district attorney in San Diego, displayed both his persuasive powers and an awareness of the importance of his post at the Union Pacific, the commission decided not to advance Milligan's name as a qualified candidate, thus forestalling her appointment. Among the names forwarded to the governor was that of Associate Justice William Hastings, and on September 2, 1987, Orr appointed Hastings to the vacancy created by Krivosha's resignation.[3]

Hastings and His Court

As was noted previously, William Hastings came to the supreme court in 1979 as the replacement for retiring justice Harry Spencer. An experienced insurance defense lawyer, Hastings had practiced with the Lincoln law firm of Chambers, Holland, Dudgeon, and Hastings until he went onto the district bench in Lancaster County in 1965, a post he occupied until his appointment to the supreme court. A fine trial judge, he was well liked by the bar and had scored an 82 percent "yes" vote in the retention election of 1982, the highest approval rating of any judge at any time during the Krivosha court.[4]

The other judges on the court when Hastings assumed the reins were Leslie Boslaugh, C. Thomas White, D. Nick Caporale, John Grant, and Thomas Shanahan. Dale Fahrnbruch, a Lancaster County district judge, was appointed to replace Hastings.

John Grant retired in 1993 and was succeeded by David J. Lanphier, who had been in private practice in the Sarpy County area south of Omaha. Lanphier's service on the court was very short-lived because he was defeated at the polls in his first retention election in 1996—the result of a well-orchestrated campaign stemming from popular dissatisfaction with the court's position on term limits.

When Thomas Shanahan was appointed as a U.S. district judge in December 1993, he resigned from the supreme court at once. John F. Wright of Scottsbluff, a member of one of Nebraska's most distinguished legal families, succeeded Shanahan.

The final member of the Hastings court, who shared only two months of service with Hastings until the chief justice retired in January 1995, was William M. Connolly of Hastings, who was elevated from the court of appeals in November 1994 to take the place of Leslie Boslaugh, who had retired after thirty-three years of service on the high court.

A Return to the Days of Yesteryear

When Hastings was elevated to the post of chief justice, the other five members of the court had all served with him as associate justices under Chief Justice Norman Krivosha. Hastings's replacement as an associate justice, Dale Fahrnbruch, had not. John Grant, the junior of the six, had served more than four years under Krivosha's leadership. All six of the justices had substantial exposure to Krivosha's management style, his penchant for publicity, and his predilection for running a one-man show. Not surprisingly, much of what Krivosha had done did not appeal to them.

It shortly became obvious to even casual observers of the court that "Krivoshaism" had become a dead letter, and the court was soon in full retreat from the openness that had marked the Krivosha years. There was no more sitting at law schools, schmoozing with lawyers, or attendance at bar functions. The court began to retreat into its own cloistered chambers and to slowly but surely expunge virtually all the innovative changes that Krivosha had foisted upon them. It was almost as though the court were saying, "He was really just a political opportunist, and now we are going back to doing the things that real judges do, in the way that real judges do them."

However, the reactionary forces at work in the court did not prove to be a panacea for its very many legal ills. The reclusive attitude of the court exacerbated the tension between the court and the bar, and even though Hastings labored valiantly to work with the bar and to pay attention to its needs and wants, the rest of his court did not. Relations soon proved to be even more dismal than they were during the Krivosha era.

But it was not the court's disdainful attitude that proved to be its ultimate downfall. Two poorly reasoned, ambiguously expressed opinions of the court heaped calumny upon the heads of the sequestered seven. The court, to put it simply, made two significant mistakes, one in the area of attorney conflicts of interest, and the other regarding the definition of murder in the second degree. When the tumult and the shouting died, the court was forced to retreat from both positions, leaving only red, egg-covered faces behind.

Krivosha had been an adamant opponent of an intermediate court of appeals. One of Hastings's first measures upon assuming office was to begin to plan for the establishment of an intermediate court.

Court of Appeals

From the time Hastings took office in September 1989 until January 1990, well over one hundred supreme court opinions were authored by retired or district judges, sitting in panels of five members each with the active supreme court judges. The idea of sitting in panels, although not new, was used extensively by former chief justice Krivosha. During his nine-year tenure, district or retired judges wrote 417 opinions, an average of forty-six opinions per year.[5]

Even with the additional help from retired or district judges and the prodigious output of the court during Krivosha's incumbency, the court kept slipping backward. When Krivosha took office at the end of 1978, the court had 525 cases pending before it. At the end of 1987, 1,010 cases were on file. Yet during Krivosha's term, 3,513 cases were disposed of by formal written opinion, and myriad others by administrative action.[6]

Bar association leaders began to worry about the number of per curiam opinions and district judge opinions that emanated from the court during the Krivosha term. Some felt that district judges might subconsciously be more likely to affirm their colleagues on the district bench, increasing the futility of appeal. In 1986 the bar association began to discuss the prospect of some kind of intermediate court of appeals, which would operate to hear the more mundane cases and relieve the supreme court of the burden of hearing every appeal. Fredric H. Kauffman of Lincoln chaired a special committee in 1988, following the earlier 1986 committee, that discussed the matter. The Kauffman committee was ultimately transmuted into the committee that assisted Chief Justice Hastings in putting together the legislation that led to the creation of the court of appeals.[7]

In the remaining months of Krivosha's tenure as chief justice, nothing concrete emerged from the bar association study committee. Chief Justice Krivosha was not enthusiastic about a court of appeals. Once Hastings assumed the chief's chair, things changed significantly. At first, he tried to create an appellate division of the district court. Retired district judge William Colwell of Pawnee City volunteered to handle the administrative task of establishing the panels and assigning cases to an appellate division, which Hastings hoped would function as an intermediate buffer between the trial court and the supreme court.[8]

However, because there was an absolute dearth of statutory authority for the creation of such a court, and because those district judges who were selected still had to handle their trial dockets at home, Hastings soon realized that an appellate division was, in reality, little better than a patch over a burgeoning rupture. He began searching for a more permanent solution to the court's expanding backlog.

Lincoln attorney Charles Thone, Republican governor of Nebraska from 1979 to 1983, and the man who had first appointed Hastings as an associate justice on the supreme court, contacted Hastings and suggested that he try to expand upon and implement the bar's idea of an intermediate court. James Bruckner, a Lincoln trial lawyer, assumed responsibility for raising money to fund the venture. Howard Olsen of Scottsbluff, chairman of the House of Delegates of the bar association, enthusiastically joined the effort, and Frederic Kauffman of Lincoln, one of the bar's eminent litigators, also assumed a leadership role.[9]

The group met frequently over the noon hour to discuss how the system would work. Hastings drafted much of the enabling legislation, assuming that voters would approve the creation of the court at the 1990 general election. The new court was approved by a vote of 337,667 to 166,185.[10] The committee was active in an electioneering role, flooding the state with advertisements spelling out the need for a new court. The committee hired public relations executive Doug Evans of Lincoln to spearhead the campaign.

After the voters had given their imprimatur, the legislature introduced and passed LB732, which created the mechanics of the court system, in its 1991 session. The court was constituted after the 1991 legislative session ended. Governor Ben Nelson appointed Richard D. Sievers of Lincoln and John F. Irwin of Bellevue on December 11, 1991, and he appointed William M. Connolly of Hastings, Lindsey Miller-Lerman of Omaha, Edward E. Hannon of O'Neill, and John F. Wright of Scottsbluff the next day. Before the end of the year, the supreme court selected Sievers to be the chief judge.

When the Nebraska State Court of Appeals was created, the Nebraska Constitution required that supreme court judges live in Lincoln. Voters subsequently removed the provision from the constitution in the general election of 1998. However, no such provision was applicable to the court of appeals, and the members, except for Hannon and John Wright, established offices in their hometowns. Hannon moved to Lincoln—where the lights were brighter than in O'Neill—as did Wright, upon the confirmation of their appointments.

Hastings, an ardent advocate of having the supreme court judges reside in Lincoln because it could promote collegiality, did not impose the same requirement on the court of appeals. The court of appeals sits around the state, frequently rotating panels of three judges. Hastings had learned from the short-lived appellate division of the district court that judges who lived outside of Lincoln, for the most part, wanted to continue to live outside of Lincoln. He therefore omitted the Lincoln residency requirement in the enabling legislation in order to guarantee the largest possible pool of applicants for the court of appeals.[11]

Panels of the court of appeals, utilizing guidelines spelled out by the supreme court in its rules and codified in Nebraska's statutes, decide which opinions of the court of appeals will be published and can be cited as authority.[12] Not all opinions are published. For example, in 1992, the first year the court sat, it issued forty-eight published opinions and eight hundred memorandum opinions and judgments on appeal. In 1993 the court of appeals issued 126 published opinions and 1,033 memorandum opinions and judgments on appeal. In 1994 it issued eighty-three published opinions. The court's first published opinion was handed down March 24, 1992, a scant three months after its judges were appointed, an example of phenomenal speed by any standard of judicial expediency.

All criminal and civil appeals, except for cases involving a death sentence, life imprisonment, or the constitutionality of a statute, are initially scheduled to be heard by the court of appeals. The supreme court has the power to remove cases from the court of appeals to its own docket in order to regulate the workload between the two courts. Appellants can also file a petition to bypass the court of appeals and go directly to the supreme court, and after the court of appeals has rendered a decision, it is possible to file a petition for further review by the supreme court.

The court of appeals has been an unqualified success. During its first ten

years of existence, up until December 31, 2001, it disposed of 10,943 cases and
has dramatically reduced the time between filing an appeal to the release of a
dispository opinion, either by the court of appeals or the supreme court.[13] Most
experienced observers of the judicial system agree that "justice delayed is justice denied" and that the court of appeals has therefore materially improved
the administration of justice in Nebraska.

Monkeying Around with Murder

A cogent aphorism, attributed to Saint Bonaventure, aptly characterizes the
performance of the supreme court in dealing with second-degree murder cases
during Hastings's term: "An example from the monkey. The higher it climbs,
the more you see of its behind." Much like the reaction to the *Hunt* case during
Krivosha's court, the decisions of the Hastings court regarding malice and
second-degree murder brought the wrath of the press and the public down
upon the its head.

It all began with *State v. Pettit*, decided in 1989.[14] Sylvester Frank Pettit was
tried for manslaughter in the death of his wife. He was found guilty and sentenced to four to twelve years in prison. Pettit claimed that his wife's death was
an accident. Nebraska's statute on manslaughter (Sec. 28-305) provided that
manslaughter occurred when A, without malice, kills B upon a sudden quarrel, or when A kills B unintentionally during the commission of an unlawful
act. Pettit appealed, and the supreme court dissected the manslaughter statute. The court determined that the real issue on the first section of the statute
was whether conviction for death during a sudden quarrel required an intent to
kill, or whether there was a form of strict liability resulting from a death on a
sudden quarrel, so that no intent to kill was necessary. The court held that killing on a sudden quarrel required intent. There was no strict liability. Because
the district court had failed to instruct the jury that intent to kill was an element of voluntary manslaughter, it had thus committed reversible error, and
Pettit's conviction had to be set aside.

Nebraska's high court, in an extensive opinion written by Judge Shanahan,
reviewed the two types of homicide at common law. Murder required malice.
Manslaughter did not. At the time courts across the country began to recognize a difference between voluntary and involuntary manslaughter. Voluntary
manslaughter was considered an intentional killing in the heat of passion and
the result of severe provocation.

Nebraska does not recognize common law crimes. All crimes in the state are statutory. In this case, the court recognized that the Nebraska manslaughter statute was somewhat deficient, defining voluntary manslaughter in the sudden quarrel section, and involuntary manslaughter in the commission of an unlawful act section. The court had to interpret the statute. Voluntary manslaughter requires an intent to kill, suddenly formed on sufficient provocation. Involuntary manslaughter is accidental but is committed during an unlawful act. The intent to kill in voluntary manslaughter is without malice.

Shanahan reasoned: "Thus, intentional criminal homicide as the result of legally recognized provocation distinguishes voluntary manslaughter 'upon a sudden quarrel' from another intentional criminal homicide, murder in the second degree, namely 'a person commits murder in the second degree if he causes the death of a person intentionally, but without premeditation.'"[15] Thus, both voluntary manslaughter and second-degree murder required intent, but provocation distinguished one from the other. Premeditation distinguished first- from second-degree murder.

Fahrnbruch dissented, starting the court down a slippery slope toward chaos. He began:

> Because the majority of the court abolishes a critical distinction between the crime of second degree murder and the crime of manslaughter committed upon a sudden quarrel, I am compelled to dissent. To be guilty of manslaughter committed upon a sudden quarrel, the majority holds, the killer must commit the slaying with intent to kill. . . .

Fahrnbruch continued:

> It is my position that common-law voluntary manslaughter was subsumed by the crime of second-degree murder. . . . In my view, Nebraska case law and Nebraska's homicide statutes reflect that Nebraska has done away with the common-law distinctions of voluntary and involuntary manslaughter. . . .
>
> Prior to the adoption of the current criminal code in 1977, the second degree murder statute required that the killing be done "purposely and maliciously," Neb. Rev. Stat. Sec. 28-402 (Reissue 1975). The new code defined second degree murder as a killing

done "intentionally but without premeditation." Sec. 28-304.
However, malice continues to be judicially required as an element
of second-degree murder.[16]

Here is where Judge Fahrnbruch went wrong. He failed to recognize that the
legislature had eliminated malice when it changed the language of the statute, and so the court could no longer require malice as an element of second-
degree murder. He also failed to realize that provocation was the essential
element differentiating voluntary manslaughter (sudden quarrel) from second-
degree murder. Fahrnbruch went on, "It is my contention that malice is a
judicially supplied essential element in second degree murder to distinguish
second degree murder from an intentional killing that is permitted by law
under certain circumstances, i.e. a person's or law enforcement officer's killing someone where legally permissible under Nebraska's justification for use
of force statutes."[17]

Fahrnbruch then moved to his final point: "Second degree murder is committed when the killing is done intentionally without just cause or excuse, i.e.
with malice; manslaughter is committed when the killing is without malice.
. . . It is logically impossible to distinguish between a killing done intentionally and one done with malice. A killing committed without malice is one committed unintentionally."[18]

White joined Fahrnbruch's dissent. Boslaugh wrote a separate dissent in
which he argued, "Malice is the intentional doing of a wrongful act without just
cause or excuse. Since manslaughter is a killing without malice, there can be
no intention to kill in committing manslaughter." Essentially all the dissenters ignored the element of provocation and focused on the notion that intent
and malice were the same thing.

The court was calm after *Pettit* for some time, until *State v. Myers* came to
the court in 1994, five years after *Pettit*, and after Judge Shanahan, the author
of *Pettit*, had resigned from the court to become a federal district judge.
Fahrnbruch wrote the majority opinion in *Myers* and succeeded in imposing
his belief about malice and second-degree murder on the entire court, without a dissenting voice.[19]

Darren L. Myers shot and killed Kevin Thomas. He was charged with first-
degree murder and convicted of second-degree murder. He was sentenced to
life imprisonment. On appeal, his conviction was reversed and he was granted

a new trial because the trial judge did not instruct the jury that malice was an essential element of second-degree murder. The court, under Fahrnbruch's tutelage, held that such an omission was plain error and did not even have to be designated as error by the appellant.

Fahrnbruch sang a familiar song: "The current code states that '[a] person commits murder in the second degree if he causes the death of a person intentionally, but without premeditation.' Neb. Rev. Stat. Sec 28-304 (Reissue 1989). It does not mention malice. However, this court has continued to require malice as an element of second degree murder."[20]

Fahrnbruch's contention on this issue was a classic case of the wish being father to the thought. The cases that he cited for his theorem were highly suspect. He proceeded, "[B]y omitting the element of malice from the second degree murder instruction, the instruction in effect became one for the crime of intentional manslaughter as defined by this court in *State v. Pettit* (citation omitted). Malice is not an essential element of manslaughter." But, of course, in *Pettit*, the majority said that intent was necessary for voluntary manslaughter. Fahrnbruch again equated malice and intent and ignored provocation. He essentially changed the holding in *Pettit* to conform to his dissent in *Pettit* and discussed "intentional" manslaughter, as opposed to Shanahan's use of "voluntary" and "involuntary" manslaughter in *Pettit*.

Attorney General Don Stenberg, harshly criticized by the court for failing to handle death penalty cases appropriately, struck back in an article in the *Creighton Law Review* in which he strongly criticized the result and effect of *Myers*.[21] Stenberg pointed out that in *State v. Williams* (1995), the court applied *Myers* retroactively, allowing defendants to raise the *Myers* theory in post-conviction proceedings. The court also found that defense lawyers who had not, in pre-*Myers* cases, objected to jury instructions that did not include "malice" were guilty of ineffective assistance to their clients. Stenberg argued that *Myers* violated the separation of powers doctrine. Nebraska has only statutory crimes, but Stenberg felt that *Myers* created a common law crime and made it retroactive. In another article in the same issue of the law review, Creighton professor Richard E. Shugrue, a criminal law expert, argued that the court was wrong because it ignored the fact that the legislature removed "malice" from the second-degree murder statute when it revised Nebraska's criminal law in 1977.[22]

Shortly after *Myers*, *State v. Grimes* (1994) came to the court, with essentially the same result as in *Myers*. Because the trial judge did not instruct on malice as an element of second-degree murder, Grimes was granted a new trial.[23] John Wright, newly elevated to the supreme court from the court of appeals as the replacement for Shanahan, dissented. He pointed out the fallacy of Fahrnbruch's reasoning in Myers. To reach the result Fahrnbruch wanted in Myers, he relied on a series of cases that held that malice was an element of second-degree murder and that were decided under the prior second-degree murder statute, in which second-degree murder was classified as a killing done purposely and maliciously but without deliberation and premeditation. This statute was amended in the 1977 criminal code, and the legislature purposely omitted the term "malice." The legislature's judiciary committee had even given its rationale, explaining, "Section 10 is comparable to Section 28-402 on second degree murder. It differs from the present section, which requires the killing to be purposely and maliciously, whereas the new code requires that the cause of death of a person need only be done intentionally."[24] Wright went on to say, "In my opinion, malice has not been an essential element of the crime of murder in the second degree since January 1, 1979."

Wright pointed out that Pettit, which had started the whole cause célèbre, was no longer law: "[W]e have since overruled the holding in Pettit that 'manslaughter is an intentional killing of another under Nebraska law. State v. Jones, 245 Neb. 821, 832, 515 N.W. 2nd 654, 660 (1994).'"[25] Wright went on to point out that Nebraska statutory law did not impose malice as a necessary ingredient of second-degree murder and that the overruling of Pettit eliminated the voluntary or involuntary manslaughter distinction. Second-degree murder only required that a murder was done intentionally. It did not require malice or premeditation. And manslaughter, because Pettit was no longer law, did not require any intent at all. Wright did not bemoan the overruling of Pettit or the junking of the sudden provocation distinction, nor did he accept what Fahrnbruch so zealously preached, that malice and intent were the same thing. His dissent, in which he merely pointed out Fahrnbruch's fallacy, did not provide a way out of the dilemma.

Hastings subsequently acknowledged that Wright was right and Fahrnbruch wrong and that Myers relied erroneously on a case decided under a pre-amendment statute. He regretted that many new trials had to be ordered and that a number of convicts convicted of second-degree murder on erroneous instructions had to be released because of problems getting witnesses to retry them.[26] The whole mess stained Hastings's regime to a very large extent. The controversy was finally resolved in *State v. Burlison*, a 1998 case decided three years after Hastings retired. Both the press and the bar were very vocal in their opposition to *Myers*, especially because of the release of prisoners.

In *Burlison*, the appellant filed a motion for post-conviction relief because the information charging him did not include malice as an element of the crime of aiding and abetting second-degree murder. The district court denied his motion for relief, and he appealed to the supreme court, which also denied him relief. In a *per curiam* opinion, the court said, "Thus, according to this line of precedent, malice is an element of second degree murder not withstanding the fact that Sec. 28-304(1) does not expressly specify it as such." The court reflected, "This rule marked a departure from our prior cases holding that under Nebraska law all crimes are statutory and no act is criminal unless the Legislature has in express terms declared it to be so. . . . Upon further consideration, we determine that our prior decisions interpreting Sec. 28-304(1) to include malice as a necessary element of the crime of second degree murder were clearly erroneous and therefore should be overruled."[27] Thus *Myers*, *Grimes*, *Jones*, and their progeny were finally laid to rest. Dissenting, Caporale argued, "[I]f the law changes based merely upon the makeup of this court at any particular time, the law loses predictability and becomes arbitrary and capricious."[28]

This statement makes one wonder why political parties and interest groups fight so vigorously to support or oppose candidates for the U.S. Supreme Court. They do so hoping that new judges will overturn existing precedent. For example, many Catholics and evangelicals want new U.S. Supreme Court nominees to be committed to overruling that court's approbation of abortion. If a decision is wrong, it should be corrected. Hew to the line, and let the chips fall where they may. But interest groups that succeed, through political pressure, in getting some of their adherents on an appellate court do not establish that prior decisions are erroneous.

The Great Wall of China

A second area in which the court became quite involved in public controversy was in the disqualification of attorneys and law firms for apparently representing both sides in the same litigation. Because the court construed its line of decisions to be very broad in scope, it put in doubt the future employability of law clerks and law students who had worked for one law firm as students and then sought employment at another firm.

The first building block in the court's reasoning was *State ex rel. Freezer Services, Inc. v. Mullen* (1990).[29] Freezer Services brought an original action for mandamus in the supreme court, requesting that District Judge J. Patrick Mullen disqualify the Omaha law firm of McGrath, North from defending a lawsuit brought by Freezer Services against Jake Waller. For years, Freezer Services had been represented by the Omaha law firm of North and Black and specifically by John North Jr. Freezer Services learned of an instance of alleged legal malpractice by North and terminated North and Black's representation. Freezer Services then hired the Lincoln law firm of Cline, Williams.

The Omaha law firm of McGrath, North represented Waller. The North in this firm was the father of John North Jr. of North and Black. McGrath, North and North and Black began merger talks. The firm of McGrath, North hired John North Jr., Black, and some of their employees. McGrath, North instituted several screening practices, commonly known collectively as a "Chinese Wall," to insure that John North Jr. did or learned nothing concerning the Freezer Services case. Such screening practices preclude the lawyer in question from doing any work on the case, seeing any of the files of the case, attending meetings or talking to other lawyers about the case, and sharing the fees attributable to the case. Cline, Williams objected to the screening practices, and on behalf of Freezer Services filed a motion to disqualify McGrath, North, because of the obvious possibility that John North Jr. would communicate information he had learned while representing Freezer Services to the McGrath, North lawyers representing Jake Waller. Following an evidentiary hearing, Judge Mullen refused to disqualify McGrath, North but specified rules for the younger North's separation from the case.

The supreme court decided that John North Jr. was clearly disqualified from doing anything on behalf of Waller, and it wrestled with the issue of whether his removal from the case disqualified the entire firm of McGrath, North. The court stated that a literal reading of Canon 5 would disqualify McGrath, North but acknowledged that McGrath, North said it had created an impenetrable Chinese Wall. The court recognized that the federal courts seemed quite willing to accept Chinese Walls, especially insofar as they allowed lawyers to move freely from one firm to another, a phenomenon becoming more common in Nebraska by the 1990s.

The court determined that McGrath, North must be disqualified and that Judge Mullen had no discretion not to disqualify the firm. Because Mullen's act was purely ministerial, the court issued the writ of mandamus. In doing so, the court said, "We therefore hold that when an attorney who was intimately involved with the particular litigation, and who has obtained confidential information pertinent to that litigation, terminates the relationship and becomes associated with a firm which is representing an adverse party in the same litigation, there arises an irrefutable presumption of shared confidences, and the entire firm must be disqualified from further representation."[30] *Freezer Services* only involved attorneys, and the court clearly seems to have decided it correctly.

Three years later, the second attorney disqualification case came down in *State ex rel. FirsTier Bank v. Buckley* (1993).[31] Original actions for writs of mandamus were filed in the supreme court to disqualify the Omaha law firm of Lieben, Dahlk, Whitted, Houghton, Slowiaczek, and Jahn from representing plaintiffs in two lawsuits: one against FirsTier Bank before Judge James Buckley, and the other against FirsTier in a case before Judge Stephen Davis.

Both situations grew out of allegedly fraudulent self-dealing by Omaha National Bank, the predecessor of FirsTier, when it bought some of its own stock for significantly inadequate consideration from trusts and estates it was handling. At the time, in the early 1970s, the Omaha law firm of Fitzgerald, Brown represented Omaha National Bank. In 1988 eight lawyers left Fitzgerald, Brown and formed the Lieben, Dahlk law firm. Only one of the eight, T. Geoffrey Lieben, had been with Fitzgerald, Brown at the time of the alleged self-dealing. All the other Lieben, Dahlk lawyers came to Fitzgerald, Brown later.

FirsTier alleged in its petition seeking mandamus that Fitzgerald, Brown had obtained the discharge of the bank, which had been serving as the executor of the estate in county court. Now, the plaintiffs in the underlying cases contested the validity of that discharge. The lawsuit did not disclose what information Lieben, Dahlk possessed as a result of its prior relationship with Fitzgerald, Brown that would be of assistance to the plaintiffs or detrimental to FirsTier.

Lieben testified that he had never worked on any of the matters while at Fitzgerald, Brown. Current Fitzgerald, Brown partners testified to the same effect. FirsTier asked whether Nebraska law permitted an attorney who belonged to a firm representing a client to later bring a suit against the client on the same matter and argue in that suit that the past representation by the first firm was ineffective or fraudulent.

The Nebraska Supreme Court reviewed at length similar cases from other jurisdictions and granted the writs of mandamus, holding that the firm of Lieben, Dahlk was disqualified. In an opinion written by Hastings, the court concluded, "[A] very real and critical consideration is the perception that the public has of the legal profession generally. It is difficult to explain to an individual client how an attorney who was once associated with a firm can leave that firm and now bring suit against that client involving the same or substantially similar subject matter formerly handled by his or her prior firm."[32]

Chief Justice Hastings worried about appearances, propriety, and criticism of the bar, and he adopted a "bright line" rule. The court determined that an attorney must avoid any representation against a former client when the matter was the same or substantially similar to one that he or his firm had previously handled for the former client. Buckley was, on its face, limited to attorneys, and again, it appears to have been decided correctly. But the court would soon demonstrate that it may be possible to have too much of a good thing.

Almost immediately after issuing Buckley, the court decided State ex rel. Creighton Univ. v. Hickman.[33] The case was another original action seeking mandamus. Creighton University sued St. Joseph's Hospital in Omaha and asked Judge Paul Hickman to disqualify the law firm of Bickel and Brewer, a Texas firm, from representing St. Joseph's. McGrath, North represented Creighton. St. Joseph's hired Bickel and Brewer, and that firm leased office space in Omaha and moved several attorneys, secretaries, and support staff to Omaha. In discovery, Creighton produced millions of pages of documents, and Bickel and Brewer realized that they needed additional clerical and paralegal help to analyze them. They turned to Celebrity Services, a temporary help agency, for assistance.

Celebrity Services sent several employees for interviewing. Among them was Leslie Walzak. Walzak had worked for McGrath, North as a clerical employee while attending law school. She then became a law clerk. After she graduated and was admitted to practice, McGrath, North hired her as an associate, and she practiced at that firm until she was disbarred approximately a year and a half later. While at McGrath, North, she spent about forty hours working on the Creighton case.

Wlazak lied to Bickel and Brewer about her knowledge of the case and her work at McGrath, North. She never admitted having been admitted to the bar or disbarred and claimed to have been a paralegal and law librarian. Bickel and

Brewer hired Walzak without checking with McGrath, North or asking their permission to hire her.

Walzak went to McGrath, North to review documents. A McGrath, North lawyer recognized her and asked her to leave, which she did. Bickel and Brewer fired her immediately after learning of her true history with McGrath, North. Creighton University then filed a motion to disqualify Bickel and Brewer. After a three-day evidentiary hearing, Judge Hickman denied the motion.

Citing FirsTier v. Buckley, the supreme court reversed the district court and disqualified Bickel and Brewer, granting the mandamus. The court recognized that Walzak was not an attorney and that she only performed clerical tasks for Bickel and Brewer, but it ruled that the "bright line" rule was still applicable.

Shortly after the court handed down the decision in Hickman, the first test of its new precedent arose from a case involving a young law student at the University of Nebraska–Lincoln. He had worked as a summer clerk for the Cline, Williams law firm of Lincoln and had been hired as a clerk for the following summer by another prominent Lincoln firm, Knudsen, Berkheimer. The two firms were often on opposing sides of transactions and litigation. The Knudsen firm told the young student that pursuant to Hickman, they did not believe they could hire him as a clerk, since he no doubt would have done research at Cline, Williams on matters that would have been adverse to some of Knudsen's clients. They paid the young student his expected summer's wages, and he did research at the law school instead, but the issue was brought to the attention of Harvey Perlman, then dean of the University of Nebraska–Lincoln College of Law.[34] Perlman recognized that if broadly construed, Hickman could make it very difficult for law students who had clerked at firms that did not hire them as associates to enter the legal practice.

Perlman discussed the matter with Knudsen, Berkheimer and then spoke with Larry Raful, who was at the time the dean of Creighton University's law school. The two agreed that they should write a letter to the court, not as a criticism of the opinion but of the court's rule-making authority for the bar, when the court acts legislatively rather than judicially. The two deans explained the predicament of the young law student and asked the court to address the problem.[35]

Hastings called Perlman and told him that the court felt the Hickman case applied to everyone, including law clerks, paralegals, and secretaries. Hastings then wrote Perlman a letter, confirming his initial interpretation. Perlman was uncertain as to what to do with the letter. It was not an opinion of the court. It was not a rule devised under the rule-making process. Essentially, it was a private communication between the court and the two deans that significantly affected the employability of the law students of Nebraska.[36]

Perlman finally concluded that the matter should be called to the attention of the bar's House of Delegates, and the bar ultimately decided to petition the court to adopt rules that would alleviate, to some degree, the implications of Hickman and the letter. The bar formed a committee to petition the court which included both Perlman and Raful. The committee fashioned two proposed rules, one for lawyers and one for non-lawyers. The rule for nonlawyers, which included clerks, would have allowed a Chinese Wall. The bar submitted the petition, assuming that the court would draft a rule, publish it, and then hold hearings on it, the normal procedure.[37]

However, the court did not follow the normal procedure. The committee received a notice from the court that the court would hear the petition on a certain day and that the committee would have twenty minutes to state its position. The committee had to file briefs by a certain date. The committee complied, and the court appeared in robes and heard the matter. No one appeared to argue against the rule, prompting one judge to say, "I guess nobody is here to argue on our behalf," a very intriguing comment. Perlman argued on behalf of a rule for nonlawyers.[38]

The court did not author a formal written opinion. It did adopt a new rule sometime thereafter, and though it was not the rule proposed by the committee, it was, in Perlman's opinion, more "mellow" than the court's position expressed in Hastings's letter.[39] Hastings, incidentally, had retired by the time the court convened to hear arguments on the rule, and C. Thomas White had become the chief justice. White was the judge who had written the court's opinion in Freezer Services and was chief justice when the court adopted the new rule.

White's court moved to repair the wrong in two cases decided after White became chief justice. In State ex rel. Wal-Mart v. Kortum (1997), Wal-Mart filed an original action seeking a writ of mandamus to compel District Judge Alfred Kortum to disqualify a Scottsbluff law firm, the Van Steenburg firm, from representing a plaintiff in a tort case against Wal-Mart because the firm had previously represented Wal-Mart in other tort cases.[40] The supreme court appointed a special master who found that the Van Steenburg firm never learned from Wal-Mart any confidential information or trade secrets when it represented the store. After the four tort cases handled by Van Steenburg had been concluded, Wal-Mart advised the firm that it would no longer represent Wal-Mart.

In an opinion written by Connolly, C. T. White's court junked the "bright line" rule and adopted instead the same test that it announced in *Freezer Services*, holding that disqualification was necessary only if the matter the attorney was handling for his new client against his former client was "substantially re-lated" to work he had done for the former client.[41] Connolly erased the "bright line": "Clearly, the 'appearance of impropriety' and attempted screening pro-cedures [Chinese Walls] do not address whether two causes are 'substantially related.'" The court concluded that there was no substantial relation between Van Steenburg's defense of prior Wal-Mart cases and its representation of new tort clients seeking damages from the store. White, concurring, thought that the sole test for disqualification should be if the lawyer or other person-nel had "worked closely with and represented the opposing party in the same litigation."[42]

On July 23, 1997, the White court adopted Canon 5, DR 5-109, of the *Code of Professional Responsibility* entitled "Support Personnel of a Law Firm—Conflict of Interest." It provided that law clerks, paralegals, and other support person-nel would be disqualified only in cases where they had acquired confidential information about a previous client, and it allowed the support personnel an opportunity to show he or she had not received any confidential information.[43] Further, even if support persons were personally disqualified, the law firm for whom they worked would not be disqualified if there was no genuine threat that the confidential material would be used against the former client.

The court obviously heard the message from the law schools and the prac-ticing bar. Support personnel would no longer disqualify a law firm from rep-resentation. The supreme court, by adopting the new rule, moved to clarify the disqualification morass and made job prospects much brighter for law students and lawyers who wanted to switch firms. The retreat from the "bright line" rule adopted by the Hastings court gives credence to Mr. Dooley's dictum that courts follow election returns. But how and why did the supreme court get itself in this mess in the first place?

Many knowledgeable observers felt that the court clearly backed away from the "bright line" rule as a response to pressure from the bar and the law schools. But the court did not meet with the bar and schools in an attempt to understand and rectify the problem. Others felt that the court retreated from the issue because they were hunkering down, under assault. Even though the bar and the law schools stressed that they were attempting to handle the matter through the court's legislative, rule-making powers, the court apparently never viewed the movement in that light.

Some of the sitting judges, according to at least one student of the court, were quite proud of the rules that the court had adopted and were anxious to return the bar back to its ethical level of the early twentieth century.[44] They did not want to engage in a conversational discussion with the bar, preferring instead to have a structured setting in which the court was asking the questions.

During Hastings's tenure, the court, until Shanahan left for the federal bench in 1993 and was replaced by John Wright, was comprised exclusively of men who had gone to law school in the 1940s and '50s, men who had a very different view of the practice of law than those who studied law from the 1970s through the 1990s. One example of the generational divide was the court's refusal to sit any longer at the two law schools. Under Krivosha, the court sat at least once a year at both the University of Nebraska and Creighton University, so that students could see justice in action without leaving their campus. The Hastings court stopped the practice, because in the words of one supreme court judge, students had the temerity to attend the session, leave when they pleased, wear their baseball caps backwards, and eat pizza and drink cokes during arguments. Whether or not one agrees with such behavior, the court was seriously out of touch with the youth of America and may have been overly impressed with its own sense of decorum. Perlman commented that the difference between the law school visits of the Nebraska Supreme Court and the Eighth Circuit Court of Appeals was the difference between night and day.[45] The Eighth Circuit was hip; the Nebraska Supreme Court was not.

A final example of the anachronistic stance of the Hastings court came in the area of bar admissions ceremonies. For many years, new Nebraska lawyers took the oath of admission to the bar in the supreme court chambers. Krivosha changed all that. He worked with the Nebraska Federal District Court to have a joint admissions ceremony in the rotunda of Nebraska's statehouse, where newly certified applicants could take the oath for both courts in an impressive ceremony. Krivosha also realized that many practicing lawyers had sons or daughters who were going to be admitted to the bar, and he followed the time-worn procedure of allowing a father who was a practicing attorney to move, or submit, the admission of his son or daughter before an omnibus motion admitted all those who were not progeny of Nebraska practitioners.

Hastings changed the practice. As soon as he took office, a doting father could no longer move the admission of his son or daughter. The court never offered an explanation for the change to the bar. The clerk's office surmised that it might have been made to save time. The court simply denied prospective movants the chance to make admission to the bar a memorable family occasion, thus earning the enmity of a significant number of experienced bar members, and apparently for no valid reason.

The Jurisprudential Output of the Hastings Court

One can only conclude that the Hastings court was overly impressed with its out-of-date sense of dignity and propriety, and its refusal to acknowledge change led it into serious difficulty. The court's pomposity may have largely been a reaction to the changes imposed by Krivosha. Like a pendulum, the court swung as far to the right as it had swung to the left under Krivosha. It should have stopped in the middle.

All courts make mistakes. The "bright line" rule was one, not because the court adopted it in the first place, in an attempt to placate public fears, but because it did not examine all of the ramifications of the rule, and once it learned of them, it refused to discuss the matter either with the bar or the law schools. The court's withdrawal into its own quarters and its adoption of an "us versus them" mentality placed in clear relief the wisdom of Krivosha's attempt to make the court, as a public body, more accessible to the public.

The Hastings court, like the courts before it, spent large amounts of time and intellectual energy on death penalty cases, struggling to define "aggravating circumstances" in such a way as to pass constitutional muster. Many of the decisions involved the same cast of characters, who would come before the court on direct appeal from a sentence of death, then on a motion for post-conviction relief, and then on habeas corpus. At least for the supreme court, the defendants became household names.

The first major death penalty case to appear before the Hastings court was *State v. Ryan* (1989).[46] Michael Ryan, leader of a criminal and religious cult near Rulo, and a man who had made a prior appearance before the court during Krivosha's term, was convicted of the murder of one of his followers. The other cultists, at Ryan's behest, had tortured the victim over a period of three days, lashing him and tying him with barbed wire, sodomizing him with a shovel handle, breaking his arm, stomping on his chest, and skinning him alive. Ryan was an active participant in most of the action. The case caused a great furor in Richardson County and, indeed, throughout the state of Nebraska. After Ryan was convicted, he moved for sentencing by a three-judge panel. The trial judge denied the motion, conducted the sentencing hearing by himself, and sentenced Ryan to death. Ryan then appealed.

In its opinion, the supreme court discussed at length the cases decided by the U.S. Supreme Court that weighed the differences between judge and jury sentencing, cases now overruled or made suspect by *Ring v. Arizona* (2002).[47] It concluded that it was within the permissible discretion of the trial judge to determine whether or not a three-judge panel should be convened.

In a companion case, also *State v. Ryan*, (1989), the court castigated the trial judge for his parsimony in allowing attorney's fees to court-appointed defense counsel.[48] The trial judge had allowed a payment of only thirty dollars per hour for the defense counsel, in an apparent effort to save money for Richardson County. Judge John Grant's words were instructive: "This case was a disaster to many, aside from the two victims of Michael Ryan. Among those afflicted are the taxpayers of Richardson County and the State. The fact remains, however, that the attorneys appointed to represent the defendants in this bestial event are not guilty of any crime. They are honorable professional people and have been appointed by a court to perform a duty required by the Constitution."[49] Accordingly, the court substantially increased the fee award over the amount allowed by the district court.

The next person to appear before the court in a death penalty case was John Joubert, the killer of two young boys, on a motion for post-conviction relief. The trial court denied his motion, and the supreme court affirmed the denial. Joubert argued that his trial counsel had been ineffective, but the supreme court pointed out that the counsel's plea bargain permitted Joubert the right to remain silent, and one of the two murder charges was dropped. Joubert also complained that the three-judge sentencing panel had received and read letters from the families of his two victims. The panel disposed of this issue, however, noting in its sentencing memorandum: "To the extent these letters have provided a catharsis for those writing them, we acknowledge receiving and reading them. Nevertheless, these letters have no probative value or weight in our determination." The supreme court added its final fillip, "[I]t is presumed that judges disregard evidence that should not have been admitted." Thus, even though the letters were detrimental to Joubert, the court did not consider them and there was no error.[50]

Harold "Willie" Otey came back to the court on a second motion for post-conviction relief, which was summarily denied. The court pointed out that such motions could not be used to ask the supreme court to revisit matters that could, and should, have been decided on the direct appeal. The court went on to tell Otey that even though the matters he raised were procedurally barred, the court had reweighed both the aggravating and mitigating circumstances in his case and found that his motion was without merit.[51]

Trying another approach, Otey asked the Board of Pardons to commute his sentence to life imprisonment. The Board refused to do so. Otey then filed a petition in Lancaster County District Court, asking that the district court deny the enforcement of the death penalty and order a new commutation hearing. The district court entered a temporary injunction. The supreme court reversed and ordered that the injunction be dissolved.

The court's decision addressed separation of powers considerations. Otey had alleged that Attorney General Donald Stenberg, one of the members of the Board of Pardons, had two of his assistants appear before the Board to oppose commutation and to present evidence against Otey, thus creating a conflict of interest. The court found none: "A commutation decision of the Nebraska Board of Pardons, a discretionary act of grace from the executive branch, does not trigger the requirements of the Due Process clause. In a death penalty case in Nebraska, it is the judicial branch of government that sentences a convicted felon to death. . . . In Nebraska, commutation of a death sentence by the State is purely a matter of grace exercised by the executive branch, and no due process rights are available to the applicant." The court said that an offender had the right to seek clemency but that the Board of Pardons had unfettered discretion whether or not to grant it.[52]

Erwin Charles Simants next appeared before the court, asking for a change in his status as a mentally ill person who was acquitted because of insanity. Simants offered testimony to the effect that he should be allowed more freedom in supervised group settings, and the Lincoln County attorney offered expert testimony to the contrary. The district judge denied Simants any change of status and revoked his privilege to leave the grounds of the Lincoln Regional

Center. Simants appealed, and the supreme court agreed with the district court, denying Simants any relief.

The supreme court took Nebraska's Attorney General Stenberg to task when *State v. Joubert* once again came to the court.[53] The supreme court had set an execution date for Joubert. The U.S. District Court had issued a stay of execution, and Attorney General Stenberg then moved the court to set a new date. Joubert filed a special appearance and also filed a motion for sanctions. The supreme court overruled all motions.

The court held that it had the inherent power to set a new execution date when it had set a previous date, and the death warrant had expired without an execution having taken place. The court then proceeded to excoriate the attorney general: "The setting of execution dates in anticipation of the termination of a stay clearly constitutes preparation for the carrying out of an execution, in violation of federal law. . . . Thus the Attorney General asks us not only to perform a useless act, he asks us to perform a lawless one. It appears he has overlooked that U.S. Const. Art. VI subjects the state of Nebraska to the 'Constitution,' and the laws of the United States and that he has sworn not only to support the Constitution of this state, but that of the United States as well."[54] The court chided the attorney general, noting that he had "no legitimate legal reason for moving for the setting of an execution date while a federal stay was pending." The court then invited Joubert to return with another plea for sanctions if Stenberg tried again.

On the same day that it determined *Joubert*, the court decided *State v. Palmer*, (1994), where again, the attorney general had moved the court to set an execution date. In Palmer's case, no federal stay was pending. The court loosed another blast at Stenberg: "Setting executions where there is no legal impediment to the execution is, by law and this court's experience, a ministerial act done routinely in order to carry out the court's judgment. . . . The Attorney General's failure to present pertinent facts and law made what had formerly been routine and ministerial, not routine and not ministerial."[55]

The court was highly critical of Stenberg and his office for asking for writs of execution before cases were in a position to proceed to that stage. Stenberg also filed boiler-plate briefs in support of his requests without differentiating between the types of cases involved, evidence either of a tremendous workload backlog or intellectual laziness.

The court made it clear that Stenberg was not going to bamboozle it without presenting a strong factual base of evidence. Such castigation of a sitting attorney general by the court is without precedent in Nebraska jurisprudence. Some observers would say that the same was true of the attorney general.

Finally, the Hastings court turned again to aggravating circumstance (1)(d), hoping to salvage something from the criticism the federal courts had previously leveled. The vehicle was *State v. Ryan* (1995), wherein Ryan appealed the order of the district court denying him post-conviction relief. He raised thirty-seven errors that he claimed had occurred at the district court post-conviction hearing, including the ineffective assistance of counsel and the unauthorized use of the insanity defense. Both the district court and the supreme court ruled against him on every issue.

The significant issue in this opinion, however, was the position the Nebraska Supreme Court took on (1)(d). The federal courts had held the first prong, which Nebraska had construed to involve torture, sadism, or sexual abuse, to be constitutionally acceptable. But the second prong, which was predicated upon the state of mind of the killer, was on much shakier ground. The U.S. Supreme Court had outlawed an Oklahoma statute that provided almost the same thing. The Eighth Circuit had found (1)(d), standing alone, to be constitutionally insufficient but had said that because the Nebraska Supreme Court could give it a more narrow construction, it was not unconstitutional per se.

The Nebraska court decided to acknowledge that the federal courts had found the second part of (1)(d), the "exceptional depravity" prong, to be unconstitutional and appeared to be in doubt concerning its continued viability. But, the court said: "Importantly, though, the Eighth Circuit held in *Harper* that *the invalidity of the second prong of (1)(d) does not vitiate the efficacy of the first prong.* We therefore hold that aggravating circumstance (1)(d) is facially constitutional to the extent that the first prong has been narrowed and defined by this court."[56]

The Hastings court demonstrated a strong penchant for law and order with the death penalty cases it considered. Ryan, Otey, Joubert, Palmer, Simants, and Moore came before the court on many occasions and were rebuffed on each attempt. The court did not spell out any new or startling rules, but it held the line on cases that had been decided by previous courts. No doubt because it kept seeing the same faces again and again, the court grew irascible when forced to confront any of them unnecessarily and severely reprimanded Attorney General Stenberg for making such reconsideration necessary.

The Hastings court gave its last word on (1)(d) in *State v. Ryan.* But it was not the Nebraska Supreme Court's last word on the statute. After Hastings retired in January 1995, the court revisited (1)(d) in *State v. Moore* (1996), after Moore had been resentenced in 1995, and approved both prongs of (1)(d).[57] The U.S. District Court then approved the *Moore* interpretation in Moore's subsequent habeas corpus case. The Eighth Circuit, by a 2–1 panel vote early in 2002, however, rejected the view of the Nebraska Supreme Court and the federal district court. But the full bench of the Eighth Circuit, in an *en banc* hearing, heard reargument on the matter during September 2002 and upheld Nebraska's construction in early 2003. The Nebraska Supreme Court stated in *Moore*, "This, the exceptional depravity component of aggravating circumstance Sec. 29-2523(1)(d) may be proved either by demonstrating the existence of one or more of the factors identified in *State v. Palmer*, 224 Neb 282, 399 N.W. 2d 706 (1986), *cert. Denied* 484 U.S. 872, 108 S.Ct. 206, 98 L.Ed 2d 157 (1987), or by demonstrating 'the killer's cold, calculated planning of the victim's death', as exemplified by experimentation with the method of causing the death or by the purposeful selection of a particular victim on the basis of specific characteristics."[58]

This statement forms the basis for interpretation of death penalty cases in Nebraska today. Clearly, under the test now approved by the Nebraska Supreme Court and the Eighth Circuit, the murder of Beverly Ramspott by Hunt would have qualified him for the death penalty had it been committed after 1996.

Separation of Powers and Other Issues

Throughout the Hastings court era, the court often found itself serving as a separation of powers referee, determining which side of state government might prevail. Its first test came before Hastings had even assumed the role of chief justice. In the interim period between Krivosha's resignation and Hastings's first day as chief justice, the senior associate justice, Leslie Boslaugh, served as chief justice *pro tem*. During that brief period, a case of substantial significance to the initiative process, *State v. Radcliffe* (1988), came before the court. Walter Radcliffe, a lawyer and at the time perhaps the most prominent lobbyist before the Nebraska Legislature, was criminally charged with hiring and paying circulators to circulate a petition for a state run lottery. The trial court sustained Radcliffe's motion to quash the information on the grounds that it violated his First Amendment free speech rights. The state took exception to the ruling. On appeal, the supreme court agreed with the district court. Citing *Meyer v. Grant*, a decision of the U.S. Supreme Court in which it held that a Colorado statute banning paid circulators was unconstitutional, the Nebraska Supreme Court recognized First Amendment rights and gave every indication of wishing to aid the initiative process, a position it would soon modify.[59]

Such initiative litigation continued once Hastings assumed the center seat on the bench, but the Hastings court displayed a less than enthusiastic populistic response. In *State ex rel. Labedz v. Beermann*, (1988), State Senator Bernice Labedz of Omaha, along with several others, sued Secretary of State Allen Beermann in district court, seeking a writ of mandamus to put an initiative measure calling for a state lottery on the ballot.[60] Beermann had rejected the initiative petitions because of inadequate signatures. The trial court refused to grant the writ, and Labedz and her cohorts appealed. The supreme court affirmed the refusal, explaining that the secretary of state's determination of the sufficiency of signatures is an administrative, not a judicial, act, and he is consequently not required to give the petition circulators notice of what he has done. The court also approved the extremely short period for filing an appeal from the secretary's determination (ten days), because of the complexity of the electoral process and the need to have ballots printed and distributed. The court did not have a controlling U.S. Supreme Court precedent to contend with, as it did in *Radcliffe*, and it thus was able to express, however veiled, its distaste for the continuing initiative efforts to further gambling.

Initiative is tried frequently in Nebraska but historically has had only minimal success. Since 1914 fifty-six proposed referendums or constitutional amendments have been put on the ballot through the initiative process. Only eighteen have passed and not been rejected by the courts, a success rate of only 32 percent.

In contrast, the legislature has submitted 249 issues to the voters, who adopted 197 of them, a success rate of 79 percent. Among the few initiative successes have been the banning of corporate farming, term limits for state senators, and a ban on same-sex marriages, but the U.S. District Court held the latter to be unconstitutional in May 2005, a position subsequently overturned by the Eighth Circuit in the summer of 2006.[61]

Another election matter came to the court but was only heard by Hastings in *State ex rel. Chambers v. Beermann* (1988).[62] Sec. 32-517 R.R.S. 1943 provides that only the chief justice can hear a special hearing in certain electoral matters. State Senator Ernie Chambers was running for reelection to the unicameral. He received a certificate of nomination from the secretary of state. Subsequently, the candidate who was nominated for the U.S. Senate by the New Alliance party—Bob Kerrey—declined his nomination, and that party nominated Chambers as his substitute. Chambers accepted the nomination. Secretary Beermann then issued an order that Chambers could not appear on the ballot as a candidate for the U.S. Senate because the same person cannot run for two offices at the same election and because Chambers had not changed his registration to the New Alliance party at least ninety days before filing his application for nomination.

In a decision worthy of Solomon, Hastings held that Chambers could be on the ballot as a candidate for the U.S. Senate because Nebraska could not constitutionally impose any requirement on a U.S. Senate candidate other than what the U.S. Constitution imposed. Hastings went on to rule that Nebraska could legitimately impose the requirement that no person could run for two offices at the same election. Unless Chambers declined to run for the U.S. Senate, his nomination for the legislature would be cancelled and his name would be on the ballot only for the U.S. Senate seat. In what was one of his few pyrrhic victories, Chambers withdrew as a candidate for the U.S. Senate.

The court returned to its populist, pro-initiative stance again in *State ex rel. Stenberg v. Beermann*, (1992), in a decision written by C. Thomas White, the sole dissenter in *Labedz*.[63] Attorney General Stenberg asked the court to hold unconstitutional LB426, a legislative effort that required every petition circulator to be of legal age and a resident of and registered voter in Nebraska. It also provided that any person circulating a petition outside the limits of the county in which he or she was a registered voter would be guilty of a misdemeanor.

The court enjoined Beermann from enforcing the law, holding that it violated the Nebraska Constitution because it was not a law facilitating the initiative and referendum as required by Article III, Section 4. Speaking for the court, White stated, "It is difficult to justify a provision that does not and cannot forbid the financing of paid circulators in the individual counties, but forbids circulation across county lines. Indeed, the effect of the law is to place impossible barriers to the economically less fortunate to successfully initiate legislation if they cannot pay local circulators and are forbidden to solicit outside their own counties."[64] White argued that the law would suppress the right of expression of the economically underprivileged.

The most compelling issue involving the functioning of government that was considered by the Hastings court concerned term limits, a subject that led to a great deal of popular dissatisfaction with the court as well as the un-seating of Justice David Lanphier at his first retention election. In 1992, by a count of 481,048 to 224,114, the people of Nebraska voted for an initiative to impose term limits on both state and federal offices.[65] Prior to the election, Joe Duggan sought to enjoin Secretary of State Beermann from putting term limits initiative 407 on the general election ballot. He raised three issues. They were: (1) the petitions did not have enough signatures; (2) they added qualifi-cations for federal offices not permitted by the U.S. Constitution; and (3) the proposed language was invalid. The trial court denied an injunction, and the matter went on the ballot.

After the election, in *Duggan v. Beermann* (1994), term limits came before the supreme court. In an opinion written by Judge Lanphier, the supreme court invalidated the election results and held that the petitions lacked sufficient signatures. The court also decided that the injunction was moot. But Duggan asked for a declaratory judgment that there were insufficient signatures, leav-ing the issue open for consideration.

Duggan took the position that Article III, Section 2 and Article III, Section 4 must be read together. Article III, Section 2 provided that in order to amend the Nebraska Constitution, which installing term limits would require, an initia-tive petition must be signed by at least 10 percent of all registered voters in the state. The initiative petitions failed to meet this standard. Article III, Section 4 said that the necessary number of signatures should be based on the vote for governor at the last general election. The court held that Article III, Section 2, which was adopted later, repealed Article III, Section 4, and that 10 percent of the registered voters needed to have signed the petition. Because the petitions had insufficient signatures, the court declared the election void.[66]

This opinion sounded the death knell for Justice Lanphier's career on the su-preme court. In the fall of 1996 he was defeated in his retention election, the only supreme court judge ever to meet that fate. A highly organized cadre of term limits supporters opposed him, citing *Duggan I* and its sequel *Duggan II* while arguing against his retention. The court decided *Duggan II* in 1996, after C. Thomas White became chief justice, and unlike *Duggan I*, *Duggan II* was a *per curiam* opinion.[67] After the supreme court decision in *Duggan I*, which was handed down in 1994, the term limits advocates attempted to place Initiative 408 on the November general election ballot. The initiative would have placed term limits on Nebraska state officials and the state's senators and congressmen. Duggan sought an injunction in the district court, which denied the injunction. The measure went on the ballot, and Nebraskans passed it with a vote of 359,774 to 171,894.[68]

In 1995 the U.S. Supreme Court held, in U.S. Term Limits, Inc. v. Thornton, that a state constitutional amendment that imposed term limits on either the U.S. Senate or House of Representatives was unconstitutional. The Nebraska court threw out the 1994 election that adopted term limits, stating, "While declining to pass on the constitutionality of the Amendments relating to state term limits, we hold that the remaining Amendments resulting from Measure #408 must also be struck down because the unconstitutional amendment was so interwoven with the other amendments that the entire measure now must fail."[69] In somewhat audacious language, the court swallowed hard: "If the people choose to amend their Constitution and comply with their self-imposed limitations, then this court will not encroach upon the people's power. Assuming these self-imposed limitations are complied with, the people of Nebraska may amend their Constitution in any way they see fit, provided the amendment does not violate the Constitution of the United States."[70]

Finally, the court and the legislature were at odds again in State ex rel. Spire v. Beermann (1990), an action filed by Attorney General Robert Spire to declare unconstitutional the legislative act that changed Kearney State College, a part of the state college normal-school network, into the University of Nebraska at Kearney. Spire had issued an opinion holding that the Nebraska Constitution barred the transfer, and he sought judicial affirmation of his position.

The supreme court disappointed him. Although four judges—Boslaugh, Caporale, Grant, and Fahrnbruch—thought it was unconstitutional for a state college to be transformed into a university by legislative fiat, Hastings, White, and Shanahan thought that the change was acceptable. Because of the rule that at least five judges were needed to find a law unconstitutional, the opinion of the triumvirate was controlling.[71] The essence of their holding was that a constitutional amendment was not necessary to change or abolish a state normal school. The court's decision explains why the legislature in Nebraska, and not the court, was the battleground for the more recent effort by Nebraska City interests to move Peru State College to Nebraska City from the village of Peru.

It is difficult to deduce a coherent pattern from the Hastings court's decisions on political matters. The court clearly did not like gambling or term limits, and it went quite far to make sure that such issues did not become law in Nebraska. The court paid lip service to the initiative process, all the while managing to strike down several attempted initiatives. But it did not seem especially enamored with the legislature, either. If it didn't like the initiative process, the court seemingly would have liked the legislature, but such did not appear to be the case.

Names Will Never Hurt Me

Although controversy may have been bubbling below the surface on the Hastings court, it rarely manifested itself in the court's opinions. Still, an occasional crack in the façade allowed thoughtful observers to speculate that all might not be well.

In the latter years of his service on the court, Justice Thomas Shanahan, now a federal district judge sitting in Omaha, preferred to work at home and come to the statehouse only when the court was sitting or having consultation. His habits provoked an occasional raised eyebrow among his colleagues. Even more so, he was frequently quite acerbic in his dissents, belaboring those in the majority more than was the usual wont of a dissenting jurist. For example, in *Broken Bow Prod. Credit Assn. v. Western Iowa Farms* (1989), a case in which a financial institution sought to enforce a lien against cattle sold by an impecunious rancher, the majority of the court held that in accordance with Nebraska statutes, a brand is only *prima facie* evidence of ownership, which may be rebutted. Shanahan peeled the hide, brands and all, off his colleagues with his dissent:

> It is quite unlikely that any Nebraska stock grower views a cattle brand as a meaningless mark rather than an indelible indicator for ownership of the animal bearing its owner's brand. . . . This court, like a loyal laboratory lackey, has assisted in loosing the monster in cattle country. . . . Under the present Sec. 54-109, some side-windin' owlhoot could rustle someone's branded cattle and wind up as the owner by being caught with the critters—a result which is bad law, east or west of the Pecos, and which violates not only the Code of the Hills but common sense as well. Somebody better fetch the marshal.[72]

State v. Rein (1990) involved a patrolman who stopped a driver for no apparent reason, only to discover that the driver was under the influence. White, in a dissent joined by Caporale, said, "As I am unable to reconcile the opinion in this case with the holding in our recent case of *State v. Carter* (citation omitted), I dissent." Shanahan, writing separately, replied, "Nor can I; therefore, so do I."[73] Such flippancy does not often sit well with one's colleagues, especially the more self-possessed members of the bench.

The Hastings court showed little sympathy for either judges or lawyers whose conduct was beyond the pale. In the case of *In re Complaint Against Staley* (1992), the judicial qualifications commission filed a five-count complaint against William Staley, the separate juvenile judge of Sarpy County. The court appointed a special master, who found that four of the counts had been proved. The commission adopted his findings as to two of the counts and dismissed the other three. The commission then recommended that Staley be given a public reprimand and that he pay all of the costs of the hearing.

Staley appealed. One count alleged that he failed to have verbatim records made of dispositive hearings. The supreme court had even commented upon this oversight in an earlier opinion. Staley had become embroiled in a shouting match with the courthouse administrator over his assigned parking spot. After the supreme court reviewed all of the counts, it agreed with the special master that four of them had been proved. Then the court stated that a reprimand was an inadequate remedy, criticized Staley harshly, and promptly removed him from office.[74]

In *Wheeler v. Nebraska State Bar Assn.* (1993), Wheeler, a former county judge in rural Nebraska, alleged that the Nebraska State Bar, in releasing its 1990 Judicial Performance Evaluations, caused him to lose his 1990 retention election. He sued the bar, alleging that it had reason to know that many of the survey responses were invalid and that it published the survey results without investigating the truth or the invalidity of the individual responses. He sued for defamation. The bar demurred, and the trial judge sustained the demurrer. Wheeler refused to plead further, and the trial court dismissed his action. Upon appeal, the supreme court affirmed the dismissal.

In an opinion written by Judge Caporale, the court accepted the validity of the ratings system: "Ratings by their very nature will reflect the philosophy of those doing the rating and are nothing more than expressions of subjective evaluations concerning a judicial candidate's qualifications. There is simply no objective method to determine the rating an individual judge should receive in any given performance category, therefore, by this very subjective nature, rating cannot imply a provably false factual assertion."[75] Caporale acknowledged that Wheeler might have been a good judge, but obviously not everyone thought so. Those who rated Wheeler had a right to their subjective views, and the bar association had the right to publish those collective impressions. Thus, even though the court had some doubt as to the validity of the responses, it was willing to grant leeway to the bar, especially in the case of a judge who might be bringing disrepute to the judicial system by his performance in office.

The court was not breaking new ground in *Wheeler*. In a very similar case some years earlier, the California Court of Appeals had reached the same result, holding that the public is well-served by public comment of a bar association regarding a judicial candidate's qualifications. The court felt that a bar association had a vested interest in aiding the public to make sound judgments concerning the abilities of prospective judges.[76]

The court also displayed a willingness to get tough with lawyers whose behavior failed to meet appropriate standards. In *State ex rel. Nebraska State Bar Assn. v. Dineen* (1990), the counsel for discipline filed a motion to disbar Dineen based on discipline against him in Maine, where he had been disbarred. Hastings wrote the opinion—a real surprise, because virtually all disciplinary opinions were *per curiam* and written by C. Thomas White. White disqualified himself from voting on matters involving discipline because he was the court member assigned to oversee the disciplinary process, but he apparently had no problem with writing the *per curiam* opinions once his colleagues had determined what action they wished to take. Presumably he did so because he was more familiar with the facts of the cases than were other members of the court and therefore could crank out the opinions in an expeditious fashion. Hastings said for the court, "The issue on this appeal is whether the court, upon receiving notice of discipline from another state, shall proceed forthwith to impose identical sanctions here, or whether due process requires something further."[77] The court concluded that due process required some form of hearing, but similarly limited the evidence that could be adduced. Such a ruling allowed the Nebraska court to impose whatever discipline it felt was warranted, without being bound by the result reached elsewhere.

The court protected the judicial selection process from public scrutiny in its opinion in *Marks v. Judicial Nominating Comm.* (1990), which was a suit for a declaratory judgment under the public meeting law. James R. Marks asked for a ruling that the action of a judicial nominating commission was void when it submitted names to the governor after reaching its decision in a closed session. The candidates were heard in a public session, where adherents and opponents were allowed to speak, but the committee, in a closed meeting, discussed the relative strengths and weaknesses of the candidates and selected names to forward to the governor. The trial court found that the statutes that governed judicial nominating commission activity, and that allowed discussion of the candidates in closed meetings, specifically trumped the open meeting statutes, and denied Marks any relief. In a brief opinion by Boslaugh, the supreme court agreed.[78]

The current dean of Nebraska's College of Law, Steven L. Willborn, wrote an article in which he was critical of the court's reasoning in *Marks*. He argued that the nominating commissions should have to cast their roll call votes on judicial candidates in public, contending that doing otherwise violated Nebraska's public meeting statutes. In *Marks* the supreme court held that the specific judicial nominating statutes overrode the general public meetings statutes and that a public roll call vote was not necessary.

Willborn contended, with little factual support, that public roll calls would result in the names of more female candidates coming to the governor's desk. He argued, without citing any sources, that there was considerable anecdotal evidence that the selection process had been manipulated to favor friends, law partners, and even relatives of the commissioners, almost always to the disadvantage of female candidates. One wonders where Willborn got his information.[79]

And finally, in a 4–3 opinion written by Shanahan, to which Boslaugh, White, and Grant dissented, the court pitched the bar association and its affiliated foundation a curve concerning the liability of the new bar headquarters building for real estate taxes. The bar made a dual argument for seeking tax exemption: it claimed that 56.3 percent of the new building (the portion used for bar activities, the balance being leased to others) was used for educational and charitable purposes, and also contended that the bar, as an integrated arm of the court, was a governmental entity. The Lancaster County Board of Equalization denied the exemption, and after the bar appealed, the district court reached the same conclusion.

The supreme court issued a comprehensive opinion reviewing most of its past precedents, and it concluded that the bar's foundation, which held title to the building, was neither charitable nor educational, and denied the exemption.[80] The supreme court declined to decide whether the property was governmental because the bar had not raised that issue before the Board of Equalization, throwing it in for the first time in the district court appeal. The dissent stoutly maintained to no avail that the foundation was educational and charitable.

The Hastings court, in all its cases dealing with the legal profession, sent a signal to the judiciary, the bar, and the public that the days of a "good old boys club" were over. The court was going to hold lawyers at arm's length, and there would be no cozy treatment of all the brothers in the fraternity. The bench and the bar were poles apart during the Hastings court.

Flotsam and Jetsam

Water law, criminal law, worker's compensation law, and tort law are all part of the daily workload of a supreme court. They are cases that have to be decided but that lack a great deal of popular appeal and are often mundane. In an important case involving water, the environment, and endangered species, the Hastings court affirmed an order of the Director of Water Resources that granted an in-stream flow appropriation for Long Pine Creek, Nebraska's premier trout fishery, to the Game and Parks Commission for the purpose of insuring that the stream's trout had an adequate supply of water.[81] The decision ran counter to the position of many irrigators in the area, who wanted to lower the allowed stream levels in order to use the excess water for their crops. The court discussed all the constitutional issues involved and then decided that water did not actually have to be diverted from the stream to be a valid appropriation, upholding the legislative scheme of providing for minimum flows in order to benefit fish and wildlife.

Some of the Hastings court's decisions in these pedestrian areas had intriguing factual patterns. In City of Lincoln v. ABC Books, Inc. (1991), the city proceeded against an adult bookstore and movie theater located on O Street, the city's main thoroughfare, in the heart of the downtown area, only blocks away from the university campus and its impressionable student masses.[82] The store had viewing rooms where a patron could secrete him or herself and view lascivious movies or television films. The booths were fully enclosed, so no one could see into them, but they all had several apertures in their walls so that people in adjoining booths could have sexual contact with each other, a frequent occurrence according to the testimony of Lincoln undercover police officers.

Lincoln had enacted an "open booth" ordinance several years earlier, which required the booths to be open. ABC had been prosecuted three times for non-compliance with the ordinance but did not change the booths. On the prosecution of the case at bar, the city was granted an injunction, banning the use of the booths until they were modified to comply with the mandate of the ordinance. The court gave short shrift to ABC's appeal, holding the booths to be a nuisance and confirming that the ordinance did not constitute a prior restraint on free speech.

Vencil v. Valmont Industries (1991) raised the thorny issue of occupational disease in a worker's compensation case. Daniel J. Vencil had, over a span of years, developed serious lower back pain because of the nature of his work, but he could give no specific cause of an injury, such as a slip, trip, or fall. There was no question that he had pain and that it was as a result of work that he had done for years. Nonetheless, the court found that his malady was not compensable, holding in line with earlier cases, in which it found that coverage could only be secured when an injury happened suddenly and violently, producing at the time objective symptoms of an injury.[83] Caporale, Boslaugh, White, and Fahrnbruch, who all concurred, felt that occupational disease coverage should be imposed on employers by legislative act and not by judicial fiat.

Shanahan and Grant both dissented, pointing out that the worker's compensation law allowed coverage for occupational disease and that there was no requirement that the disease precipitate an injury. Shanahan, loosing another jibe at his brethren, said, "[T]he accident test currently used by this court is a symptom of occupational diseases in the judiciary: retinitis pigmentosa statutorum and decisional dyslexia."[84]

Crewdson v. Burlington Northern R.R. Co. (1990) was an object lesson in just how conservative the Hastings court could be. Dan Crewdson, a young, soon-to-be married man still living at home, was hit by a Burlington Northern train at the Emerald crossing just west of Lincoln. His view of the crossing was blocked by a coal train parked at it, in violation of railroad regulations. Crewdson's father sued for his son's wrongful death, and a jury awarded him $510,000 in damages. Burlington Northern appealed, and although the supreme court affirmed the verdict with regard to the liability, it remanded the case for a new trial on the issue of damages, holding that the jury verdict "shocks the conscience." The court said that the amount was clearly excessive but that it was unable to determine the extent of the excess. Grant and Shanahan dissented, arguing that because there was no objective justification for setting aside the award of damages, the verdict should have been sustained.[85] Logically, they were correct. What test could the court have used to determine that the amount was excessive that would have not also told them how excessive it was?

Summary of the Hastings Court's Jurisprudence

The Simmons court elicited little public criticism, and the White court received scrutiny because of its activities outside of the cases it decided. The Krivosha court, and to an even larger extent, the Hastings court, however, received a great deal of criticism because of the decisions they rendered. The U.S. Supreme Court is accustomed to being in the white glare of the public and the media spotlight; the Nebraska Supreme Court is not. But if nothing else, the Nebraska Supreme Court, during its periods of public scrutiny, might have been pleased that its efforts to explain and interpret the law were being read and evaluated by so many Nebraskans.

The Hastings court attempted to refine the death penalty rules that had so troubled the court under Krivosha. Its efforts did not always meet with approval by the federal courts that reviewed its work product on habeas corpus petitions. But its *Palmer* decision, spelling out factors constituting exceptional depravity, along with the court's last *Moore* decision, both seemed to have given the aggravating circumstances prong at least a fighting chance to win approbation from the entire bench of the Eighth Circuit, an approval given by the *en banc* court in 2003. The 2002 decision of the U.S. Supreme Court in *Ring v. Arizona* means that juries, rather than judges, must determine whether enough aggravating factors exist to justify sentencing a felon to death, but the jury has to apply some statutory guidelines that spell out what factors warrant the death penalty, and the Hastings court did a good job of articulating the scope of those guidelines.[86]

Hastings and his colleagues demonstrated a strong desire to monitor the performance of both the bar and the judiciary. In their relationships with the bar, especially in the "bright line" or Chinese Wall cases, however, the judges showed a desire not to discuss change but to mandate it. Such rigidity was one of the major weaknesses of the court under Hastings's leadership. His penchant for argumentation, as manifested by his motion behavior while a trial judge, is consistent with the aloof attitude taken by the court in regard to the bar and its needs and wishes. The Hastings court was also quite willing to find fault with legislative and municipal activity when fault was present. The court

Table 14. Decisions of the Hastings court, 1987–95

Total cases	2,609
Civil cases	1,799
Criminal cases	810
% of civil cases	68.95
% of criminal cases	31.04
Total cases, no. of affirmances	1,645
Total cases, % of affirmances	63.05
Criminal cases, no. of affirmances	604
Criminal cases, % of affirmances	74.56
Total cases, no. of reversals	595
Total cases, % of reversals	22.80
Criminal cases, no. of reversals	129
Criminal cases, % of reversals	15.92

did not often practice platitudinous deference to either legislators or city councils when it believed that the other bodies had erred.

For the most part, the Hastings court avoided the spotlight of publicity that the Krivosha Court had encountered in *Hunt* and *ConAgra*. It went about its tasks in a workmanlike fashion. But it did bring much criticism down upon its head when it began to legislate judicially in the second-degree murder and malice cases and in the Chinese Wall cases, never escaping from the quagmire while Hastings remained at its helm.

Work of the Court

Hastings was appointed as chief justice in September 1987. The court of appeals began its work in January 1992. So for more than half his tenure, Hastings and his court labored by themselves, although retired or district judges produced 162 opinions during Hastings's incumbency, an average of approximately forty opinions a year until the court of appeals was off and running. During his more than seven years at the helm of the court, Hastings and his colleagues averaged 352 opinions per year.

Table 14 shows the numerical output of the Hastings court, and table 15 shows the opinion production of each member of the court. Hastings ranked fourth in opinions written, averaging 2.90 opinions per month. When one considers his administrative duties, even with the two law clerks, he more than held up his end of the workload. C. T. White, the most prolific author in every category, wrote 306 opinions over Hastings's term, or about one-half an opinion per month more than his chief.

Table 15. Hastings court opinions, 1987–95

JUDGE	NO. CONTRIBUTED[a]	% OF 2,609	RANK
Hastings[b]	258	9.88	4
Boslaugh[b]	249	9.54	5
C. T. White[b]	306	11.72	1
Caporale[b]	301	11.53	2
Shanahan	227	8.70	6
Grant	225	8.62	7
Fahrnbruch	278	10.65	3
Lanphier	69	2.64	8
Wright	28	1.07	9
Connolly	3	0.11	10
Per curiam	501	19.20	
Retired and district judges	162	6.20	
Total	**2,607[c]**		

[a]Does not include dissents or concurrences.
[b]On court for entire period of Hastings's incumbency.
[c]The court wrote two opinions on matters not involving an actual case decision.

Although the court of appeals took many cases off the hands of the supreme court, during Hastings's tenure his court heard eighty-six appeals from the court of appeals, which in essence doubled the judicial labor on those cases. The supreme court was not generous to its fledgling offshoot, affirming only twenty-one, or 24.41 percent, of the appeals. It reversed fifty-four of the appeals, while eleven, or 12.79 percent, met some other fate.

Criminal cases constituted virtually one-third of the court's opinions, a rather startling percentage when one thinks of the often highly praised "good life" of Nebraska. All who praise the wonderful work ethic of Nebraskans can refer to the number of miscreants energetically involved in criminal activity in the state. And although the Hastings court affirmed slightly less than two-thirds of all the appeals coming to it, it affirmed the result in criminal cases 75 percent of the time.

Hastings obviously believed that a chief justice should have a low dissent rate, very unlike Simmons and Krivosha, both of whom led their courts in dissents. Hastings dissented twenty-six times out of 2,607 opinions, or 0.99 percent of the time, as is shown in table 16. During Krivosha's term, Hastings dissented 1.39 percent of the time. Only Fahrnbruch, who came to the court to

Table 16. Chief Justice Hastings dissents, 1987–95

Total Hastings dissents	26
Dissents as % of total cases heard by the court	0.99
No. of dissents in which Hastings wrote an opinion	4
% of dissents in which Hastings wrote an opinion	15.38
Total Hastings sole dissents	1
Sole dissents as % of total Hastings dissents	3.84

replace Hastings when the latter became chief justice, had a lower dissent rate than Hastings among the longer-serving judges.

When Hastings did dissent, he almost always did so in the company of others. He was the sole dissenter in only one of his twenty-six dissents. In only four of the dissents did he write an opinion, choosing rather to go along with the written opinions of other members of the court.

Hastings's example must have influenced his colleagues, for the Hastings court had an 8.70 percent dissent percentage, second lowest of the four courts studied. No supreme court in Nebraska can be noted for dissent, but both the White and Krivosha courts had dissent rates in excess of 10 percent. Table 17 sets out the dissents of the Hastings court.

Somewhat surprisingly, C. Thomas White was the most frequent dissenter. From the tone of some of Shanahan's dissents, one might surmise that his disagreements with his colleagues would have led him to dissent more than anyone else, but he wrote substantially less than White. Shanahan left the court in December 1993, so his tenure was over thirteen months shorter than White's, but because Shanahan averaged approximately eight dissents a year, it is highly unlikely that he would have moved up in the ranks of dissenters had he stayed for Hastings's full term. At least by his example, Hastings tried to encourage collegial, unanimous decisions by his colleagues. How much of his court's low dissent rate was attributable to his model is impossible to quantify, but it undoubtedly made some difference.

Facing the Voters

In 1990 and 1992 six of the members of the Hastings court faced the voters in retention elections. No justice stood before the voters in 1994 because of election scheduling. The six elections that were held did not reveal overwhelming public approval of the court's performance. In contrast with elections during the White and Krivosha years, the scores for the Hastings court were rather low.

Table 17. Dissents by members of the Hastings court, 1987–95

JUDGE	DISSENTS	% OF TOTAL CASES	RANK
Hastings[a]	26	0.99	6
Boslaugh[a]	52	1.99	3–4
White[a]	96	3.67	1
Caporale[a]	52	1.99	3–4
Shanahan	71	2.72	2
Grant	30	1.14	5
Fahrnbruch	19	0.72	7
Lanphier	16	0.61	8
Wright	12	0.45	9
Connolly	1	0.03	10

Note:

Total cases decided by Hastings court	2,609
No. of total cases in which there was a dissent	227
% of total cases in which one or more judges dissented	8.70

[a]On court for entire period of Hastings's incumbency.

After his court appointment, Hastings was approved by the voters for the first time in 1982. His "yes" retention percentage was 82.04 percent, although he was running from the first supreme court district. In 1990, running statewide as chief justice, his "yes" percentage was 75.70 percent. Paul White faced the voters twice as chief justice: in 1968, when his "yes" percentage was 82.35 percent; and in 1974, when it dropped to 78.65 percent. Krivosha was only voted upon once, in 1982, when his approval percentage was 77.48 percent. Hastings thus scored lower as chief justice than either of his two predecessors.

All the members of the Hastings court who also served under at least one other chief justice scored lower under Hastings, with the exception of Shanahan, who went virtually sideways. Boslaugh faced the voters five times. In 1966, under White, his "yes" rating was 81.27 percent. In 1972, also under White, he scored 79.80 percent. In 1978, still under White, he scored 80.14 percent. In 1984, under Krivosha, his "yes" rating was 75.64 percent. In 1990, under Hastings, it was 75.30 percent. C. Thomas White faced three retention elections. In 1980, under Chief Justice Krivosha, his "yes" percentage was 77.24 percent. In 1986, also under Krivosha, it was 59.30 percent, but that figure was an anomaly, clearly attributable to voter reaction to Hunt. In 1992, under Chief Justice Hastings, his "yes" vote was 70.04 percent. Caporale faced the voters twice. In 1986, under Krivosha, he received a 71.49 percent approval rating. In 1992, under Hastings, it declined to 69.11 percent. Shanahan also survived two elections. In 1986, under Krivosha, his favorable vote was 71.03 percent. In 1992, under Hastings, it was 71.79 percent.

It appears that the court went through a gradual decline in "yes" votes from White's incumbency to that of Hastings. Some of the decline is no doubt attributable to the general decline in admiration and respect for the court by the public, especially the public dissatisfaction with the second-degree murder and malice fiasco.

During the second half of the twentieth century, the nation experienced a growing disrespect for governmental institutions, and Nebraska was no exception. From the late 1960s to the mid-1990s, electors showed increasing disdain for judges. Perhaps some of them were following the lead of the Nebraska bar, which also lowered its ratings of supreme court judges.

Seven Fat Years or Seven Lean Years?

In the Genesis story recounting Joseph's captivity in Egypt, Joseph interprets the Pharaoh's dream as presaging seven years of plenty followed by seven years of famine. There was no melding. First there were seven fat years, and then there were seven lean years. There were no average years. Such absolutes seldom occur, and they did not in the seven and a half years of William Hastings's tenure as chief justice.

Hastings had a number of triumphs, chief of which was the creation of the court of appeals. Although many judges, including Paul White and Krivosha, did not favor the creation of an intermediate appellate court, the court of appeals got off to a fast start and began to reduce significantly the backlog that had been clogging the supreme court. Some have suggested that the backlog was only transferred to the docket of the court of appeals, but in fact the two courts, whether working in tandem or not, have very significantly increased the number of cases decided by written opinion each year and reduced the amount of time it takes for a case at issue to be heard on oral argument.

But Hastings also had some failures. The second-degree murder and malice cases weakened the prestige of the court, loosed several criminals back into society, and brought a barrage of editorial criticism down upon the head of the court. Relationships with the bar began to sour, especially over the "bright line" rule and the court's refusal to discuss issues of common concern in anything other than a judicial setting. The court ended its pattern of sitting at the law schools, and the judges did not participate in bar activities.

The Hastings court did nothing of great pith and moment as far as marking its jurisprudential legacy. It remained, for the most part, a stolid, sober, conservative Plains court, reflecting the attitudes and aspirations of the constituency it served.

6. Is the Law an Ass? An Idiot?

A New Twist on the Court's Efforts

Over the span of fifty-seven years, from 1938 to 1995, more than half a century, the judges of the Nebraska Supreme Court attempted to resolve legal disputes, establish a coherent body of precedent, and instill a sense of confidence in Nebraska's citizens that justice would be theirs upon resort to the state's legal system. Their efforts in doing so, including their successes as well as their failures, have been the subject of this book.

The central argument in the preceding chapters is that the status and reputation of the court slipped backward from 1938 to 1995. There is considerable evidence to document this conclusion. Over the years the public gave judges seeking retention lower favorable votes with virtually each succeeding election. For example, in the 1960s and 1970s, Leslie Boslaugh received favorable percentages of 81.27 percent, 79.80 percent and 80.14 percent, an average of 80.40 percent favorable. By the 1980s, Boslaugh's percentage had dropped to 75.64 percent. In 1990, it was 75.30 percent. D. Nick Caporale dropped from 71.49 percent in 1986 to 69.11 percent in 1992. William Hastings had a "yes" retention percentage of 82.04 percent in 1982, when he was an associate justice. As chief justice in 1990, his favorable vote was 75.7 percent.

In a comprehensive newspaper feature on the court in the *Lincoln Journal Star* in 1996, former state district judge Samuel Van Pelt was quoted as saying that in thirty-five years as a lawyer and judge, he had not heard as much criticism of the Nebraska Supreme Court as he was hearing at that time. In addition to Van Pelt, many other lawyers were quoted to the same effect. Principal points of anger were the *Myers* case on second-degree murder and malice; the "bright line" rule in attorney disqualification cases; and the refusal of supreme court judges to participate in bar association activities.[1]

In approval polls conducted by the Nebraska State Bar Association, Boslaugh's favorable retention votes dropped from 84.7 percent in 1984 to 75.8 percent in 1994. Hastings's scores declined from 84.7 percent in 1984 to 79.5

percent in 1994. C. Thomas White's ratings went from 90.8 percent in 1984 to 61.1 percent in 1996, a shocking decline. Dale Fahrnbruch had a rating of 93.1 percent in 1990; by 1996 it was at 65.7 percent.

The Public Policy Center of the University of Nebraska was part of a research team led by the National Center for State Courts in 1999. The group surveyed 1,826 adults nationwide to determine the level of trust and confidence citizens had in their courts. The message from the survey was clear: citizens are not happy with the way courts in America operate.[2] Frances K. Zemans, then head of the American Judicature Society, stressed that it was imperative that the judiciary spend time educating the public about the need for judicial independence in a democracy.[3]

Scholars are entitled to apply their own criteria to any evaluative process and to reach conclusions independent of those reached by others. In this instance, however, the evidence allows only one conclusion: the court did decline in both public and professional acceptance and, more importantly, in the quality of its work product. As of 2006 the court's reputation has improved, and it appears headed back to a position of general acceptance and approbation.

Overly Formal

One of the reasons for the court's difficulties was that it relied too much on the concept of legal formalism, using rules and precedent that appeared to have been ordained on high and that could be mechanically applied to virtually any factual situation. The court did not easily adapt to changing conditions or to new ideas. Yet when it did, it found itself in difficulty as well. There seemed to be no way for the court to satisfy everyone. The most concrete example of the court's futility is the Hastings court's problems with the definition of second-degree murder. The court relied on outmoded precedent that had been jettisoned by legislative amendment, never really realizing that the legislative arm of government had rendered some of the court's prior pronouncements anachronistic.

Law really is a product of society. As society changes, the law and the judges must change as well. Lawrence Friedman, describing courts in the terms of legal realism, argues that very few cases are decided by the use of formal legal rules. More subtle factors are involved: economics, the prejudices and personalities of judges, political currents, and the prevailing culture of the day.[4] The court led by Norman Krivosha, more than any of the other courts, seemed to rely on legal realism to form its opinions, which did not earn it high marks. Yet Krivosha stated that his was a formalistic court.[5]

Robert Simmons led the supreme court into the modern era. Despite the significant societal changes that occurred during the twenty-five years of Simmons's tenure as chief justice, his court did not move forward with much alacrity. Nationally, tort law, in a movement led by California lawyer Melvin Belli and his notions of "demonstrative evidence," exploded into a significance that few could have imagined. Across the land, after World War II and the Korean conflict, state government began to grow, as national notions of the welfare state started trickling down to Nebraska. Citizen conflicts with government began appearing on the court's docket.

The Simmons court was ambivalent in its response to new ideas about the law. In *Commonwealth Trailer Sales, Inc. v. Bradt* (1958), a case decided toward the end of Simmons's tenure, Simmons criticized the other members of the court for following a rule of law that the court itself had established some years earlier.[6] The rule, in light of societal changes, was outmoded, and Simmons argued that it should have been changed. For his pains, he was taken to task by justices Carter and Chappell, who said that if the pronouncements of the court were to be changed, only the legislature could do so. Yet only a few weeks later, in *Gillespie v. Hynes* (1959), Carter wrote that earlier cases setting out a rule opposed to what he was announcing were erroneous and were overruled. On this occasion, Simmons pointed out that the court was arbitrarily abolishing some of its own precedents, making it very difficult for the lower courts to follow, and picking and choosing precedent on an ad hoc basis to support its decision in a particular case.[7]

One can argue, with some justification, that what the Simmons court was really doing in these two cases was demonstrating the dilemma that all judges have. They want to do the right thing and decide cases based on their notions of the societal benefit to be gained, but they must avoid any appearance of being another legislature, responding to the needs and wishes of the populace. To do otherwise would risk running afoul of the constitutional doctrine of separation of powers among the three branches of government. Consequently, judges must cloak their intentions in the mechanical application of formal legal rules, and occasionally they are hoisted by their own petard when the rules they have and the end they seek are in conflict.

Courts cannot satisfy everyone, and they should not try to satisfy anyone but themselves. Sometimes they fail there. They often fail to satisfy the bar and the public, two entities with different standards. On the one hand, the bar wants to be able to advise clients how the court is likely to rule in future cases, and so it favors predictability, especially in matters involving property. On the other hand, the public wants to be convinced of the validity of the court's result. Does the decision satisfy common sense? Is it in accord with prevailing notions of justice? Even new and sweeping changes can meet with public approval if they seem to lead to the right results.

Ruehle v. Ruehle (1956) provides another example of the masking problem for the Simmons court.[8] Justice Carter had to know that the precedent he was criticizing—that of calling up district judges to sit with the court in other than constitutionally permitted instances—had been going on for years and was well accepted by both the bench and bar. Indeed, he had been called up himself. But he didn't like the result the court reached in Ruehle with the sitting district judge. Instead of saying that the court had reached a poor result and the public should be aware of just how badly Mr. Ruehle had been treated, he resorted to formalistic criticism of the method the court had employed to reach that result, thus setting off a bitter intramural quarrel that occupied much of the time and energy of the Simmons court over the ensuing three years. Unfortunately, to uphold the doctrine of stare decisis and the role of the court in our tripartite constitutional system, judges sometimes are compelled to act aggressively.

The court led by Paul White displayed some of the same ambivalence shown by the Simmons court. In Stadler v. Curtis Gas, Inc. (1967), the court held that the Board of Regents could be liable in tort when acting in a proprietary capacity, thus taking a giant step toward abrogating the doctrine of governmental immunity from tort liability.[9] White himself pointed out in his dissent, "What we are doing today is responding to the 'felt necessities of the time,' under the guise of judicial power. The end does not justify the means and an objective born of judicial impotence should not be accomplished by judicial usurpation."[10]

In Prendergast v. Nelson (1977), the White court reviewed all of the questions of constitutionality raised by the Nebraska Hospital–Medical Liability Act, even though many of the constitutional issues were not really involved, as the result of the manner in which the case reached the court.[11] The decision was perilously close to being an advisory opinion, running contra to the well-established doctrine that courts decide only actual cases or controversies, but as some of the dissenters said, "This court would have been guilty of a disservice to the public if it had refused to decide the issues presented."[12]

Yet in four death-penalty cases—State v. Stewart (1977), State v. Rust (1977), State v. Holtan (1977), and State v. Simants (1977)—the White court carefully followed legislative guidelines laid down to determine when the death penalty was warranted in first-degree murder cases.[13] The court made no attempt to impose its own notions of appropriate standards. The legislature had acted, and the court applied the law.

In its most significant cases, the Krivosha court could be said to have junked established precedent and to have relied on its own notions of right and wrong. By wandering afield and applying its own ideas regarding when the death penalty was justified, the Krivosha court spurred great controversy, triggering vast amounts of media criticism of the court's misbegotten effort in State v. Hunt (1985).

The Krivosha court had to deal with a large number of first-degree murder cases, and in almost all of them, Chief Justice Krivosha reiterated his belief that the death penalty was warranted in only the most unusual case. The legislature had set out the standards, standards carefully applied by the White court, but the judges on the Krivosha court did not interpret those standards as easily as their predecessors.

In State v. Hunt, one of the most despicable schemes for the killing of a human being ever devised came before the court.[14] Interpreting the suffering of the victim as opposed to the nature of the scheme to be critical in establishing whether the killing was "especially heinous" and indicative of "exceptional depravity," the court reversed the imposition of the death sentence.

In most of the other first-degree murder cases considered by the Krivosha court, the court applied the standards more rationally, upholding the death sentences, but Krivosha dissented in almost all these cases. His leadership position, coupled with the force of his intellect and his well-constructed dissents, created for the bar uncertainty as to the status of Nebraska law. They created nothing but public disdain for Krivosha and his colleagues, especially after Krivosha's extremely well-publicized colloquy with Chicago columnist Mike Royko over Royko's indignation at the result in Hunt.

Krivosha's court adopted a rule in a civil case of first impression in Nebraska that also touched off a great deal of media criticism. In ConAgra, Inc. v. Cargill, Inc. (1986) the court was given the opportunity to clothe its notions of appropriate corporate behavior in the formalism of a rule because the factual situation involved had not been the previous subject of litigation in Nebraska.[15] After the court took a huge money judgment away from Omaha food conglomerate ConAgra, the disappointed leader of ConAgra assailed the court in the media. In that particular case, the court did not have to overturn any prior precedent to reach the end it desired. It was free to pick and choose among precedent from other jurisdictions where the issue had arisen before.

The Krivosha court departed from established Nebraska precedent in *James v. Lieb* (1985), when it allowed spouses or family members to recover for emotional distress if they witnessed a victim being seriously injured or killed as the result of a defendant's negligence.[16] The rule seemed to make sense to the public. The plaintiff's bar was ecstatic. But the insurance industry and the defense bar were very much opposed to the court's abrogation of prior precedent.

Finally, the Krivosha court refused to abolish established precedent in the case of *Kreifels v. Wurtele* (1980) and eschewed the opportunity to declare Nebraska's auto guest statute unconstitutional.[17] The court slyly avoided the necessity for doing so by finding the defendant's conduct to be gross negligence, an exception to the guest statute. Krivosha invited the bar to continue to try to overturn the statute, suggesting that the court was seriously divided on the issue and that it might junk the statute if court personnel changed or the right case came along. Of course, the suggestion angered the defense bar, the insurance industry, and some members of Krivosha's court, who felt that his candor revealed too much of the inner workings of the court. Members of the plaintiff's bar who thereafter took guest statute cases to the supreme court, only to lose on appeal, may have been disenchanted by his comments as well. Thus, neither formalism nor realism seemed to be the answer as to how to placate the public and the practitioners. A court's reputation may all come down to personalities and impressions.

The Krivosha court certainly did pay more than lip service to formalism in three major cases. In *State v. Ellis* (1981), a circumstantial evidence case if there ever was one, the court upheld a rather tenuous manslaughter conviction.[18] In the impeachment trial of Attorney General Paul Douglas, the court followed well-known rules in determining that Douglas should not be impeached. And in *Vacek v. Ames*, (1985), to almost everyone's surprise, the court breathed new life into outworn concepts of criminal conversation and alienation of affections.[19]

But the court of Chief Justice William Hastings brought the most wrath down upon its head through its misuse of formalism. In State v. Myers (1994) and its progeny, the Hastings court relied on a series of cases which were decided under a statute that had been subsequently repealed and replaced to reach the conclusion that malice was an element of second-degree murder.[20] The legislature had specifically said that malice was not, but Judge Dale Fahrnbruch, writing for the court, adhered to prior precedent, ignoring the change, and threw out a whole series of second-degree murder cases. Essentially, Fahrnbruch decided the issue that he wanted to decide, not the issues the parties had raised. He had wanted to do so since his dissent in State v. Pettit (1987) seven years earlier. He tried to correct what he thought was an error, misconceiving the new role of the supreme court as a doctrinal court after the advent of the court of appeals. Because some of the convicted killers could not be retried, they had to be freed. The bar, press, and public all responded indignantly, with the press severely criticizing the court.[21] The Myers case was ultimately overruled, but not before substantial damage had been done to the court's reputation.

The Hastings court turned away from formalism and adopted a new rule in lawyer disqualification cases, a rule that went much further than existing Nebraska precedent and that the court on its own, without input from the bar, believed to be necessary. The court had obviously failed to consider all the ramifications of its action, and both the bar and the law schools rose up in anger, blaming the court for unnecessarily complicating the movement of lawyers and law students between places of employment. Neither formalism nor realism worked. Neither the bar nor the public respected the court's work product. And then the court, without notice or reason, further alienated the bar when it removed predictability from bar admissions ceremonies and refused to let parents move the admission of their offspring.

None of the Nebraska courts had much success in simply applying abstract rules of law to any given factual situation in order to obtain the result the court wanted. So much for legal realism. Neither did they have much success in taking well-known rules of law and applying them to a set of facts to gain a result without regard to what the public wanted. So much for formalism. In the heightened glare of public scrutiny in which courts operate today, in all probability neither approach offers much hope for success.

Today, newspapers, radio stations, and television stations all vie to be first with a story, to explain it with all its ramifications, and to dissect it down to the smallest detail. The chances of any court successfully escaping such scrutiny would seem to be miniscule. Courts are very important players in today's world. Editors and columnists point out with great regularity the import of judicial decisions. As society increasingly divides into special interest groups, each with its own agenda, courts will find it harder and harder to maintain the image of dispensing wisdom and justice from above the fray. Familiarity breeds contempt, and Nebraska's court, like all the rest, is discovering that truism.

Ad Hominem

Most of the criticism of twentieth-century Nebraska courts focused on the opinions that they issued, the decisions that they made, and the results that they reached. More needs to be said about who reached those decisions, what their attributes were, or how well they judged. And what has been the impact of the Missouri Plan since 1962?[22] Has Nebraska had better judges since they were appointed rather than elected? Although there has not been much written about the Missouri Plan in Nebraska, it is widely praised across the country.

One can only make a subjective judgment when comparing elected, pre-1962 judges with appointed, post-1962 judges. There are really no objective standards for comparing elected to appointed judges, except for the reversal rates of cases reaching the supreme court. The Simmons court, which ended at the same time the Missouri plan took effect, reversed lower courts 33.45 percent of the time, including both civil and criminal cases.[23] The White court, which followed it, had a reversal rate of 19.21 percent.[24] The White court reviewed on appeal some judges who were electoral holdovers. The Krivosha court, starting in 1978, examined the work only of judges who had been initially appointed, with two or three exceptions, yet the reversal rate of the Krivosha court was 21.43 percent.[25] The Hastings court, the last of the four courts, had a reversal rate of 22.80 percent.[26] At least part of this rating, however, has to be attributed to the second-degree murder chaos resulting from the *Myers* decision. The supreme court reversed the decisions of trial judges who followed the statute rather than the supreme court's unfortunate reliance on outdated precedent, although it should not have. Thus it would appear that appointed judges fared better on appeal than their elected predecessors, but the appointed appellate judges were not so fortunate.

No woman had served on either the district court or supreme court bench prior to 1972, when Betty Peterson Sharp of Nebraska City was appointed to be a district court judge. In 2006 Nebraska had nine women trial judges—Vicky Johnson, Karen Flowers, Jodi Nelson, Sandra Dougherty, Patricia Lamberty, Mary Gilbride, Teresa Luther, Terri Harder, and Kristine Cecava—out of fifty-four, one woman judge—Frankie Moore of North Platte—out of six judges on the court of appeals, and one woman—Lindsey Miller-Lerman—out of seven on the Supreme Court.[27] Nebraska's trial (district court) judges deal with cases involving rape, custody disputes, protection orders, child support amounts, and divorce. In 2002 approximately 30 percent of the Nebraska bar consisted of women. Women are thus seriously underrepresented on Nebraska's judicial rosters. A Gender Fairness Task Force, appointed by Chief Justice William Hastings in 1991, recommended the appointment of women judges in representative numbers relative to the population, calling it critical to achieving gender fairness in the Nebraska courts.

Nebraska had not had a black or Hispanic judge at the district court or appellate court levels until a black district judge—Marlin Polk—was appointed in Omaha in April 2005. One black female judge—Edna Atkins—served on the county court bench in Douglas County, two more are currently serving there, and two black judges—Wadie Thomas and Vernon Daniels—are serving on the juvenile bench. Although Nebraska does not have a substantial minority population, the minority population in the state has increased in recent years, and still those of non-Caucasian descent are unrepresented in the ranks of judicial officers. Most modern state supreme courts are quite diverse. Nebraska has failed to keep pace with the trend.[28]

Outstanding Judges

By reversing or affirming the work of the district judges, the supreme court has, in effect, rated them. The court also has had several favorites, whom it called to Lincoln frequently to sit with it.[29] Except in those rare instances where the federal courts have examined the work of the Nebraska Supreme Court in criminal matters, as on writs of habeas corpus, nobody has affirmed or reversed the work of the supreme court. How the judges have performed over the years is therefore something of a mystery, though since 1984 the bar association has rated the supreme court judges on a number of points. But no rating exists for those judges on the Simmons and White courts who served prior to 1984.

Appellate judges can be rated on a variety of factors, including longevity on the bench, acceptance by the public and the practicing bar, quality of written opinions, willingness to take a stand in dissents or concurrences, output of work, and intellectual leadership. If these factors are applied to the twenty-six judges who served under the four chief justices—Simmons, White, Krivosha, and Hastings—seven judges can be rated as outstanding, twelve as acceptable, four as unsatisfactory, and three served so briefly that they did not establish a record for ranking.

The seven judges who have been outstanding justices, in chronological order of their initial ascension to the bench, are William B. Rose, George A. Eberly, Edward F. Carter, Adolph E. Wenke, Harry A. Spencer, Leslie Boslaugh, and Hale McCown. Three of the seven—Rose, Carter, and Boslaugh—were the longest-serving judges in the history of the Nebraska court. Carter served thirty-six years, Rose thirty-four, and Boslaugh thirty-three.[30] Each judge was a prodigious worker. Carter wrote over 1,100 opinions while he was on the court, Boslaugh wrote 1,189, and Rose contributed 999. Carter led the Simmons court in opinions and in concurrences and was second in dissents. Boslaugh dissented 295 times over his career and concurred 205 times.

Carter was never opposed for office after he was elected in 1934. The one time he had a retention election, in 1964, his favorable retention percentage was 84.84 percent. Rose was never seriously challenged at the polls. Boslaugh experienced only retention elections. In five of them, he averaged a favorable vote of 78.43 percent.

Rose was an acknowledged expert on evidence. The bench and the bar alike praised Carter's opinions. Chief Justice Simmons mentioned Rose's intellectual leadership in his dissent in *Ruehle v. Ruehle*.[31] Chief Justice Krivosha spoke of Boslaugh's vast knowledge of Nebraska law in his interview.[32] So did journalist Dick Herman.[33] Carter was the acknowledged leader of the conservative bloc on the court all during the Simmons years and was venerated by the great bulk of the practicing bar.

All three were willing to dissent when necessary. Witness Rose's dissent in *State ex rel. Ralston v. Turner*, when he questioned the inherent powers of the court, or Carter's dissent in *Ruehle v. Ruehle*, or Boslaugh's powerful dissent in *State v. Hunt*.[34]

Rose wrote careful, thoughtful opinions. Boslaugh's never said more than was necessary in reaching a decision. Carter was more prolix than either of the others, but his opinions were very hard to challenge either legally or logically. Rose and Carter worked without clerks to aid them for all of their careers, and Boslaugh worked alone as well in his early years on the court.

George A. Eberly served with Simmons only until 1942. Appointed to the court in 1925, he was never opposed for reelection. Immensely popular with the practicing bar, he wrote very crisp, cogent opinions. The bulk of his seventeen years of service occurred before the Simmons era began, but his reputation, coupled with his popularity with the public and the bar, and combined with the fine mind displayed in his written work during the Simmons era, certainly stamp him as one of the best.

Adolph E. Wenke came to the supreme court to replace Eberly in 1942. He won his initial election by 407 votes out of 61,023 votes cast, a margin of three-quarters of one percent.[35] Thereafter, in three more elections, he ran unopposed. His entire service on the court took place during the Simmons regime, as he died in office in 1961. He wrote 411 opinions, dissented twenty-seven times, and concurred on twenty-one occasions. He was the leader of the liberal bloc on the court. One judge who worked with both Wenke and Edward F. Carter said that the court was polarized between Carter, leader of the conservatives, and Wenke. It was that judge's opinion that Carter was much easier to work with, more friendly, and more tolerant of opposing views. Wenke had a tendency to put down those who disagreed with him with comments like, "No one in their right mind would believe that." But Wenke appeared to have strong public acceptance in northeast Nebraska, and his outstanding athletic and activities achievements at the University of Nebraska–Lincoln carried over into his professional life, as he was quite popular with the bar.

Wenke wrote well, and his influence among his colleagues over a span of eighteen years shaped many of the decisions of the court. He was definitely a force in moving the court into the modern world, especially in regard to the political philosophy of President Franklin D. Roosevelt. Interestingly enough, Wenke did not dissent in any of the *Johnson v. Radio Station wow* cases or in *Hawk v. Olson*, cases in which the Nebraska court attacked the federal judiciary that had become the capstone of modern Democratic philosophy after the U.S. Supreme Court switched directions in response to Roosevelt's abortive court-packing plan.[36]

Harry A. Spencer and Hale McCown complete the roster of outstanding judges. Spencer was a no-nonsense conservative, a veteran of both the county and district courts, and an untiring worker. He was politically astute and very careful and cautious in his off-the-bench behavior. McCown came to the court with no prior judicial experience but with a long and glittering record of bar as-

sociation activities. An avid Democrat, he expressed a strong liberal concern
for the rights of the poor, prisoners, and the under-privileged. Both Spencer
and McCown spent eighteen years on the court. Spencer was elected in 1960,
winning by a large majority, and scoring 84.69 percent and 84.12 percent in
his two subsequent retention elections. McCown was the first supreme court
judge appointed under the Missouri plan, and in his two retention elections he
averaged 77.25 percent in favorable votes.

Both Spencer and McCown worked very hard. Spencer wrote 861 opinions in
his years on the court, while McCown wrote 665. McCown dissented 217 times
and concurred on 107 occasions, while Spencer dissented 154 times and concurred on fifty-three occasions. McCown's dissents were extremely well written and made him the darling of the *Lincoln Journal* and the *Lincoln Star*, both of
which frequently commented upon his being the conscience of the court. Both
in the amount and quality of their output, the two judges deserve encomiums
from the public and the bar alike.

McCown's intellectual courage, his willingness to take a stand on difficult
issues, earned him the respect and admiration of the bar. He was well known
and highly regarded among lawyers, as he had done a great deal of association
work, serving as president of the Nebraska State Bar Association in 1961. In
addition, McCown's gracious demeanor, gentlemanly behavior, and strong
character earned him friends wherever he went. He was an outstanding individual and was in this author's opinion the single most outstanding judge
during the period studied.

The Rank and File

Twelve judges fall within the "acceptable" category of Nebraska Supreme
Court judges. In chronological order, they are Bayard H. Paine, Frederick W.
Messmore, John W. Yeager, Elwood B. "Jimmy" Chappell, Paul E. Boslaugh,
Robert C. Brower, Donald Brodkey, C. Thomas White, D. Nick Caporale,
Thomas M. Shanahan, John T. Grant, and David J. Lanphier.

These twelve functioned adequately during their service on the court.
Messmore, the longest serving of the twelve, may have been intellectually over-
matched by some of his colleagues, but he had excellent political skills and
faced an opponent only in the final election of his career, when he eked out a
narrow victory over another well-known Democrat in his district.[37] Paine was
a solid if somewhat prolix workman. Yeager was extremely popular with the

Omaha bar. A small man, he could not be pushed around. He authored some very cogent dissents that were polite but very firm in tone.

Chappell was a masterful politician who made much of his service in World War I and his American Legion connections. He was fond of announcing at political rallies, "I'm Jimmy Chappell, your nonpartisan Republican candidate for the supreme court." Paul Boslaugh was the soul of moral rectitude, a man of imposing presence and great dignity. Robert Brower, a bright and friendly country lawyer, spent only six years on the court because he was advanced in age when appointed, but he brought prior legislative experience to the court's deliberations.

Donald Brodkey was quite intellectual, but he suffered from the belief that his opinions had to cover every conceivable issue from every conceivable vantage point. C. Thomas White, a bright and capable champion of the underdog, alienated much of the bar because of his irascibility and liberal bias. D. Nick Caporale was exceptionally intellectual, but some felt that he fell short in the area of common sense. He was very meticulous and precise, almost to the point of compulsiveness. Thomas Shanahan was popular among lawyers but angered his colleagues with biting personal attacks and strange work habits. His stinging dissents and penchant for the trenchant phrase made him a favorite with the print media. John Grant was well liked by everyone and a very competent arbiter. David Lanphier had just begun to establish himself when term-limits advocates voted him out of office after he wrote an opinion throwing out a favorable vote on such limits.

The Rank

Four judges—Robert L. Smith, John E. Newton, Lawrence M. Clinton, and Dale E. Fahrnbruch—fell short of the mark as "acceptable" judges, either because of the quality of their work product, their behavior toward the bar, or their detrimental impact on the court's collegiality.

Smith may have been a thoughtful and perceptive judge. It is very difficult to ascertain, because his opinions were so hard to read and comprehend that the bar, press, and public struggled to decipher them. It was as though he were writing in Sanskrit much of the time. Appellate judges must not only decide issues properly but also state their arguments in language that can be easily comprehended. Smith failed utterly with the writing aspect. Because of his nocturnal work habits, he was virtually an unknown to most people, and his early retirement from the bench went unlamented.

Newton would never have been on the supreme court had lawyers of greater ability been willing to take the job. At the time of Newton's appointment, the northeastern quadrant of the state, from which he came, seemed deficient in legal talent. Governor Norbert T. Tiemann selected Newton virtually by default. He was no intellectual, and he was brusque and overbearing in his treatment of lawyers. He preferred the golf course to the library, and his opinions were off-the-cuff, shoot-from-the-hip efforts that did a better job of setting out his political and philosophical points of view than of educating the trial bench and the bar as to the law. On one occasion, when the legislature was in the process of redistricting the court, Newton told a representative of the media that the boundary line for his district had to end at the Douglas County line "because I don't want any niggers in my district."[38] Taking him all in all, Newton would have to be ranked as the least capable of the entire aggregation.

Lawrence Clinton was capable, but he was extremely difficult for his colleagues to deal with. One judge pointed out that Clinton refused to go along with any innovative efforts of the chief justice and court administrator's office, and that Clinton, who died in office of a heart attack, killed himself by "just being mean."[39] Clinton was described as an "angry man." He was a devout Catholic and fought bitterly with his colleagues over the court's refusal to authorize the expenditure of public funds for Catholic schools.

The court construed Article VII, Section 11 of the constitution in two cases in 1976, and in both instances it struck down legislative aid to private schools and colleges because the constitutional language barred the appropriation of public funds to "any sectarian or denominational school or college."[40] The state constitution was slightly changed by the 1969–70 Constitutional Revision Commission, and in the primary election of 1972, voters approved a new wording that allowed federal funds to be channeled to parochial students rather than to the institutions themselves. Clinton gleefully wrote the opinion in a case approving such payment, delighting in rubbing his cohort's nose in the result.[41]

Dale Fahrnbruch was another capable judge, but one whose refusal to decide anything other than what he wanted to decide led the court into the slough of despond. Fahrnbruch wrote the ill-starred opinion in State v. Myers, the second-degree murder case that started the Hastings court down the slippery slope to disaster.[42] Fahrnbruch had dissented in State v. Pettit, the manslaughter case decided several years previously, and he seized upon *Myers* as the vehicle for making his views about second-degree murder the law.[43] In doing so, he relied upon a string of prior cases that had been repealed by subsequent legislative changes. The weak precedent made no difference to him; he said what he wanted to say, and let the devil take the hindmost. As a trial judge, Fahrnbruch had irritated all who had to deal with him by his unfailing refusal to accept the work product of the bar. No order or judgment was ever submitted to him for approval without coming back for redrafting, covered with Fahrnbruch's emendations. When he reached the supreme court, he could not correct the parties' briefs, so he showed what he thought in the language of his opinions. Unfortunately, he did not always consider the ramifications of his actions.

One court official recounted a conversation with a member of the supreme court who was distressed over the ratings that Fahrnbruch, then a district judge, received in the bar polls. The judge could not understand the ratings because Fahrnbruch was a smart man and a very hard worker. The court official replied that the prevailing position of the bar was that Fahrnbruch deserved low ratings because of the terrible way he treated lawyers, both in court and in chambers.[44]

The court did not have to jettison the second-degree murder rule in *Myers*. Had Fahrnbruch and his colleagues stopped to realize that they were going to free a number of convicted murderers by saying that the failure to instruct on malice was clear error, they could have set the matter down for reargument on their own motion and sought the position of the parties regarding the retroactive impact of the new rule. But Fahrnbruch would brook no such niceties; he had spoken, and in his mind the law was as he announced it.

Rookies?

Three judges—Harvey M. Johnsen, John F. Wright, and William M. Connolly—served so briefly during the four supreme courts in question that it is not possible to rank them intelligently. After leaving the Nebraska court in 1940 for a career on the bench of the U.S. Court of Appeals for the Eighth Circuit, Johnsen went on to establish himself as one of the outstanding federal appellate judges in the country. Nebraska's loss was America's gain. And both Wright and Connolly, in the years that have elapsed since the end of the Hastings court, have proven to be very capable judges, writing cogent opinions and winning the approbation of the public and the bar in polls and retention elections.

Hail to the Chiefs

Utilizing the same criteria for the four chief justices as for their brethren, one can, with intellectual honesty, deem all four of them to have been outstanding. Each chief justice made a significant impact on his court, the bar, and the law. But it is appropriate to go beyond that categorization and rank them in order of their impact, their attributes, and their legacy. Rated against a mixture of objective and subjective factors, Krivosha ranked first, Hastings and Simmons tied for second and third, and White finished last.

Krivosha, while demonstrating more interest in administrative matters than White or Hastings, managed to lead his court in opinions written, dissents, and concurrences. He wrote all his own opinions and read the briefs in every case filed to determine if the case should be heard *en banc* or if it could be heard by a five-judge panel. There is no question that he was the hardest worker of anyone on the court in the modern era. He gave over two hundred public addresses each year, speaking in such diverse places as bar meetings, service club luncheons, and high school and college graduations.

Krivosha was very bright and an excellent writer. His powerful dissent in *Sporhase*, a case in which he was the only dissenter, was adopted almost *in toto* by the U.S. Supreme Court.[45] His dissents in death penalty cases led federal courts to stay executions in almost all his dissenting cases, permitting only Harold Otey and Robert Williams to go to the electric chair. Krivosha concurred in the opinion in the John Joubert case, arguing that there was only one valid prong in aggravating circumstance (1)(d), the "exceptionally heinous" prong. The federal Eighth Circuit narrowly accepted the validity of the second prong, however, in 2003 in *Moore v. Kinney*.[46]

Krivosha started the practice of meeting with bar leaders to discuss common concerns. He took the supreme court on the road, sitting at both the University of Nebraska and Creighton University law schools. He instituted a joint admission ceremony with the federal district court. More than anything else, Krivosha lifted the veil of secrecy from the work of the court. Especially in a state with as strong a tradition of Populism as Nebraska, government should operate in the public arena as frequently as possible, and Krivosha certainly told both the public and the bar what the court was doing and what it was likely to do in the future.

Of course, there were problems with the Krivosha administration. His colleagues resented his frequent speaking ventures. They showed no willingness to follow his lead on administrative matters. He was unable to carry his excellent relationship with bar leaders over to the rank and file of the bar. And he unwisely became embroiled in a very public controversy with Mike Royko concerning the *Hunt* case.

But all in all, whether using legal formalism or legal realism, Krivosha pulled his court further into modernity than did any of his peers in the post of chief justice. His court was often contentious. Although the court led by Paul White dissented most, Krivosha led all of the chief justices in the number of dissents, the percent of dissents, the number of dissenting opinions written, and most importantly, in the number of times he was the sole dissenter. His performance runs counter to the leadership notions of scholars Tarr and Porter and Ducat and Flango, who argue that chief justices with high individual and court dissent rates were displaying deficiencies in leadership. Krivosha, and to a considerable extent Robert Simmons, both utilized the dissent as an educational device to show conservative courts how the law was changing, even out on the hustings.

The Nebraska Supreme Court is obviously different than the courts studied by political scientists. All the judges who consented to be interviewed—Krivosha, Hastings, McCown, and Boslaugh—stated that the historical pattern in Nebraska has been for the chief justice not to pressure or attempt to influence his colleagues to reach a certain result. All the persuasion is open and aboveboard and takes place in the presence of all the court members, either at the case conference held immediately after a case is argued—when the judge assigned the opinion, rather than the chief justice, solicits the thoughts of the other judges concerning the case—or sometimes later, at the opinion conference, when the judge who has written the opinion presents it to the rest of the court for approval. Apparently, not even much discussion or persuasive activity takes place in the interim between the first and second conferences, while the opinion is being drafted.

This pattern is very different from the routine followed on the U.S. Supreme Court, where justices jockey for position all the time. If a Nebraska chief justice, for reasons of practice, tradition, or otherwise, feels constrained in attempting to persuade his colleagues during the decisional process, a dissent is virtually his only avenue to demonstrate to them their errancy and attempt to change their thinking for future cases.

It is difficult to differentiate between the effectiveness of Hastings and

Simmons. Hastings had one major triumph—the formation of the court of appeals—and a lesser one, in the Gender Fairness Task Force. But he also had two significant setbacks: the second-degree murder mess, and the worsening of relations with the bar and law schools over the "bright line" rule. Simmons enjoyed cordial relations with the bar, but his court engaged in fruitless raillery against the U.S. Supreme Court. In a rather protracted period of intramural name-calling as the result of *Ruehle v. Ruehle*, the court found it hard to shake off the stultifying effects of six judges of similar background serving together for eighteen years.

Simmons was spared dealing with an inquisitive press. In his day the press never acknowledged that Franklin Roosevelt was crippled or that Dwight Eisenhower had a mistress, or that John Kennedy was a philanderer of epic proportions. No untutored television news anchors distilled major opinions into thirty-second sound bites. Simmons was blissfully spared the burdens Hastings had to bear in dealing with the media. Perhaps if *Myers* had been decided in 1954 instead of 1994, no one would have noticed but a few prosecutors.

Simmons dealt with a much smaller bar than did Hastings, a bar that was recently integrated and spared from legislative oversight by supreme court action. Continuing legal education, a thorn in Hastings's flesh, was virtually unknown in Simmons' day. The number of women practicing in the entire state in the Simmons years could fit comfortably in the supreme court's cramped courtroom. Conditions were much easier and more pleasant for Simmons than for Hastings.

The Hastings court tried to deflect criticism from individual judges by adopting the use of the *per curiam* opinion in 19.20 percent of its cases, a total of 501 such opinions. In contrast, seven of the 4,065 opinions issued by the Simmons Court were *per curiam*.

Virtually untroubled by outside elements, the Simmons court took summers off, cranked out an average of 162.6 cases a year (less than half as many as Hastings and his colleagues decided), and faced new legal concepts and techniques only toward the end of its era. Because of the very dissimilar periods in which they worked, the Simmons court judges, who generated little if no controversy, cannot be rated above the hardworking but sometimes overwhelmed members of Hasting's court. But even though they were often engulfed by their caseload, discordant elements in the bar, and society at large,

Table 18. Court statistics

	SIMMONS	WHITE	KRIVOSHA	HASTINGS
Years as chief	25	16	9	8
Av. no. cases per year	162.60	259.25	390.33	326.12
Total cases decided	4,065	4,148	3,513	2,609
Total cases affirmed	2,264	3,033	2,380	1,645
% of total cases affirmed	55.69	73.11	67.74	63.05
Total cases reversed	1,360	797	753	595
% of total cases reversed	33.45	19.21	21.43	22.80
Criminal cases as % of all cases	9.30	29.82	25.93	31.04
Criminal cases affirmed	250	1,081	694	604
% of criminal cases affirmed	66.13	87.38	76.18	74.56
Criminal cases reversed	98	104	90	129
% of criminal cases reversed	25.92	8.40	9.87	15.92
Total cases with dissents	265	470	379	227
% of total cases with dissents	6.51	11.33	10.78	8.70
Total cases with concurrences	90	302	432	162
% of total cases with concurrences	2.21	7.28	12.29	6.20
Per curiam opinions	7	57	621	501
% of per curiam opinions	0.17	1.37	17.67	19.20

the Hastings court had an obligation to get it right, and on at least two major occasions, they fell short. Accordingly, by weighing the two courts in the balance, the scales do not tip in either direction.

The least successful of the four courts was the one headed by Paul White, not because of the poor quality of its work, but because of the unfortunate personal peccadilloes of its leader. White's personality quirks—his fondness for strong drink, noxious cigars, and interminable accounts of irrelevant minutiae—made him the butt of many lawyer jokes.

White's court enjoyed acceptable relations with the organized bar until it began to show disapproval of making continuing legal education mandatory. The court was reluctant to entertain any such idea because of perceived difficulty in enforcing compliance.

The White court had the highest dissent rate of any of the four courts examined. White dissented ninety-seven times, or 2.33 percent of the cases heard by his court, but he only wrote thirty-nine dissenting opinions, preferring to join in the opinions of others. He frequently complained about the administrative burdens he was forced to assume midway through his term. Both colleagues on the court and subordinates in the court administrator's office expressed the

Table 19. Decisional efforts of chief justices

	SIMMONS	WHITE	KRIVOSHA	HASTINGS
Total cases decided	4,065	4,148	3,513	2,609
Opinions written	529	545	386	258
Opinions as % of total cases	13.01	13.13	10.98	9.88
Rank on court in opinions	3	3	1	4
Total dissents	75	97	139	26
Dissents as % of total cases	1.84	2.33	3.95	0.99
Dissenting opinions written	60	39	106	4
% of dissenting opinions written	80	40.20	76.25	15.38
Total sole dissents	33	2	63	1
% of dissents as sole dissenter	44	2.06	45.32	3.84
Rank on court in dissents	1	4	1	6

view that White shunned administrative details as though they were the plague and wanted to bother only with cases of the utmost gravity.

Civility among members of the White court appeared to be strained, if the potshots court members took at each other in their opinions can be utilized as evidence. It was not at all uncommon for members to respond to dissents or concurrences with *ad hominem* blasts at the offending dissenter. White judges threw in personal statements or concurred with their own opinions on more than one occasion, circumstances that did not show up on the other three courts.

Finally, despite the opinion output of the White court (4,148 total), the court began to sink under the weight of the hundreds of cases being appealed every year. During White's tenure, the length of time between filing a case and deciding it expanded exponentially. The court's efforts toward expediting the process appeared to fail.

Tables 18 and 19 offer a factual comparison of the four courts. Table 18 sets out statistics for the courts; table 19 shows the decisional efforts of the four chief justices.

Conclusion

How should one rate the performance of the Nebraska Supreme Court as an institution, rather than as a collection of individuals, over the years from 1938 to 1995? The court declined in the opinion of the public and the legal profession over that span of time. But was the decline justified?

Judges must play the hands they are dealt. They cannot go into the community and look for issues to decide. They rule only on actual cases or controver-

sies. The bar has a responsibility in the development of any body of jurisprudence, a charge that is shared with the appellate courts. The bar must push for
new and innovative rules that reflect the needs of society and present issues to
the courts for them to hand down new precedents.

The Simmons court may be criticized for its lack of innovation, because it
simply tried to maintain the status quo over a quarter of a century. But if the
bar did not ask for new rules and sweeping change, the court cannot take all
the blame. The Simmons court satisfied the needs and reflected the mood of
mid-century Nebraskans, serving a society that had not yet come to grips with
the reality of societal change.

Societal and cultural change enveloped Paul White's court. In its decisions
in *Stadler v. Curtis Gas Inc.* and *Prendergast v. Nelson*, it showed some signs of
accommodating innovation.[47] But the White court showed a marked reluc-
tance to move forward when it upheld the guest statute in *Botsch v. Reisdorff*.[48]
In criminal cases it approved virtually every death penalty case it got its hands
on and generally followed the conservative bent of its leader, who decried the
result in *Stadler*.

The Krivosha court mirrored society. The court's rulings in *Sporhase* and
Little Blue N.R.D., both civil cases, had to please agricultural interests by pro-
tecting water from out of state interests and making it more available to in-
state users.[49] The U.S. Supreme Court's reversal of *Sporhase* cannot be attributed
to Nebraska's judges, other than Krivosha himself. The decision in *ConAgra*
had to please Nebraska's stockholders, angering only Charles "Mike" Harper
and a few other acquisition-minded corporate moguls.[50] Criminal cases were
another story. The excruciatingly minute scrutiny of death penalty appeals,
mandated by the U.S. Supreme Court, revealed a serious philosophical schism
on the court, and the *Hunt* decision, arguably the court's worst ever, pleased no
one and angered almost all who learned of it.[51]

The Hastings court was caught in the same civil-criminal dichotomy as the
Krivosha court. Its civil jurisprudence, with the exception of the "bright line"
rule that attempted to return the court to the glories of yesterday, was quite
modern and straightforward.

Discussing the "bright line" rule, Harvey Perlman stated that at least a
"couple of judges" on the Hastings court were quite proud of the ethical rules
that they had developed and wanted ethics to be as they were years before,
prior to the huge increase in the number of lawyers.[52] Bernard Schwartz, one

of America's leading legal historians, theorizes that judges often carry the attitudes of an prior generation because of the way they are chosen and the average length of their tenure. Because legislators are elected at shorter intervals, their viewpoint is more likely to reflect that of the younger generation. Judges have their roots in the past more than others in public life, and as a consequence, they may be slow to accept change, a view that would appear to be sustained by the "bright line" rule.[53] Still, the Hastings court's leadership role in promoting an intermediate court of appeals was significant and did much to relieve the backlog of cases that denied justice because of delay.

When Nebraska created the court of appeals, there were almost one thousand five hundred cases on the appellate docket, and litigants were waiting up to three years to have cases decided. By the summer of 2001 there was a backlog of only one hundred cases, and most cases were being heard within six months of being filed. In the first ten years of its existence (1992–2001) the court of appeals disposed of 6,032 cases without opinions and issued 4,911 opinions, both published and unpublished.[54]

In criminal matters, the court was another story. In the *Myers* case and its offshoots, the court confused the law regarding second-degree murder, angering the public, the press, and the bar.[55] The accomplishments of the court vanished in the firestorm of criticism that followed its ill-considered opinions.

But over the years, the decisions of the court reflected the work of good people, with just a handful of notable exceptions, trying hard. The *Myers* case was the result of the misconception of one judge who ignored reality to reach the decision he wanted. The opinions of the U.S. Supreme Court made the *Hunt* case and the other sentencing cases necessary.

Thus, the court cannot be seriously faulted for what it did not do. Perhaps more criticism is warranted for what it did do. Most critically of all, it fell short of the mark in instilling public and professional confidence in the justice system. If the people do not want to turn to the courts to resolve their disputes, what is left? Trial by combat?

As a product of society, law constitutes an effort to codify and explain the needs and the wants of the populace. But the supreme court can struggle to ascertain those needs and wants and accommodate them, if in doing so the rights of the minority segments of society are trampled upon. The public may think, like Mr. Bumble, that the law is an ass or an idiot. But the unfortunate man convicted of rape who is subsequently freed because of DNA evidence might not think so.

Judges may never be able to escape entirely from bad press and public outrage. Courts must try their best to remain open to new and innovative theories and to balance the needs of society with the protection of minorities. To do so, judges must be realists, not legal formalists. They need to know the implications of each decision. The court can then pick and choose from existing precedent to clothe its action. The Nebraska courts studied here did not often consider the societal implications of their decisions. If they did consider the wider ramifications on occasion, they refused to admit it to anyone. All the Nebraska judges interviewed state that the Nebraska court was a formalistic court, one that simply applied precedent to each factual situation it confronted. But the court does not have to follow this pattern. In making their decisions, judges are entitled to consider information that anyone would know; they may resort to common sense.[56]

Had the Nebraska judges been more aware of the impact of their decisions on society, they might well have been more accepted by the public. A court need not cast aside its existing rules, having enough precedents to manage most of the situations it will face. If the court encounters an issue that it has never considered, it can decide the case as it sees fit. But in any event, the court should consider all the ramifications of its action before making a decision, and then it can choose a rule from among existing precedents that will bring about the desired result. Predictability is cast aside only when the court refuses to apply any existing precedent. Nebraska's judges, like Procrustes, should be able to tailor a solution to fit any situation. After all, America is a common-law country, and judges in common-law countries make the rules. Even though legislatures pass laws, judges interpret them, and while judges say that they defer to the legislature, they do not always do so. A determined court can turn even the most clearly written law upside down.[57]

Had the Nebraska judges followed Procrustes' lead in the past half century, the public and the bar would have been more accepting of them. And it is that acceptance, that willingness on the part of the citizenry to submit disputes to others to decide in an orderly and peaceful fashion, that is the hallmark of a rational and peaceful society. *Salus populi suprema est lex*: the people's good is the highest law.

Appendix 1

Associate Justices of the Nebraska Supreme Court, 1938–95

William B. Rose, 1909–43

Rose came to Nebraska in 1888, after having been admitted to the Pennsylvania bar. From 1890 to 1908, he was an assistant attorney general. In 1908 the size of the court increased from three to seven judges, and Rose was one of four new members appointed by Governor George L. Sheldon. The increase in the size of the court was an attempt to lessen railroad influence over it. Sheldon, a Republican, campaigned on what appeared to be a Populist platform, assailing the railroad's influence over the court and legislature through its distribution of the free railroad pass. He won the election of 1906 handily and was no doubt pleased to appoint Rose, who had been chairman of the Republican State Committee in 1906, and who had been instrumental in having the GOP convention nominate Sheldon for the gubernatorial seat. While on the court Rose authored 999 signed opinions, eighty signed dissents, and seven concurrences. In 1936 William Wigmore, dean of the Northwestern University Law School, named him one of the twenty-two best state court judges in the country on the law of evidence.

George A. Eberly, 1925–43

Eberly was appointed to fill a vacancy on the court in 1925 and was never challenged in an election until he retired in January 1943. He was a graduate of the University of Michigan Law School and practiced in Stanton, his hometown, until he was appointed to the court. During the Spanish-American War, Eberly was a sergeant in Grigsby's Rough Riders cavalry troop. He rose to the rank of colonel in the Nebraska National Guard and commanded the Fourth Nebraska Infantry on the Mexican border in 1917.

Bayard H. Paine, 1931–49

Bayard Paine moved to Grand Island with his parents from Painsville, Ohio, when he was one year old, and he resided in Grand Island until his death over eighty years later. He graduated from Northwestern University and taught school for a short time, read law in a Grand Island law office, and spent one year at the University of Michigan Law School. He became a state district judge in Grand Island in 1916 and served until he was elected to the Nebraska Supreme Court in 1930. He served on the supreme court for eighteen years, retiring in January 1949. A Methodist, Paine for years served as a trustee of both Nebraska Wesleyan University and Southern Methodist University in Dallas. A voracious reader, he maintained a very extensive personal library, wrote a small volume of Nebraska history entitled "Pioneers, Indians and Buffaloes" in 1935, and also contributed some law-related articles to *Nebraska History*.

Edward F. Carter, 1935–71

Edward F. Carter, the longest serving judge in the history of the Nebraska Supreme Court, had a thirty-six year stint on the court, and for twenty-two of those years he was the senior judge in point of service. After his military service in World War I, he practiced in Bayard until he was elected to the state district bench in 1926. When he took office on the supreme court in January 1935, he was the youngest member of the court in the history of the state. He wrote some eleven hundred opinions while on the court, and his colleagues praised the clarity and cogency of his writing. He served as president of Cornhusker Boys State for thirty-three years. He was never challenged in an election during his service on the court.

Frederick W. Messmore, 1937–65

Frederick Messmore, an Iowa native, graduated from Creighton University School of Law in 1912 and began a law practice in Beatrice. He became county attorney in 1914 and served until 1918, when he enlisted in the army. Prior to entering public service, he was active in Democratic Party affairs. While in the army he contracted influenza and became very ill, but he recovered in time to be discharged in 1919. Returning to Beatrice, he was elected county judge in 1920 and district judge in 1928. In 1937 he was appointed to the Nebraska Supreme Court by Governor Cochran to fill the vacancy left by the death of Judge Edward Good. He served until January 1965, when he retired. His only electoral challenge came in 1958, when he defeated Hebron attorney W. O. Baldwin, a Democratic stalwart, by a vote of 22,751 to 20,023.

Harvey M. Johnsen, 1939–49

Harvey M. Johnsen served on the court only briefly. A native Nebraskan, he graduated from the University of Nebraska College of Law in 1919. He practiced in Omaha after graduation and was president of the Omaha Bar Association in 1931. In 1937 he was selected as the first president of the newly integrated (unified) Nebraska State Bar Association. Governor Cochran appointed him to the supreme court in November 1938 to fill the vacancy caused by the death of Judge L. B. Day, but he delayed taking the bench until he finished his term as president of the bar. In 1940 Franklin D. Roosevelt appointed him to the U.S. Court of Appeals for the Eighth Circuit, where he served as an active judge until 1965 and thereafter on senior status, until his death in 1976.

John W. Yeager, 1941–65

John W. Yeager, a district judge from Omaha, ran unopposed in 1940 to fill Harvey Johnsen's seat. A native of Indiana and Texas, he came to Omaha in 1915. He interrupted his practice to serve in the U.S. Army during World War I. He joined the Douglas County Attorney's office in 1921 and served there for twelve years, becoming chief deputy in 1931. In 1933 he was elected a district judge in Omaha, and he served as a district judge until he was elected to the supreme court.

Elwood B. Chappell, 1943–61

Elwood B. Chappell, who replaced William Rose on the court, came to the court from the district bench in Lancaster County in January 1943. Chappell was a graduate of the University of Nebraska, earning both a bachelor of arts and a degree in pharmacy. He supported himself during his college years by working part-time as a barber. He graduated from the University of Nebraska College of Law in 1916. He practiced in Lincoln until enlisting in the service during World War I. He returned to Lincoln after the war and resumed his practice. In 1920 he served as commander of Lincoln's American Legion Post. In 1923 he was appointed police judge and then became the first judge of Lincoln's municipal court in 1925. He was elected to the district court in 1928 and served there until his election to the supreme court. In 1940 he served as president of the Nebraska State Bar Association.

Chappell's 1928 campaign for district judge showed his political acumen. He ran against the incumbent, Mason Wheeler. During the campaign, Wheeler made a speech in the rural county town of Bennet, in which he said that as a judge he made sure that everyone, from the banker to the barber, received justice. Chappell had retained his barber's union card from his university days. He and his campaign manager, Guy Chambers, one of Lincoln's finest lawyers, spread the word to barbers throughout the county that Wheeler had insulted them. Every barbershop in the county backed Chappell to the hilt. Wheeler's position grew worse when, speaking at Hallam, he tried to rectify the mistake by saying that he meant "banker to bricklayer" rather than "banker to barber." He thus earned the enmity of all the bricklayers, and Chappell won in a walk. He served as a district judge until he was elected to the supreme court in 1942.

Adolph E. Wenke, 1943–61

Adolph E. Wenke, who filled George Eberly's seat on the bench, was a resident of Stanton like Eberly. Wenke graduated from the University of Nebraska College of Law in 1923 after a stellar college career in which he played tackle on several powerful Nebraska football teams, participated in track, and was elected to the Innocents Society. After he graduated from law school and passed the bar, he played a year of professional football with Milwaukee's team in the National Football League.

Wenke went to Stanton in 1924 to practice and served as county attorney, city attorney, a member of the school board, a trustee of Doane College, and commander of the Stanton American Legion post. In 1936 he was an alternate delegate to the Democratic Party's national convention. He was appointed a district judge in February 1938, and he served there until his election to the supreme court in November 1942. In 1943 he was president of the University of Nebraska Alumni Association. During his terms on the supreme court he often served as a referee for the National Railway Adjustments Board and the Railroad System Board of Adjustment and as a member of the Presidential Railroad Emergency Board. He died in office in March 1961.

Paul E. Boslaugh, 1949–61

Paul Boslaugh, who was elected to the supreme court in 1948 when Bayard Paine declined to run again, became the oldest judge ever to sit on the court. He was too old to serve in World War I. Like Chappell and Harvey Johnsen, Boslaugh was a past president of the Nebraska State Bar Association and was a member of the 1937 committee that successfully recommended the integration of the Nebraska bar. He was a member of the House of Delegates of the American Bar Association from 1942 to 1954. He served on the supreme court until January 1961, when his son, Leslie, succeeded him. Paul Boslaugh graduated from the University of Nebraska College of Law in 1903 and began to practice in Harvard, Nebraska, the same year.

Leslie Boslaugh, 1961–94

Leslie Boslaugh graduated *cum laude* from Nebraska's law school in 1941 and served as an assistant attorney general and a member of the Statute Revision Commission until he entered military service in World War II. An army officer in the European theater, he was discharged in August 1946 and returned to the attorney general's office. When his father was elected to the supreme court in 1948, Leslie went back to Hastings and practiced with his father's partner, Lester Stiner. In 1960 he was elected to the supreme court to succeed his father. Leslie Boslaugh belonged to the American Legion, Veterans of Foreign Wars, and a number of Masonic bodies, although he was not the inveterate joiner that many of his colleagues were. He was a great railroad buff and collector of model railroad cars and brass engines. He retired from the court in 1994, having served thirty-three years, the third longest tenure of any judge on the Nebraska Supreme Court.

Harry A. Spencer, 1961–79

Harry A. Spencer, who succeeded E. B. Chappell in January 1961, was born in Bishops Walton, England. His family shortly thereafter came to Nebraska, where he graduated from Omaha South High School, the University of Nebraska, and, in 1930, from Nebraska's College of Law (*cum laude*). He practiced in Lincoln for a number of years before he was elected county judge in 1945. In 1951 he was elected to the district bench, where he served until his election to the supreme court in November 1960. Spencer was a delegate to the Republican Party's National Convention in 1936 and again in 1940. He was an active member of Kiwanis, having held a regional leadership position in the club, and participated in all the Masonic bodies. Involved in bar association activities, Spencer served as a member of the House of Delegates of the American Bar Association for a number of years, representing the judicial administration section. Spencer retired from the court in 1979. As senior associate judge, he served as acting chief justice for a brief period between Paul White's retirement and Norman Krivosha's appointment in 1978.

Robert C. Brower, 1961–67

Brower came to the court after Adolph Wenke's death in March 1961, and he served until his retirement in 1967. Brower graduated from the University of Michigan School of Law in 1919 and practiced railroad law in Kalispell, Montana, until 1922, when he returned to Fullerton after his father's death. He served on the Fullerton school board, as Nance County Attorney during World War II, and as a Nebraska state legislator from 1953 to 1957. He was an active Democrat, and Governor Frank Morrison appointed him to keep a good Democrat in Wenke's seat. He was a member of the Elks and the Eagles lodges.

Hale McCown, 1965–83

McCown was a Democrat, the leading lawyer in Beatrice, and the head of its most prestigious firm. He was a graduate of Duke Law School, where he had been a friend and classmate of Richard Nixon. McCown's undergraduate education was at Hastings College. He practiced in Portland, Oregon, from 1937 to 1942, and then served as an officer in the U.S. Navy until 1945. He returned to Beatrice to practice after his military service, where he was active in civic affairs, holding several leadership positions in the local Presbyterian church and serving as president of the Nebraska State Bar Association in 1961.

Robert L. Smith, 1965–73

Smith was the son of Seymour Smith, one of Omaha's most beloved lawyers. He was a graduate of Southern Methodist University and Creighton Law School and served as a state district judge in Omaha from 1961 to 1965. He served only briefly on the supreme court, resigning in 1973.

John W. Newton, 1967–77

A very conservative justice, Newton became a state district judge in 1956. He was Dakota County Attorney from 1928 to 1956. He was a close personal friend of Paul White. Newton died in 1984 after leaving the court in 1977. White gave a glowing eulogy of Newton at memorial services held by the court in 1984, far different than the repetitive remarks he made at services for other departed judges when he was chief justice.

Lawrence M. Clinton, 1971–82

After serving in World War II and graduating from Creighton's law school, Clinton practiced law in Sidney, Nebraska. He came directly to the supreme court from his law practice. He suffered heart trouble for several years before he died in office in 1982.

Donald Brodkey, 1974–82

Brodkey was a South Dakota native. He graduated from the University of South Dakota and the University of Iowa College of Law. He began practicing in Omaha in 1933 and served as a district judge in Omaha from 1960 until 1974, when Governor Exon appointed him to the supreme court. He was a friendly, warm, and garrulous personality, an inveterate photographer, and was both intelligent (a member of Phi Beta Kappa, the Order of the Coif, and the *Iowa Law Review*) and reasonable. His one flaw as a judge was the length of his opinions. His scholarly approach prompted him to consult and cite every conceivable authority.

C. Thomas White, 1977–98

White was a native of Humphrey, Nebraska. He graduated from the Creighton University Law School in 1952 and began practicing in Columbus. He served as Platte County Attorney from 1955 to 1965. Governor Morrison appointed him to the district bench in 1965, and Governor Exon placed him on the supreme court in 1977. A Roman Catholic, White served in the U.S. Army during 1946–47. Even as a young district judge, White manifested a stern, gruff demeanor on the bench. The bar viewed him as plaintiff-oriented, especially in cases where insurance companies represented the defendants.

D. Nick Caporale, 1982–98

Caporale, a brilliant man, attended law school after service as an officer in the U.S. Army. He was awarded the Bronze Star for his service in Korea from 1952–54. From the time he graduated from law school at the University of Nebraska until he was appointed to the district bench in 1979, he had a fine career as an excellent trial lawyer with a prestigious Omaha law firm. A man of slight stature, he was extremely cordial and well liked and respected by his peers.

Thomas M. Shanahan, 1983–93

Shanahan was a graduate of Notre Dame and the Georgetown University School of Law. He practiced with a leading law firm in Ogallala from 1959 until his appointment to the court. He was a very capable lawyer and had been very active in the work of the state bar. He was serving on its executive council at the time of his appointment.

Shanahan's work habits were similar to those of Robert Smith. He often stayed at home during the day and worked in his capitol office at night. He was a frequent dissenter, and his dissents often contained barbs aimed at his colleagues, a practice that did not make him many friends. Several members of the court pointed toward Shanahan's criticisms when he was being considered for appointment to the U.S. District Court, a position he won in 1993.

John T. Grant, 1983–93

Grant, a charming and affable jurist, loved golf. He had practiced in Omaha since his graduation from Creighton Law School in 1950. He was appointed to the district bench in Omaha in 1974. Before assuming his seat on the district bench, he was very active in the work of the Omaha bar and served as its president. An accomplished storyteller with a rollicking sense of humor, Grant was very popular with lawyers and maintained his interest in bar activities.

Dale E. Fahrnbruch, 1987–96

Fahrnbruch, a Lincoln native, received his law degree from Creighton University in 1951 and then served as a reporter for the *Lincoln Journal* from 1951–53, during which time he received the Pulitzer Prize for an extensive series on flood control. After reporting for the paper he became an assistant county attorney, serving in that post until 1959, when he joined an established Lincoln firm. In 1973 he was appointed to the district court in Lincoln, and he served there until he replaced William Hastings on the supreme court in 1987, after Hastings was promoted to chief justice. A member of the Kiwanis club, Fahrnbruch had served as president of Lincoln's Child Guidance Center before assuming the bench.

David J. Lanphier, 1993–97

Lanphier was an Omaha native who graduated from Creighton University in 1967. He attended Fordham University Law School, attaining his JD in 1971. From 1972 until 1992, he practiced law in Omaha.

Lanphier served on the Omaha City Personnel Board from 1984 to 1989 and was chair of the board during 1988–89. He also was a member of the Nebraska Crime Commission in 1992.

John F. Wright, 1994–

Wright graduated from the University of Nebraska College of Law in 1970 and then joined his family's firm in Scottsbluff. His father, Floyd, and his uncle, Flavel, who practiced in Lincoln, had both been presidents of the Nebraska State Bar Association. Wright was active in bar work himself, serving as president of the Western Nebraska Bar Association in 1986. He served a number of years on the Scottsbluff school board and twice as its president. An elder and deacon in the Presbyterian Church, he was a member of the Scottsbluff Rotary Club until he moved to Lincoln in 1992 after his appointment as one of the six original members of the Nebraska Court of Appeals.

William M. Connolly, 1994–

A gregarious, red-haired Irishman, Connolly graduated from Creighton Law School in 1963 and went to Hastings, where he took a post as deputy county attorney from 1964–66. He served as county attorney from 1967–72 and then joined one of Hastings's better law firms, where he practiced until he was appointed to the court of appeals in 1992 as one of the original six members. He was president of the county attorney's association in 1972, served in the House of Delegates of the state bar association, and was a member of the bar's executive council at the time of his appointment to the court of appeals.

Appendix 2
Letter to Charles M. Harper

March 14, 1986

Charles M. Harper, Chairman
ConAgra, Inc.
ConAgra Center
One Central Park Plaza
Omaha NE 68102

Dear Mr. Harper:

On Saturday, March 8, 1986, the *Omaha World-Herald* carried a news story in which you commented upon the supreme court decision in *ConAgra v. Cargill*. You were quoted as having made some statements about the quality of justice in Nebraska and Chief Justice Norman Krivosha, which I believe to be inaccurate and harmful to the public's understanding of the judicial process. As a consequence, on behalf of the Nebraska State Bar Association, I feel impelled to set forth my position.

First, let me say that I can understand your disappointment, and even anger, at the reversal of the judgment in ConAgra's favor. Almost every lawyer who practices frequently before the supreme court has had the experience of losing a hard-won verdict in the lower court. It is often a shattering blow. But it is inherent in the nature of the appellate process that a reviewing court can disagree with, and reverse, the decision of the trial court. There is no more presumption that the higher court was wrong than there is that the lower court was right.

I do regret that an executive of your ability and experience, exposed daily to the highly competitive world of corporate activity, would give vent to your frustration by suggesting that the decision was a miscarriage of justice, and by implying that Chief Justice Krivosha was in some way influenced by your notion as to what the Eastern financial community desired.

The decision was obviously a difficult one for the court. Seven judges considered it for many months and split four to three. Both the majority and minority opinions contain comprehensive discussions of the facts and citations of precedent. Although you do not agree with the result, I find nothing in the opinion to justify your assertion that the opinion was a miscarriage of justice.

I have great difficulty in understanding your remarks about Chief Justice Krivosha. Although it is true that he grew up in Detroit—a city I never thought of as "Eastern"—he has lived in Nebraska for over thirty years. He attended college and law school at the University of Nebraska. He has practiced law or been a judge in Lincoln since after his graduation. I would be very interested to learn what, if any, evidence you possess that leads you to conclude that (a) there was a position concerning this lawsuit adopted by Eastern financial interests; (b) that Chief Justice Krivosha was aware of such a position, if it existed; or (c) that he acted upon that knowledge in order to further the "Eastern" position. Yet such is the clear import of your statement.

Further, the opinion of the court was *per curiam*, and the author was not identified. There is nothing in the opinion that identifies the author to me. Although the chief justice was obviously in the majority, he possesses only one vote, and if he, in your opinion, did anything improper to influence the other three judges who also voted in the majority, you should bring that information to the attention of the Judicial Qualifications Commission. Your suggestion that the two district judges who sat with the court would be open to undue influence or pressure, or might decide the case on some basis other than the dictates of their conscience, is a slur upon their honesty and integrity. I seriously doubt you could find a lawyer or judge in Nebraska, who knows either of the lower court judges, who would believe they would be subject to any improper influence.

Finally, I am distressed by your comments that ConAgra will remember the decision when next it reviews the location of the corporate headquarters. Although it is quite common and entirely appropriate for a corporation to suggest moving when it seeks something in the legislative arena, it is entirely out of place to suggest that any judge should consider citizenship in rendering a decision. Justice is blindfolded, and properly so. No citizen of Nebraska should prevail in a case simply because he, she, or it resides in Nebraska. Appellate judges review only the record made in the court below. They do not, and should not, consider the identity of the parties. To suggest otherwise is to impair public confidence in the courts.

I believe that all Nebraskans have been impressed with the skill and expertise you have brought to the management of ConAgra. You have clearly established yourself a position as an outstanding member of the Omaha, and Nebraska, community. Unfortunately, it is precisely that position which, in my judgment, lends underserved weight to your remarks.

I would hope that once the anguish of defeat has subsided, and you have had an opportunity for mature reflection upon what you have said, you will publicly acknowledge that it emanated from your sense of anger and disappointment, and that your innuendos are without substance or foundation in fact. By doing so, you would continue your outstanding record of public service to Nebraska and its populace.

Yours truly,
James W. Hewitt

Appendix 3
Chief Justice Paul White Memorial Speeches, 1968–70

The following speeches are all taken from volumes of the Nebraska Reports.

John W. Yeager
January 8, 1968

There is little that I can add to what has already been said in honor of our brother, Justice John Yeager. Using John's diction, it could well be said that there are a multitude of others, besides the distinguished gathering here, who are of the same attitude and disposition as we are here this A.M.

To one, like myself, who has fallen into the line of march quite recently, Justice Yeager has meant a lot. He was a real physician of applied liberty. With intellect, dispassionate temperament, and courageous resolution of decision, he spelled out in his record a clear concept of the law and of the judicial power. He was to me, and will be in the future, a continuing reminder of the proper posture of a judge and his proper attitude toward both the responsibilities and self-imposed limitations on judicial power.

As a judge, in Socrates' terms, he heard courteously, answered wisely, considered soberly, and decided impartially. His hallmark was the same as Coke's, "That when the case should be, he would do that which should be fit for a judge to do."

Elwood B. Chappell
May 26, 1969

There is little that I can add to what has already been said. It must be said that there are a multitude of others besides the distinguished gathering here this morning, who are of the same attitude and disposition.

To one, like myself, who has fallen into the line of march quite recently, Justice Chappell has meant a lot. He was a real physician of applied liberty. With intellect, dispassionate temperament, and courageous resolution of decision, he spelled out in his record a clear concept of the law and of the judicial power.

As a judge, in Socrates' terms, he heard courteously, answered wisely, considered soberly, and decided impartially. His hallmark was the same as Coke's, "That when the case should be, he would do that which should be fit for a judge to do."

We idealize a government of law rather than men, but the revelation must come from the lips and the character of an individual human, and the personification of our ideals, be they religious, ethical or legal, is of the essence of humanness. The law becomes a jeering cacophony of tongues unless it has its cultural transmission and respect of the people in the integrity and character of the individual, be he a priest, a lawyer, an Egyptian scribe or vizier, a prophet, or a judge.

Before this group of friends this morning, all of this image is personified in Judge Chappell. In personal appearance, in conduct and demeanor, and in his speaking of the law, he exemplified a sanctified dedication to the law and the moral principles it implements. He knew that only the majesty of the law could transcend the dictator, the monarch, or the whims of a transient innovating oligarchy.

Frederick W. Messmore
April 6, 1970

There is little that I can add to what has already been said. There are many others besides the distinguished gathering here this morning who are of the same attitude and disposition.

We idealize a government of law rather than men, but the revelation must come from the lips and the character of an individual human, and the personification of our ideals, be they religious, ethical, or legal, is of the essence of humanness. The law becomes a jeering cacophony of tongues unless it has its cultural transmission and receives the respect of the people in the integrity and character of the individual, be he a priest, a lawyer, an Egyptian scribe or vizier, a prophet, or a judge.

Before this group of friends meeting to honor him this morning, all of this image is personified in Judge Messmore. In personal appearance, in the dignity of his conduct and demeanor, and in his speaking of the law, he exemplified a sanctified dedication to the law and the moral and cultural principles it implements.

He placed his faith in the American principle that only the majesty of the law could transcend the dictator, the monarch or the whims of a transient innovating oligarchy.

Robert G. Simmons
May 4, 1970

There is little that I can add to what has already been said. It must be said that there is a multitude of other citizens across the breadth and length of this great state besides the distinguished gathering here this morning, who are of the same attitude and disposition.

We idealize a government of law rather than men, but revelation must come from the lips and the character and the ability of an individual human, and the personification of our ideals, be they religious, ethical, or legal, is of the essence of humanness. The law becomes a jeering cacophony of tongues unless it has its cultural transmission and invites the respect of the people in the integrity and character of the individual judge.

Bob Simmons, as a judge and as a man, had the wisdom of knowing that the majesty of the law lies not alone in the principles it applies and expounds, but in the certainty that furnishes a guide to the people in the security of law and order. He knew that only the majesty of the law could transcend the dictator, the monarch, or the whims of a transient innovating oligarchy. In Judge Simmons we find the personification of the traditions of the law that in some way we must transmit to each generation if ordered liberty is to survive.

Judge Simmons was a real physician of applied liberty. With intellect, dispassionate temperament, and a courageous resolution, he spelled out in his record a clear concept of the law and of the judicial power.

Notes

1. An Introduction to the Nebraska Supreme Court

1. Friedman, *History of American Law*; Friedman, *American Law in the 20th Century*; Hall, *Magic Mirror*; Horwitz, *Transformation of American Law* (1780–1860 and 1870–1960).
2. See, for example, *Gideon v. Wainright*, 372 U.S. 335 (1963); *Miranda v. Arizona*, 384 U.S. 436 (1966); *Apodaca v. Oregon*, 406 U.S. 404 (1972); *Batson v. Kentucky*, 476 U.S. 79 (1986); *Mapp v. Ohio*, 367 U.S. 643 (1961).
3. Horwitz, *Transformation of American Law, 1780–1860*, 30. See also Hurst, *Law and Economic Growth*.
4. *Charles River Bridge v. Warren Bridge*, 11 Pet. (36 U.S.) 420 (1837).
5. Hall, *Magic Mirror*, 221–22; Hurst, *Law and Social Order*, 163–64.
6. Hall, *Magic Mirror*, 223–24.
7. Hall, *Magic Mirror*, 224.
8. Friedman, *American Law in the 20th Century*, 491.
9. Norman Krivosha, interview by author, Lincoln NE, 12 June 2002 and 13 August 2002. Transcript in author's possession.
10. Friedman, *History of American Law*, 126–27.
11. Friedman, *History of American Law*, 126–27.
12. Friedman, *American Law in the 20th Century*, 476; *Republican Party of Minnesota v. White*, 536 U.S. 765 (2002).
13. Gray, "State's Response," 163–64.
14. Krivosha, interview, 24.
15. Grodin, *In Pursuit of Justice*, 182–83.
16. Sheldon, *Century of Judging*, 27–29.
17. Vile, "Selection and Tenure," 96–100.
18. Nebraska Constitution, Art. V, Sec. 2.
19. Vile, "Selection and Tenure," 100.
20. Tarr and Porter, *State Supreme Courts*.
21. Tarr and Porter, *State Supreme Courts*, 261, 267–68. The elevation of an aggressive individual, one with a clear agenda, to the chief justiceship can transform a court.
22. Sheldon, *Century of Judging*, 249; Tarr and Porter, *State Supreme Courts*, 240–41.
23. Ducat and Flango, *Leadership in State Supreme Courts*.
24. Ducat and Flango, *Leadership in State Supreme Courts*, 21; Friedman et al., "State Supreme Courts," 773–86.
25. Ducat and Flango, *Leadership in State Supreme Courts*, 11.
26. Jaros and Canon, "Dissent on State Supreme Courts," 322–46, 324.

27. Jaros and Canon, "Dissent on State Supreme Courts," 322–46, 324.

28. Sheldon, *Century of Judging*, 296.

29. Sheldon, *Century of Judging*, 296.

30. Homer, "Territorial Judiciary," 349–51.

31. Nuernberger, "Letters from Pioneer Nebraska," 18.

32. Homer, "Territorial Judiciary," 351–52. See also Nebraska Legislature, *Nebraska Blue Book*, 2000–01.

33. Homer, "Territorial Judiciary," 351–52.

34. Nebraska Legislature, *Nebraska Blue Book*, 2000–01, 206.

35. Nebraska Constitution, Art. V, Sec. 21; Nebraska Legislature, *Nebraska Blue Book*, 2000–01, 262.

36. Nebraska Constitution, Art. V, Sec. 21; Nebraska Legislature, *Nebraska Blue Book*, 2000–01, 262.

37. Nebraska Constitution, Art. V, Sec. 21; Nebraska Legislature, *Nebraska Blue Book*, 2000–01, 262.

38. Berge, *Free Pass Bribery System*, 5–8; Hewitt, "Public Be Damned," 17–18.

39. Olson and Naugle, *History of Nebraska*, 232.

40. Olson and Naugle, *History of Nebraska*, 232; *State ex rel. Thayer v. Boyd*, 31 Neb. 682 (1891).

41. *Boyd v. State of Nebraska*, 143 U.S. 135 (1892).

42. *Bush v. Gore*, 531 U.S. 98 (2000).

43. *Meyer v. Nebraska*, 107 Neb. 657 (1922); *Meyer v. Nebraska*, 262 U.S. 390 (1923).

44. *Meyer*, 107 Neb. 657, 667–69.

45. Nebraska Legislature, *Nebraska Blue Book*, 2000–01, 256.

46. Nebraska Constitution, Art. I, Sec. 23.

47. Orfield, "Supreme Court of Nebraska," 241–301; Nebraska Legislature, *Laws of Nebraska*, 1893, chap. 16, p. 150; Nebraska Legislature, *Laws of Nebraska*, 1895, chap. 3.

48. Nebraska Legislature, *Laws of Nebraska*, 1901, chap. 25; Orfield, "Supreme Court of Nebraska," 278–79.

49. Nebraska Legislature, *Laws of Nebraska*, 1903, chap. 37; Nebraska Legislature, *Laws of Nebraska*, 1905, chap. 56. See also *Williams v. Miles*, 68 Neb. 463 (1903); *Lancaster County v. McDonald*, 73 Neb. 453 (1905).

50. Nebraska Legislature, *Nebraska Blue Book*, 2000–01, 259.

51. Nebraska Legislature, *Laws of Nebraska*, 1915, chap. 184; Orfield, "Supreme Court of Nebraska," 278–79.

52. Nebraska Legislature, *Laws of Nebraska*, 1925, chap. 76; Nebraska Constitution, Art. V, Sec. 2.

53. Nebraska Supreme Court Rules 2E(4), 2E(6).

2. "The Judicial Mowing Machine Thus Cuts a Wide Swath"

1. Nebraska Legislature, *Nebraska Blue Book*, 2000–01.

2. Luebke, *Nebraska: An Illustrated History*, 279.

3. Luebke, *Nebraska: An Illustrated History*, 280.

4. Luebke, *Nebraska: An Illustrated History*, 280.

5. Nebraska Legislature, *Nebraska Blue Book*, 2000–01, 421.

6. Olson and Naugle, *History of Nebraska*, 326.

7. Olson and Naugle, *History of Nebraska*, 329–30.

8. Olson and Naugle, *History of Nebraska*, 345–47.

9. *In Memoriam, Elwood B. Chappell*, 184 Neb. xxv (1969).

10. Olson and Naugle, *History of Nebraska*, 326.

11. *In Memoriam, Robert Glenmore Simmons*, 185 Neb. xxxv (1970).

12. *In Memoriam, Robert Glenmore Simmons*, 185 xxxiv.

13. Secretary of State of Nebraska, "Abstracts of Votes Cast in General Elections" (facsimile transmission from office of the Secretary of State of Nebraska): November 5, 1940; November 3, 1942; November 7, 1944; November 5, 1946; November 7, 1950; November 4, 1952; November 6, 1956; November 4, 1958.

14. "Abstract of Votes," November 2, 1948; November 2, 1954.

15. "Abstract of Votes," November 8, 1960; November 6, 1962.

16. *Ruehle v. Ruehle*, 161 Neb. 691 (1956).

17. *Ruehle*, 161 Neb. 691.

18. *Ruehle*, 161 Neb. at 730.

19. *Capitol Bridge Co. v. County of Saunders*, 164 Neb. 304 (1957).

20. *Capitol Bridge Co.*, 164 Neb. at 319.

21. *Commonwealth Trailer Sales, Inc. v. Bradt*, 166 Neb. 1 (1958).

22. *Commonwealth Trailer Sales*, 166 Neb. at 16.

23. *Commonwealth Trailer Sales*, 166 Neb. at 18.

24. *Hartman v. Drake*, 166 Neb. 87 (1958).

25. *Gillespie v. Hynes*, 168 Neb. 87 (1958).

26. *Lutcavish v. Eaton*, 166 Neb. 268 (1958).

27. *Lutcavish*, 166 Neb. at 292–93.

28. *Baker v. Baker*, 166 Neb. 306 (1958).

29. *Baker*, 166 Neb. at 319.

30. *Wischmann v. Raikes*, 168 Neb. 728 (1959).

31. Robert B. Crosby, interview by author, Lincoln NE, February 6, 1995. Transcript in author's possession.

32. *State ex rel. Ralston v. Turner*, 141 Neb. 556 (1942).

33. *Ralston*, 141 Neb. 556.

34. *Ralston*, 141 Neb. at 573.

35. *Johnson v. Radio Station WOW, Inc.*, 144 Neb. 406 (1944); *Johnson*, 144 Neb. 406, 432; *Johnson v. Radio Station WOW, Inc.*, 146 Neb. 429 (1945).

36. *Johnson*, 144 Neb. 406, 432.

37. *Johnson*, 146 Neb. 429.

38. *Johnson*, 146 Neb. 429.

39. *Johnson*, 146 Neb. at 435.

40. *Hawk v. Olson*, 146 Neb. 875 (1946).

41. *Hawk*, 146 Neb. at 881.

42. *Reller v. Ankeny*, 160 Neb. 47 (1955).

43. Van Pelt, "What Psalm-Singing Son," 63–64.

44. Van Pelt, "What Psalm-Singing Son," 64.

45. *Reller*, 160 Neb. 47.

46. *Johnson v. Johnson*, 141 Neb. 239 (1942).

47. *State ex rel. Johnson v. Hagemeister*, 161 Neb. 475 (1958).

48. *MacAvoy v. State*, 144 Neb. 827 (1944).

49. Nebraska newspaper coverage of MacAvoy's execution varied widely. The *Lincoln Star* made it the lead story on its front page on Friday, March 23, 1945. Not one word of the execution appeared in the *Lincoln Journal*. The *Omaha World-Herald* had a one-paragraph story on page 2 on Saturday, March 24, 1945.

50. *Lincoln Star*, December 1, 1948.

51. *Iron Bear v. State*, 149 Neb. 634 (1948).

52. *Iron Bear*, 149 Neb. at 651.

53. *Sundahl v. State*, 154 Neb. 550 (1951).

54. *Starkweather v. State*, 167 Neb. 477 (1958).

55. Van Pelt "What Psalm-Singing Son," 232–33.

56. Van Pelt "What Psalm-Singing Son," 231.

57. *Starkweather*, 167 Neb. 477.

58. *Griffith v. State*, 157 Neb. 448 (1953).

59. *Grandsinger v. State*, 161 Neb. 419 (1955).

60. *State ex rel. Nebraska State Bar Association v. Fisher*, 170 Neb. 483 (1960).

61. *Schluter v. State*, 151 Neb. 284 (1949).

62. *Armstead v. State*, 161 Neb. 13 (1955).

63. *Armstead*, 161 Neb. at 21.

64. *Peery v. State*, 163 Neb. 628 (1957).

65. *Peery v. State*, 165 Neb. 752 (1958).

66. *Peery v. State*, 199 Neb. 656 (1977).

67. *Parker v. State*, 164 Neb. 614 (1957).

68. *Parker v. State*, 178 Neb. 1 (1964).

69. *Parker*, 178 Neb. at 7.

70. *Kroger v. Kroger*, 153 Neb. 265 (1950).

71. *In re Petition of Ritchie*, 155 Neb. 824 (1951).

72. *Drabbels v. Skelly Oil Co.*, 155 Neb. 17 (1951).

73. *Drabbels*, 155 Neb. at 23.

74. *Smith v. Columbus Community Hospital*, 222 Neb. 776 (1986).

75. Tarr and Porter, *State Supreme Courts*, 139.

76. Jaros and Canon, "Dissent on State Supreme Courts," 322–46.

77. Jaros and Canon, "Dissent on State Supreme Courts," 324.

78. Orfield, "Supreme Court of Nebraska," 241–301.

79. Ruehle, 161 Neb. at 753.

80. Friedman, *American Law in the 20th Century*, 535.

81. Friedman, *American Law in the 20th Century*, 517.

3. "A Real Physician of Applied Liberty"

1. "Abstract of Votes," November 6, 1962.

2. Nebraska Legislature, *Nebraska Blue Book*, 1968.

3. James E. Dunlevey, Sun City CA, letter to author, Lincoln NE, undated 2001, in author's possession.

4. Nebraska Legislature, *Nebraska Blue Book*, 2000–01.

5. Judge Leslie Boslaugh, interview by author, Lincoln NE, March 20, 1997. Transcript in author's possession.

6. Dunlevey, letter, undated 2001.

7. *United Mineral Products Co. v. Nebraska Railroads*, 178 Neb. 640 (1965).

8. Nebraska Legislature, *Nebraska Blue Book*, 2000–01, 262.

9. Flavel A. Wright, interview by author, Lincoln NE, November 7, 1994. Transcript in author's possession.

10. Nebraska Constitution, Art. V, Sec. 21(4).

11. Friedman, *American Law in the 20th Century*, 476–77.

12. Nebraska Legislature, *Nebraska Blue Book*, 2000–01, 256.

13. Nebraska Legislature, *Nebraska Blue Book*, 2000–01, 263.

14. Nebraska Legislature, *Nebraska Blue Book*, 2000–01, 265.

15. James E. Dunlevey, interview by author, Lincoln NE, August 15, 2001. Transcript in author's possession. See also Smith and Fellman, "State Supreme Courts' Non-Judicial Tasks," 304–9.

16. Nebraska Constitution, Art. V, Sec. 2.

17. For a critical analysis of the requirement that five judges must hold an act unconstitutional in Nebraska, see Madgett, "'Five-Judge' Rule," 329.

18. Dunlevey, letter, undated 2001.

19. Nebraska Supreme Court, *Nebraska Reports*, volumes 174–77 (1963–64), 198–201 (1977–78).

20. *Gideon*, 372 U.S. 335; *Miranda*, 384 U.S. 436.

21. *Gideon*, 372 U.S. 335.

22. *Miranda*, 384 U.S. 436.

23. Nebraska Commission on Law Enforcement and Criminal Justice, *Crime in Nebraska—1991*.

24. See tables 3 and 6.

25. See tables 3 and 6.

26. *Furman v. Georgia*, 408 U.S. 238 (1972).

27. *Gregg v. Georgia*, 428 U.S. 153 (1976). See also *Woodson v. North Carolina*, 428 U.S. 280 (1976).

28. *State v. Stewart*, 197 Neb. 497 (1977); *State v. Rust*, 197 Neb. 528 (1977); *State v. Holtan*, 197 Neb. 544 (1977); *State v. Simants*, 197 Neb. 549 (1977).

29. Nebraska Legislature, *Revised Statutes of Nebraska, 1943*, Sec. 29-2523.

30. *Stewart*, 197 Neb. 497.

31. *Stewart*, 197 Neb. 497.

32. Dunlevey, letter, undated 2001.

33. James E. Dunlevey, Sun City CA, letter to author, Lincoln NE, May 9, 2001, in author's possession.

34. Dunlevey, letter, undated 2001.

35. Judge Hale McCown, interview by author, Lincoln NE, October 13, 2000, 5. Transcript in author's possession.

36. Van Pelt, "What Psalm Singing Son," 92, 95.

37. Judge, interview conducted in confidentiality by author, Lincoln NE, October 8, 1995.

38. Van Pelt, "What Psalm Singing Son," 95.

39. McCown, interview, 4.

40. Dunlevey, interview, 24–25.

41. *State v. King*, 179 Neb. 511 (1965).

42. *State v. Miller*, 179 Neb. 510 (1965).

43. *King*, 179 Neb. 510, 513–14.

44. *State v. Alvarez*, 182 Neb. 358 (1967); *State v. Alvarez*, 185 Neb. 557 (1970); *State v. Alvarez*, 189 Neb. 281 (1972).

45. *State v. Nokes*, 192 Neb. 844 (1975).

46. *State v. Simants*, 182 Neb. 491 (1968).

47. *DeBacker v. Brainard*, 183 Neb. 491 (1968).

48. *In re Gault*, 387 U.S. 1 (1967).

49. *McMullen v. Geiger*, 184 Neb. 581 (1969).

50. *Pedersen v. Schult*, 185 Neb. 514 (1970).

51. *State v. Walker*, 189 Neb. 124 (1972).

52. *State v. Little Art Corp.*, 189 Neb. 681, 687 (1973).

53. *Little Art Corp.*, 189 Neb. 681, 687.

54. McCown, interview, 21.

55. *State v. Micek*, 193 Neb. 379 (1975).

56. *Orleans Education Assn. v. School District of Orleans*, 193 Neb. 675 (1975).

57. *Halligan v. Cotton*, 193 Neb. 331 (1975).

58. *Kimball County Grain Cooperative v. Yung*, 200 Neb. 233 (1978).

59. *Spiker v. John Day Co.*, 201 Neb. 503 (1978).

60. *Board of Regents of University of Nebraska v. Exon*, 199 Neb. 146 (1977).

61. *State ex rel. Morris v. Marsh*, 183 Neb. 521 (1968).

62. *Morris*, 183 Neb. at 536.

63. *Morris*, 183 Neb. at 537.

64. *Morris*, 183 Neb. at 546.

65. *Hanna v. State Board of Equalization and Assessment*, 181 Neb. 725 (1967).

66. *State ex rel. Meyer v. Steen*, 183 Neb. 297 (1968).
67. *State ex rel. Belker v. Board of Educational Lands and Funds*, 184 Neb. 621 (1969).
68. *State ex rel. Belker v. Board of Educational Lands and Funds*, 185 Neb. 270 (1970).
69. *Banks v. State*, 181 Neb. 106 (1966).
70. *State v. Cavitt*, 182 Neb. 712 (1968).
71. *Lincoln Journal Star*, May 4, 2002.
72. *Prendergast*, 199 Neb. 97.
73. *Prendergast*, 199 Neb. at 134.
74. *Stadler v. Curtis Gas, Inc.*, 182 Neb. 6 (1967).
75. *Stadler*, 182 Neb. at 22.
76. *Scudder v. Haug*, 197 Neb. 638 (1977); *Scudder v. Haug*, 201 Neb. 107 (1978).
77. Hairston, Hanson, and Ostrom, "Work of State Appellate Courts," 17–27.

4. The Norman Conquest

1. Nebraska Legislature, *Nebraska Blue Book*, 1978–79, 801.
2. Dunlevey, letter, undated 2001.
3. Krivosha, interview, 18.
4. Krivosha, interview, 19.
5. Dick Herman, interview by author, Lincoln NE, April 25, 2001, 33. Transcript in author's possession.
6. Krivosha, interview, 51.
7. Krivosha, interview, 2.
8. Krivosha, interview, 6.
9. *State v. Williams*, 205 Neb. 56, 88 (1979).
10. *State v. Palmer*, 224 Neb. 282 (1986).
11. *Palmer*, 224 Neb. at 314.
12. *State v. Hunt*, 220 Neb. 707 (1985).
13. *Hunt*, 220 Neb. 707.
14. *Hunt*, 220 Neb. 707.
15. *Hunt*, 220 Neb. at 725.
16. *State v. Reeves*, 216 Neb. 206 (1984).
17. *State v. Holtan*, 197 Neb. 544 (1977).
18. *Hunt*, 220 Neb. at 725.
19. *Omaha World-Herald*, August 30, 1985.
20. Krivosha, interview, 45.
21. *Omaha World-Herald*, September 22, 1985.
22. *Omaha World-Herald*, October 2, 1985.
23. *Lincoln Journal*, August 12, 1985; *Norfolk Daily News*, August 10, 1985.
24. *Omaha World-Herald*, August 16, 1985; *Omaha World-Herald*, August 18, 1985; *Norfolk Daily News*, August 15, 1985; *Lincoln Journal*, August 13, 1985; *Lincoln Journal*, August 16, 1985; *Lincoln Journal*, August 17, 1985.
25. *Omaha World-Herald*, June 20, 1999.

26. "Abstract of Votes," November 2, 1982.

27. "Abstract of Votes," November 4, 1980; November 4, 1986; November 3, 1992.

28. "Abstract of Votes," November 4, 1986; November 3, 1992.

29. "Abstract of Votes," November 2, 1982; November 6, 1990.

30. *State v. Simants*, 202 Neb. 828 (1979).

31. *Simants*, 202 Neb. at 835.

32. *State v. Simants*, 213 Neb. 638 (1983).

33. *State v. Holtan*, 205 Neb. 314 (1980).

34. *State v. Holtan*, 216 Neb. 594 (1984).

35. *State v. Peery*, 205 Neb. 271 (1980).

36. *State v. Peery*, 208 Neb. 639 (1981).

37. *State v. Peery*, 223 Neb. 556 (1986).

38. *State v. Williams*, 205 Neb. 56 (1979).

39. *Williams*, 205 Neb. at 76–77.

40. *Williams*, 205 Neb. at 88.

41. *State v. Otey*, 205 Neb. 90 (1979).

42. *State v. Otey*, 212 Neb. 103 (1982).

43. *State v. Anderson and Hochstein*, 207 Neb. 51 (1980).

44. *Anderson*, 207 Neb. at 73–74.

45. *Harper*, 208 Neb. 568.

46. *Harper*, 208 Neb. at 587.

47. *Reeves*, 216 Neb. 206.

48. *State v. Reeves*, 258 Neb. 511 (2000).

49. *Lincoln Journal Star*, September 8, 2001.

50. *Ring v. Arizona*, 536 U.S. 584 (2002).

51. *State v. Joubert*, 224 Neb. 411 (1986).

52. *Joubert*, 224 Neb. 411.

53. *Joubert*, 224 Neb. at 434.

54. *Joubert*, 224 Neb. at 443.

55. *State v. Moore*, 210 Neb. 457 (1982).

56. *Moore v. Kinney*, 278 F.3d 774 (8th Cir. Neb. 2002).

57. *Moore v. Kinney* 320 F.3d 767 (8th Cir. Neb. 2003), reversing *Moore*, 278 F.3d 774.

58. *State v. Ellis*, 208 Neb. 379 (1981).

59. *Ellis*, 208 Neb. 379.

60. *State v. Nokes*, 209 Neb. 293 (1981).

61. *State v. Ryan*, 222 Neb. 875 (1986).

62. *Ryan*, 222 Neb. 875.

63. *ConAgra Inc. v. Cargill Inc.*, 222 Neb. 136 (1986).

64. *ConAgra*, 222 Neb. at 155.

65. *Omaha World-Herald*, March 8, 1986.

66. John C. Burke, letter to Daniel D. Jewell, March 17, 1986, letter in author's possession.

67. James W. Hewitt, letter to Charles M. Harper, March 14, 1986.

68. *McCook (NE) Gazette* March 12, 1986; *Lincoln Journal*, March 16, 1986; *Omaha World-Herald*, March 14, 1986.

69. Santoni, "Integration of Contract," 317–34.

70. *Lincoln Journal*, March 16, 1986.

71. *ConAgra Inc. v. Cargill, Inc.* 223 Neb. 92 (1986).

72. *James v. Lieb*, 221 Neb. 47 (1985).

73. *Lieb*, 221 Neb. at 59–60.

74. *Lieb*, 221 Neb. at 60.

75. *Kreifels v. Wurtele*, 206 Neb. 491 (1980).

76. *Botsch v. Reisdorff*, 193 Neb. 165 (1975).

77. *Kreifels*, 206 Neb. at 497.

78. *Smith v. Columbus Community Hospital Inc.*, 222 Neb. 776 (1986).

79. *Smith*, 222 Neb. at 780.

80. Nebraska Legislature, *Laws of Nebraska, 2003*, LB 294.

81. *Vacek v. Ames*, 221 Neb. 333 (1985).

82. *Vacek*, 221 Neb. 333.

83. Nebraska Legislature, *Revised Statutes of Nebraska, 1943*, LB 25–21, 188.

84. *Casey's General Stores Inc. v. Nebraska Liquor Control Commission*, 220 Neb. 242 (1985).

85. *Casey's General Stores*, 220 Neb. at 245.

86. *Doyle v. Union Insurance Co.*, 202 Neb. 599 (1979).

87. *Doyle*, 202 Neb. 599.

88. *Occidental Savings and Loan Assoc. v. Jenco Partnership*, 206 Neb. 469 (1980).

89. *Occidental Savings and Loan*, 206 Neb. at 485.

90. *Little Blue N.R.D. v. Lower Platte North N.R.D.*, 206 Neb. 535 (1980).

91. *State ex rel. Douglas v. Sporhase*, 208 Neb. 703 (1981).

92. *Sporhase*, 208 Neb. 703.

93. *State ex rel. Douglas v. Sporhase*, 213 Neb. 484 (1983).

94. *State v. Douglas*, 217 Neb. 199 (1984).

95. *Douglas*, 217 Neb. at 219.

96. *Douglas*, 217 Neb. at 222.

97. *University Police Officers Union Local 567 v. University of Nebraska*, 203 Neb. 4 (1979).

98. *University Police Officers*, 203 Neb. 4.

99. *Nebraska ex rel. Douglas v. Thone*, 204 Neb. 836 (1979).

100. *Thone*, 204 Neb. 836.

101. *State ex rel. Douglas v. Beermann*, 216 Neb. 849 (1984).

102. *State ex rel. Bryant v. Beermann*, 217 Neb. 632 (1984).

103. *Jaksha v. State*, 222 Neb. 690 (1986).

104. *Jaksha*, 222 Neb. at 698.

105. *State ex rel. Nebraska State Bar Association v. Michaelis*, 210 Neb. 545 (1982).

106. *Michaelis*, 210 Neb. 545.

107. *State ex rel. Nebraska State Bar Association v. Duchek*, 224 Neb. 777 (1987).

108. *State ex rel. Nebraska State Bar Association. v. Green*, 210 Neb. 878 (1982).

109. In re Complaint against Kneifl, 217 Neb. 472 (1984).

110. Kneifl, 217 Neb. at 485–86.

111. In re Complaint against Kelly, 225 Neb. 583 (1987).

112. Kneifl, 217 Neb. 472; Kelly, 225 Neb. 583; In re Complaint against Staley, 241 Neb. 152 (1992); In re Complaint against Empson, 252 Neb. 433 (1997); In re Complaint against Jones, 255 Neb. 1 (1998); In re Complaint against Krepela, 262 Neb. 85 (2001).

113. State ex rel. Douglas v. Sileven 207 Neb. 802 (1981), 817.

114. Sileven v. Tesch, 212 Neb. 880 (1982) at 886.

115. Ring, 536 U.S. 584; State v. Gales, 265 Neb. 598 (2003); State v. Lotter, 266 Neb. 245 (2003).

116. Krivosha, interview, 35–36.

117. Herman, interview, 15.

118. Krivosha, interview, 13.

119. Figure provided by the Nebraska Court Administrator's office, August 26, 2002.

120. Krivosha, interview, 15–16.

121. Krivosha, interview, 3.

122. Gray, "Ode on a Distant Prospect," 7–11.

123. Krivosha, interview, 45.

124. Krivosha, interview, 54.

5. "With Malice toward None"

1. Nebraska Court Administrator's Office, "Membership of Nominating Commission for Chief Justice, 1987" (facsimile transmission, August 26, 2002).

2. Nebraska Court Administrator's Office, "Membership of Nominating Commission."

3. Nebraska Legislature, Nebraska Blue Book, 2000–01, 823.

4. "Abstract of Votes," November 2, 1982.

5. See table 11.

6. See table 10.

7. See Groot, "Effects of an Intermediate Appellate Court," 548–72; Flango and Blair, "Creating an Intermediate Appellate Court," 74–84.

8. Chief Justice William C. Hastings, interview by author, Lincoln NE, February 24, 2000, 48. Transcript in author's possession.

9. Hastings, interview, 4–5.

10. Nebraska Legislature, Nebraska Blue Book, 2000–01, 269.

11. Hastings, interview, 48.

12. Nebraska Supreme Court Rule 2E(6); Nebraska Legislature, Revised Statutes of Nebraska, 1943, Sec. 24-1104(2).

13. Figures provided by the Nebraska Court Administrator's Office, August 26, 2002.

14. State v. Pettit, 233 Neb. 436 (1987).

15. Pettit, 233 Neb. at 460.

16. Pettit, 233 Neb. at 470.

17. Pettit, 233 Neb. at 474–75.

18. *Pettit*, 233 Neb. at 476.

19. *State v. Myers*, 244 Neb. 905 (1994).

20. *Myers*, 244 Neb. at 908–9.

21. Stenberg, "Malice in Wonderland," 15–27.

22. Shugrue, "Second Degree Murder Doctrine," 27–66.

23. *State v. Grimes*, 246 Neb. 473 (1994).

24. *Grimes*, 246 Neb. at 487.

25. *Grimes*, 246 Neb. at 488.

26. Hastings, interview, 22, 69.

27. *State v. Burlison*, 255 Neb. 190 (1998).

28. *Burlison*, 255 Neb. at 200.

29. *State ex rel. Freezer Services, Inc. v. Mullen*, 235 Neb. 981 (1990).

30. *Freezer Services*, 235 Neb. at 993.

31. *State ex rel. FirsTier Bank v. Buckley*, 244 Neb. 36 (1993).

32. *FirsTier Bank*, 244 Neb. at 45.

33. *State ex rel. Creighton Univ. v. Hickman*, 245 Neb. 247 (1994).

34. Harvey Perlman, interview by author, Lincoln NE, January 31, 2002, 2–3. Transcript in author's possession.

35. Perlman, interview, 9.

36. Perlman, interview, 9–10.

37. Perlman, interview, 12–13.

38. Perlman, interview, 14.

39. Perlman, interview, 15.

40. *State ex rel. Wal-Mart Stores v. Kortum*, 251 Neb. 805 (1997).

41. *Wal-Mart Stores*, 251 Neb. 805.

42. *Wal-Mart Stores*, 251 Neb. at 814.

43. Canon 5, DR 5-109, *Code of Professional Responsibility*, "Support Personnel of a Law Firm—Conflict of Interest."

44. Perlman, interview, 19.

45. Perlman, interview, 20.

46. *State v. Ryan*, 233 Neb. 74 (1989).

47. *Ring*, 536 U.S. 584.

48. *Ryan*, 233 Neb. at 151.

49. *Ryan*, 233 Neb. at 159.

50. *State v. Joubert*, 235 Neb. 230 (1990).

51. *State v. Otey*, 236 Neb. 915 (1991).

52. *State v. Otey*, 240 Neb. 813, 824–25 (1994).

53. *State v. Joubert*, 246 Neb. 287 (1994).

54. *Joubert*, 246 Neb. at 304.

55. *State v. Palmer*, 246 Neb. 305, 308 (1994).

56. *State v. Ryan*, 248 Neb. 405, 445–52 (1995).

57. *State v. Moore*, 250 Neb. 805 (1996).

58. *Moore*, 250 Neb. at 817. The Eight Circuit panel jettisoned the second prong in *Moore*, 278 F.3d 774, but the full court restored it, overruling the panel, in *Moore*, 520 F.3d 767.

59. *State v. Radcliffe*, 228 Neb. 868 (1988).

60. *State ex rel. Labedz v. Beermann*, 229 Neb. 657 (1988).

61. *Lincoln Journal Star*, August 29, 2002.

62. *State ex rel. Chambers v. Beermann*, 229 Neb. 595 (1988).

63. *State ex rel. Stenberg v. Beermann*, 240 Neb. 754 (1992).

64. *Stenberg*, 240 Neb. at 757.

65. Nebraska Legislature, *Nebraska Blue Book*, 2000–01, 270.

66. *Duggan v. Beermann*, 245 Neb. 907 (1994).

67. *Duggan v. Beermann*, 249 Neb. 411 (1996).

68. Nebraska Legislature, *Nebraska Blue Book*, 2000–01, 270.

69. *Duggan*, 249 Neb. 411.

70. *Duggan*, 249 Neb. at 422.

71. *State ex rel. Spire v. Beermann*, 235 Neb. 384 (1990).

72. *Broken Bow Production Credit Assn. v. Western Iowa Farms Co.*, 232 Neb. 357 (1989).

73. *State v. Rein*, 234 Neb. 917 (1990).

74. *In re Complaint Against Staley*, 241 Neb. 152 (1992).

75. *Wheeler v. Nebraska State Bar Assn.*, 244 Neb. 786 (1993).

76. *Botos v. L.A. County Bar Association*, 151 Cal. App. 3d 1083 (1984).

77. *State ex rel. Nebraska State Bar Assn. v. Dineen*, 235 Neb. 363 (1990).

78. *Marks v. Judicial Nominating Comm.*, 236 Neb. 429 (1990).

79. Willborn, "Off the Mark," 277–305.

80. *Nebraska State Bar Foundation v. Lancaster County Bd. of Equalization*, 237 Neb. 1 (1991).

81. *In Re Application A-16642*, 236 Neb. 671 (1990).

82. *City of Lincoln v. ABC Books, Inc.*, 238 Neb. 378 (1991).

83. *Vencil v. Valmont Industries, Inc.*, 239 Neb. 31 (1991).

84. *Vencil*, 239 Neb. at 41.

85. *Crewdson v. Burlington Northern R.R. Co.*, 234 Neb. 31 (1990).

86. *Ring*, 536 U.S. 584.

6. Is the Law an Ass? An Idiot?

1. *Lincoln Journal Star*, November 17, 1996.

2. Oursland, "Public Trust and Confidence," 14–17.

3. Zemans, "From Chambers to Community," 62–63; Janowitz, *The Last Half-Century*, 383.

4. Friedman, *American Law in the 20th Century*, 490.

5. Krivosha, interview, 7.

6. *Commonwealth Trailer Sales, Inc.*, 166 Neb. 1.

7. *Gillespie*, 168 Neb. 49.

8. *Ruehle*, 161 Neb. 691.

9. *Stadler*, 182 Neb. 6.

10. *Stadler*, 182 Neb. at 18.

11. *Prendergast*, 199 Neb. 97.

12. *Prendergast*, 199 Neb. at 134.

13. *Stewart*, 197 Neb. 497; *Rust*, 197 Neb. 528; *Holtan*, 197 Neb. 544; *Simants*, 197 Neb. 549.

14. *Hunt*, 220 Neb. 707.

15. *ConAgra*, 222 Neb. 136.

16. *James*, 221 Neb. 47.

17. *Kreifels*, 206 Neb. 491.

18. *Ellis*, 208 Neb. 379.

19. *Vacek*, 221 Neb. 333.

20. *Myers*, 244 Neb. 905.

21. See, for example, *Lincoln Journal Star*, November 17, 1996.

22. See Krivosha, "In Celebration of the 50th Anniversary," 128–32; Glick, "Promise and the Performance," 509–40; Daugherty, "The Missouri Non-Partisan Court Plan," 315–43.

23. See table 3.

24. See table 6.

25. See table 10.

26. See table 14.

27. Nebraska Legislature, *Nebraska Blue Book, 2002–03*, 828, 824, 805.

28. See Bonneau, "Composition of State Supreme Courts," 26–31.

29. Dunlevey, letter, May 9, 2001.

30. Nebraska Legislature, *Nebraska Blue Book, 2000–01*, 823.

31. *Ruehle*, 161 Neb. 691, 731–32.

32. Krivosha, interview, 9–10.

33. Herman, interview, 14.

34. *Ralston*, 141 Neb. 556; *Ruehle*, 161 Neb. 691; *Hunt*, 220 Neb. 707.

35. "Abstract of Votes," November 3, 1942.

36. *Johnson*, 144 Neb. 406; *Johnson*, 146 Neb. 429; *Hawk*, 146 Neb. 875.

37. "Abstract of Votes," November 4, 1958.

38. Herman, interview, 25.

39. Judge, interview, conducted in confidentiality.

40. *Rogers*, 192 Neb. 125; *Gaffney*, 192 Neb. 358.

41. *Lenstrom v. Thone*, 209 Neb. 783.

42. *Myers*, 244 Neb. 905.

43. *Pettit*, 227 Neb. 218.

44. Joseph Steele, interview by author, Lincoln NE, February 7, 2001, 30. Transcript in author's possession.

45. *Sporhase*, 208 Neb. 703; *Sporhase v. Nebraska*, 458 U.S. 941 (1982).

46. *Moore*, 320 F.3d 767.

47. *Stadler*, 182 Neb. 6; *Prendergast*, 199 Neb. 97.

48. *Botsch v. Reisdorff*, 193 Neb. 165 (1975).

49. *Sporhase*, 208 Neb. 703; *Little Blue*, 206 Neb. 535.

50. *ConAgra*, 222 Neb. 136.

51. *Hunt*, 220 Neb. 707.

52. Perlman, interview, 19.

53. Schwartz, *Book of Legal Lists*, 85–86.

54. Figures provided by Nebraska Court Administrators Office, August 26, 2002.

55. *Myers*, 244 Neb. 905.

56. Daynard, "Use of Social Policy," 919–50, 935.

57. Friedman, *American Law in the 20th Century*, 4.

Bibliography

Abel, Richard L. *American Lawyers*. New York: Oxford University Press, 1989.

Abraham, Henry J. *Freedom and the Court: Civil Rights and Liberties in the United States*. New York: Oxford University Press, 1980.

Aldisert, Ruggerio J. "Philosophy, Jurisprudence and Jurisprudential Temperament of Federal Judges." *Indiana Law Review* 20 (Spring 1987): 453–515.

American Bar Association Committee on the Federal Judiciary. *Formal Report on Thomas M. Shanahan*. N.p., n.d.

Aspin, Larry T., and William K. Hall. "Retention Elections and Judicial Behavior." *Judicature* 77 (May–June 1994): 306–15.

———. "Campaigning for Retention in Illinois." *Judicature* 80 (September–October 1996): 84–87.

———. "Trends in Judicial Retention Elections, 1964–1988." *Judicature* 83 (September–October 1999): 79–81.

Auerbach, Jerold S. *Unequal Justice: Lawyers and Social Change in Modern America*. New York: Oxford University Press, 1976.

Bakken, Gordon Morris. "Judicial Review in the Rocky Mountain Territorial Courts." *American Journal of Legal History* 15 (1971): 56–65.

———. *The Development of Law on the Rocky Mountain Frontier: Civil Law and Society, 1850–1912*. Westport CT: Greenwood Press, 1983.

Beard, Charles A. *An Economic Interpretation of the Constitution of the United States*. New York: Macmillan, 1935.

Beiser, Edward N. "The Rhode Island Supreme Court: A Well-Integrated Political System." *Law and Society Review* 8 (Winter 1973): 167–86.

Berge, George W. *The Free Pass Bribery System*. Lincoln NE: Independent Publishing Company, 1905.

Bickel, Alexander M. *Politics and the Warren Court*. New York: Harper and Row, 1965.

Billikopf, David M. *The Exercise of Judicial Power*. New York: Vantage Press, 1973.

Black, Charles L., Jr. *The People and the Court: Judicial Review in a Democracy*, New York: Macmillan, 1960.

Bond, Carroll T. *The Court of Appeals of Maryland: A History*. Baltimore: Barton Gillett Co., 1928.

Bonneau, Chris W. "The Composition of State Supreme Courts 2000." *Judicature* 85 (July–August 2001): 26–31.

Borowire, Walter A. "Pathways to the Top: The Political Careers of State Supreme Court Justices." *North Carolina Law Review* 7 (1976): 280–85.

Boslaugh, Leslie. Interview by Centennial Committee. Nebraska State Bar Association. December 12, 1995.

Brace, Paul, and Melinda Gann Hall. "Comparing Courts Using the American States." *Judicature* 83 (March–April 2000): 250–69.

Canon, Bradley C. "Characteristics and Career Patterns of State Supreme Court Justices." *State Government* 45 (1972): 34–41.

———. "The Impact of Formal Selection Processes on the Characteristics of Judges— Reconsidered." *Law and Society Review* 6 (1972): 579–93.

Carbon, Susan B. "Judicial Retention Elections: Are They Serving Their Intended Purpose?" *Judicature* 64 (November 1980): 210–33.

Cardozo, Benjamin N. *The Nature of the Judicial Process.* New Haven CT: Yale University Press, 1921.

Casey, Pam. "Measuring Success: Examining Court Performance." *Texas Bar Journal* 56, no. 2 (September 1993): 842–50.

Cohan, Leon S. "Surprise! A Merit Selection Process that Works." *Michigan Bar Journal* 75 (September 1996): 914–17.

Connor, Christopher C. "Partisan Elections: The Albatross of Pennsylvania's Appellate Judiciary." *Dickinson Law Review* 98 (Fall 1993): 1–23.

Cox, Archibald. "The Role of the Supreme Court in American Society." *Marquette Law Review* 50 (June 1967): 575–93.

Crosskey, William W. *Politics and the Constitution in the History of the United States.* Chicago: University of Chicago Press, 1953.

Currie, David P. "The Constitution in the Supreme Court: The Protection of Economic Interests, 1889–1910." *University of Chicago Law Review* 52 (1985): 324–88.

D'Alemberte, Talbot. "Searching for the Limits of Judicial Free Speech." *Tulane Law Review* (February 1987): 611–52.

Danielski, David J. "The Influence of the Chief Justice in the Decisional Process." In *Courts, Judges and Politics,* edited by Walter F. Murphy and C. Herman Pritchett, 695–703. New York: Random House, 1979.

Daugherty, Jay A. "The Missouri Non-Partisan Court Plan: A Dinosaur on the Edge of Extinction or a Survivor in a Changing Socio-Legal Environment?" *Missouri Law Review* 62 (1997): 315–43.

Davis, Horace A. *The Judicial Veto.* New York: Da Capo, 1971.

Daynard, Richard A. "The Use of Social Policy in Judicial Decision-Making." *Cornell Law Review* 56 (1971): 919–50.

Diamond, Allan J. *The Superior Court of Massachusetts, Its Origin and Development.* Boston: Little, Brown, 1960.

Dillow, Ted E. "Minutes of Meeting with Chief Justice Krivosha and Bar Officers." Nebraska State Bar Association. 12 June 1981.

Ducat, Craig, and Victor Flango. *Leadership in State Supreme Courts: Role of the Chief Justice.* Beverly Hills: Sage Publications, 1976.

Ellis, Mark R. "For the Advancement of the Honor and Dignity of Our Profession: The

Nebraska State Bar Association, 1900–2000." *The Nebraska Lawyer* (December 1999–January 2000): 7–16.

Ely, James W., Jr. *Railroads and American Law.* Lawrence: University Press of Kansas, 2001.

Flango, Victor, and Nora F. Blair. "Creating an Intermediate Appellate Court: Does It Reduce the Caseload of a State's Highest Court?" *Judicature* 64 (August 1980): 74–84.

Frankfurter, Felix, and James M. Landis. *The Business of the Supreme Court.* New York: Macmillan, 1927.

Frederick, David C. *Rugged Justice: The Ninth Circuit Court of Appeals and the American West, 1891–1941.* Berkeley: University of California Press, 1994.

Friedman, Lawrence M. *A History of American Law.* 2nd ed. New York: Simon and Schuster, Inc., 1985.

———. *American Law in the 20th Century.* New Haven CT: Yale University Press, 2002.

Friedman, Lawrence M. Robert A. Kagan, Bliss Cartwright, and Stanton Wheeler. "State Supreme Courts: A Century of Style and Citation." *Stanford Law Review* 33 (May 1981): 773–818.

Gailie, Peter J. "The Other Supreme Courts: Judicial Activism among State Supreme Courts." *Syracuse Law Review* 33 (Summer 1982): 731–93.

Gilmore, Grant. *The Death of Contract.* Columbus: Ohio State University Press, 1974.

Glick, Henry R. "The Promise and the Performance of the Missouri Plan: Judicial Selection in the Fifty States." *Miami Law Review* 32 (1978): 509–40.

Goldman, Sheldon. *Picking Federal Judges.* New Haven CT: Yale University Press, 1997.

Gray, Cynthia. "The State's Response to Republican Party of Minnesota v. White." *Judicature* 86 (November–December 2002): 163–64.

Gray, Thomas. "Ode on a Distant Prospect of Eton College." In *The Complete Poems of Thomas Gray.* Mt. Vernon NY: Peter Pauper Press, n.d.

Griffin, Kenyon N., and Michael J. Horan. "Merit Retention Elections: What Influences the Voters." *Judicature* 63 (August 1970): 78–88.

———. "Patterns of Voting Behavior in Judicial Retention Elections for Supreme Court Judges in Wyoming." *Judicature* 67 (August 1983): 68–77.

Grodin, Joseph R. *In Pursuit of Justice: Reflections of a State Supreme Court Justice.* Berkeley: University of California Press, 1989.

Groot, Roger D. "The Effects of an Intermediate Appellate Court on the Supreme Court Work Product: The North Carolina Experience." *Wake Forest Law Review* 7 (1971): 548–72.

Guice, John D. W. *The Rocky Mountain Bench: The Territorial Supreme Courts of Colorado, Montana and Wyoming, 1861–1890.* New Haven CT: Yale University Press, 1972.

Hairston, Steven E., Roger A. Hanson, and Brian J. Ostrom. "The Work of State Appellate Courts." *State Court Journal* 17 (Spring 1993): 17–27.

Hall, Kermit L. *The Magic Mirror: Law in American History.* New York: Oxford University Press, 1989.

Hall, Kermit W. "Hacks and Derelicts Revisited: American Territorial Judiciary, 1787–1959." *Western Historical Quarterly* 12 (July 1981): 270–83.

Hastings, William C. Interview by Richard Shugrue, Nebraska State Bar Association. January 29, 1998.

Heiberg, Robert A. "Social Backgrounds of the Minnesota Supreme Court Justices, 1858–1968." *Minnesota Law Review* 53 (1969): 901–37.

Heller, Francis H. "The Justices of the Kansas Supreme Court, 1861–1975: A Collective Portrait." *University of Kansas Law Review* 24 (1975): 521–35.

Hewitt, James W. "The Public Be Damned: Railroads, the Free Pass System and the Nebraska Supreme Court, 1875–1911." Master's thesis, University of Nebraska–Lincoln, 1994.

Homer, Michael W. "The Territorial Judiciary: An Overview of the Nebraska Experience, 1854–1967." *Nebraska History* 63 (Fall 1982): 349–62.

Horwitz, Morton J. *The Transformation of American Law, 1780–1860.* New York: Oxford University Press, 1992.

———. *The Transformation of American Law, 1870–1960.* New York: Oxford University Press, 1992.

———. *The Warren Court and the Pursuit of Justice.* New York: Hill and Wang, 1998.

Hurst, James Willard. *The Growth of American Law: The Law Makers.* Boston: Little, Brown, 1950.

———. *Law and Economic Growth: The Legal History of the Lumber Industry in Wisconsin, 1836–1915.* Cambridge: Harvard University Press, 1964.

———. *Law and Social Order in the United States.* Ithaca NY: Cornell University Press, 1977.

Jackson, Donald W., and James W. Riddlesperger Jr. "Money and Politics in Judicial Elections: The 1988 Election of the Chief Justice of the Texas Supreme Court." *Judicature* 74 (December–January 1991): 184–89.

Jackson, Percival. *Dissent in the Supreme Court.* Norman: University of Oklahoma Press, 1949.

Janowitz, Morris. *The Last Half-Century: Societal Change and Politics in America.* Chicago: University of Chicago Press, 1978.

Jaros, Dean, and Bradley C. Canon. "Dissent on State Supreme Courts: The Differential Significance of Characteristics of Judges." *Midwest Journal Political Science* 15 (1971): 322–46.

Kagan, Robert A., Bliss Cartwright, Lawrence M. Friedman, and Stanton Wheeler. "The Business of State Supreme Courts, 1870–1970." *Stanford Law Review* 30 (November 1977): 121–56.

———. "The Evolution of State Supreme Courts." *Michigan Law Review* 76 (May 1978): 961–1005.

Kagan, Robert A., Bobby D. Infelise, and Robert R. Detlefsen. "American State Supreme Court Justices, 1900–1970." *American Bar Foundation Research Journal* (1984): 371–417.

Kalish, Stephen E. "Legal Education and Bar Admissions: The Nebraska Experience." *Nebraska Law Review* 55 (1976): 596–636.

Kalven, Harry. *A Worthy Tradition: Freedom of Speech in America.* New York: Harper and Row, 1988.

Kaufman, Irving R. "Maintaining Judicial Independence: A Mandate to Judges." *American Bar Association Journal* 66 (April 1980): 470–72.

Kaye, Judith S. "Changing Courts in Changing Times: The Need for a Fresh Look at How Courts are Run." *Hastings Law Journal* 48 (1997): 851–66.

Kennedy, Edwin. "How Does Your Court Perform?" *State Court Journal* 11 (Spring 1987): 4–13.

Koebel, C. Theodore. "The Problem of Bias in Judicial Evaluation Surveys." *Judicature* 67 (November 1983): 225–33.

Krivosha, Norman. "In Celebration of the 50th Anniversary of Merit Selection." *Judicature* 74 (October–November 1990): 128–32.

Lazarus, Edward. *Closed Chambers: The Rise, Fall and Future of the Modern Supreme Court.* New York: Penguin Books, 1998.

Leuchtenburg, William E. *The Supreme Court Reborn: The Constitutional Revolution in the Age of Roosevelt.* New York: Oxford University Press, 1995.

Lewis, Anthony. *Gideon's Trumpet.* New York: Random House, 1964.

Linowitz, Sol M. *The Betrayed Profession: Lawyering at the End of the Twentieth Century.* New York: Charles Scribner's Sons, 1994.

Lozier, James E. "The Missouri Plan a.k.a. Merit Selection: Is it the Best Solution for Selecting Michigan's Judges?" *Michigan Bar Journal* 75 (September 1996): 918–28.

Luebke, Frederick C. *Nebraska: An Illustrated History.* Lincoln: University of Nebraska Press, 1995.

Madgett, Paul W. "The 'Five-Judge' Rule in Nebraska." *Creighton Law Review* 2 (1969): 329.

Mahoney, Anne R. "Citizen Evaluation of Judicial Performance: The Colorado Experience." *Judicature* 72 (December–January 1989): 210–16.

Maltz, Earl M. *The Chief Justiceship of Warren Burger, 1969–1986.* Columbia: University of South Carolina Press, 2000.

Martin, Albro. *Railroads Triumphant: The Growth, Rejection, and Rebirth of a Vital American Force.* New York: Oxford University Press, 1992.

Mason, Alpheus T. "Judicial Activism: Old and New." *Virginia Law Review* 55 (April 1969): 385–426.

McClellan, Madison B. "Merit Appointment versus Popular Election: A Reformer's Guide to Judicial Selection Methods in Florida." *Florida Law Review* 43 (July 1991): 529–60.

Melone, Albert P., and George Mace. "Judicial Review: The Usurpation and Democracy Questions." *Judicature* 71 (December–January 1988): 202–10.

———. *Judicial Review and American Democracy.* Ames: Iowa State University Press, 1988.

Monkkonen, Eric. "Can Nebraska or Any State Regulate Railroads? Smyth v. Ames, 1898." *Nebraska History* 54 (1973): 365–82.

Murphy, Walter F. "Marshalling the Court: Leadership, Bargaining and the Judicial Process." *University of Chicago Law Review* 29 (Summer 1962): 640–72.

Nebraska Commission on Law Enforcement and Criminal Justice. *Crime in Nebraska—1991*. Lincoln, 1991.

Nebraska Legislature. *Laws of Nebraska, 1893*. Lincoln: Secretary of State.

———. *Laws of Nebraska, 1895*. Lincoln: Secretary of State.

———. *Laws of Nebraska, 1901*. Lincoln: Secretary of State.

———. *Laws of Nebraska, 1903*. Lincoln: Secretary of State.

———. *Laws of Nebraska, 1905*. Lincoln: Secretary of State.

———. *Laws of Nebraska, 1915*. Lincoln: Secretary of State.

———. *Laws of Nebraska, 1925*. Lincoln: Secretary of State.

———. *Laws of Nebraska, 2003*. Lincoln: Secretary of State.

———. *Revised Statutes of Nebraska, 1943*. 1995 Reissue. Lincoln: Revisor of Statutes.

Nebraska Legislature. Clerk of the Legislature's Office. *Nebraska Blue Book, 1968*. Edited by Helen Griess. Lincoln, 1968.

———. *Nebraska Blue Book, 1970*. Edited by Helen Griess. Lincoln, 1971.

———. *Nebraska Blue Book, 1978–79*. Edited by Lois A. Sasso. Lincoln, 1979.

———. *Nebraska Blue Book, 1980–81*. Edited by Lois A. Sasso. Lincoln, 1981.

———. *Nebraska Blue Book, 1990–91*. Edited by Robert H. Fraas. Lincoln, 1991.

———. *Nebraska Blue Book, 2000–01*. Edited by Kasey Kerber. Lincoln, 2001.

———. *Nebraska Blue Book, 2002–03*. Edited by Ashley D. Anderson. Lincoln, 2003.

Nebraska Supreme Court. *Code of Professional Responsibility*. Canon 5, DR 5-109, July 23, 1997.

———. *Nebraska Reports*. Vol. 135–248. Lincoln: State of Nebraska, 1938–91.

Neely, Richard. *How Courts Govern America*. New Haven CT: Yale University Press, 1980.

Nuernberger, Ruth K. "Letters from Pioneer Nebraska by Edward Randolph Harden." *Nebraska History* 27 (1946): 18–27.

Oakley, John B., and Robert S. Thompson. *Law Clerks and the Judicial Process: Perceptions of Qualities and Functions of Law Clerks in American Courts*. Berkeley: University of California Press, 1980.

Olson, James C., and Ronald C. Naugle. *History of Nebraska*. 3rd ed. Lincoln: University of Nebraska Press, 1997.

Orfield, Lester B. "The Supreme Court of Nebraska: Procedure, Organization, Selection and Tenure." *Nebraska Law Bulletin* 19 (October 1940): 241–301.

Oursland, Kevin, and the University of Nebraska Public Policy Center. "Public Trust and Confidence in the Courts." *The Nebraska Lawyer* (November 1999): 14–17.

Perlman, Harvey. "Interference With Contract and Other Economic Expectancies: A Clash of Tort and Contract Doctrine." *University of Chicago Law Review* 49 (Winter 1982): 61–129.

Posner, Richard A. "The Meaning of Judicial Self-Restraint." *Indiana Law Journal* 59 (1983): 1–24.

Powe, Lucas A., Jr. *The Warren Court and American Politics*. Cambridge: Harvard University Press, 2000.

Rakove, Jack N. *Original Meanings: Politics and Ideas in the Making of the Constitution.* New York: Alfred A. Knopf, 1996.

Ranney, Joseph A. "Practicing Law in 20th Century Wisconsin: The Courts and the Bar Grapple with Growth." *Wisconsin Lawyer* 70 (March 1997): 14–24.

Reed, Traciel V. "The Politicization of Retention Elections." *Judicature* 83 (September–October 1999): 68–77.

Reid, John. *Law for the Elephant: Property and Social Behavior on the Overland Trail.* San Marino CA: Huntington Library, 1980.

Robbins, Ira P. "Concurring in Result without Written Opinion: A Condemnable Practice." *Judicature* 84, no. 3 (November–December 2000): 118–19, 160–65.

Ross, William G. "The Ratings Game: Factors that Influence Judicial Reputation." *Marquette Law Review* 79 (Winter 1996): 401–44.

Santoni, Roland J. "The Integration of Contract, Corporate and Tort Law Principles: ConAgra Inc. v. Cargill Inc." *Creighton Law Review* 20 (1986–87): 317–34.

Schwartz, Bernard. *A Book of Legal Lists: The Best and Worst in American Law.* New York: Oxford University Press, 1997.

———. *The Fourteenth Amendment.* New York: New York University Press, 1970.

———. *Super Chief: Earl Warren and His Supreme Court.* New York: New York University Press, 1983.

Scheb, John M. "State Appellate Judges Attitude toward Judicial Merit Retention: Results of a National Survey." *Judicature* 72 (August–September 1988): 170–72.

Scheurman, Kurt F. "Rethinking Judicial Elections." *Oregon Law Review* 72 (Summer 1993): 459–85.

Schwartz, Gary T. "Tort Law and the Economy in Nineteenth-Century America: A Reinterpretation." *Yale Law Journal* 90 (1981): 1717–75.

Sheldon, Charles H. *A Century of Judging: A Political History of the Washington Supreme Court.* Seattle: University of Washington Press, 1988.

Shugrue, Richard E. "The Second Degree Murder Doctrine in Nebraska." *Creighton Law Review* 30 (1996): 27–66.

Smith, Christopher G., and Heidi Fellman. "State Supreme Courts' Non-Judicial Tasks." *Judicature* 84 (May–June 2001): 304–9.

Smith, R. R., and R. D. Ingram. "Stop the Fighting: Bench and Bar Relations." *Georgie Bar Journal* 2 (June 1997): 10–13.

Spears, Franklin S. "Selection of Appellate Judges." *Baylor Law Review* 40 (Fall 1988): 501–25.

Stenberg, Don. "Malice in Wonderland." *Creighton Law Review* 30 (1996): 15–27.

Stover, John F. *American Railroads.* 2nd ed. Chicago: University of Chicago Press, 1997.

———. *The Life and Decline of the American Railroad.* New York: Oxford University Press, 1970.

Tarr, G. Alan, and Mary C. A. Porter. *State Supreme Courts in State and Nation.* New Haven CT: Yale University Press, 1988.

Trogdon, Gary A. "For the Advancement of the Honor and Dignity of Our Profession:

The Nebraska State Bar Association: The 1930s to the Present." *The Nebraska Lawyer* (October 2000): 24–34.

Urofsky, Melvin I., and Paul Finkleman. *A March of Liberty: A Constitutional History of the United States.* 2nd ed. New York: Oxford University Press, 2002.

———. *Division and Discord: The Supreme Court Under Stone and Vinson, 1941–1953.* Columbia: University of South Carolina Press, 1997.

Van Pelt, Samuel. *"What Psalm-Singing Son of a Bitch Said That?": A Collection of Legal and Political Reminiscences.* Hickman NE: Privately published by Samuel Van Pelt, 2001.

Vile, John R. "The Selection and Tenure of Chief Justices." *Judicature* 78 (September–October 1994): 96–100.

Vose, Clement E. "Interest Groups, Judicial Review and Local Government." *Western Political Quarterly* 1 (March 1966): 85–100.

Wasmann, Eric, Nicholas P. Lovrich Jr., and Charles H. Sheldon. "Perceptions of State and Local Courts: A Comparison Across Selection Systems." *The Justice System Journal* 11 (Fall 1986): 168–85.

Weifing, John B. "State Supreme Court Justices: Who Are They?" *New England Law Review* 32 (Fall 1997): 49–100.

White, G. Edward. *The American Judicial Tradition.* New York: Oxford University Press, 1978.

———. *Tort Law in America: An Intellectual History.* New York: Oxford University Press, 1980.

———. *The Constitution and the New Deal.* Cambridge MA: Harvard University Press, 2000.

Wice, Paul B. "Court Reform and Judicial Leadership: A Theoretical Discussion." *The Justice System Journal* 17 (Spring 1995): 309–21.

Willborn, Steven L. "Off the Mark: The Nebraska Supreme Court and Judicial Nominating Commissions." *Nebraska Law Review* 70 (1991): 277–305.

Williams, Jane. "Survey of State Court Opinion Writing and Publication Practices." *Law Library Journal* 83 (Winter 1991): 21–49.

Winters, Glenn R. "A Half Century in Retrospect." *Judicature* 72 (August–September 1988): 92–97.

Wiecek, William M. *The Lost World of Classical Legal Thought: Law and Ideology in America, 1886–1937.* New York: Oxford University Press, 1998.

Wold, John T., and John H. Culver. "The Defeat of the California Justices: The Campaign, the Electorate, and the Issue of Judicial Accountability." *Judicature* 70 (April–May 1987): 348–55.

Wunder, John R. *Inferior Courts, Superior Justice: A History of the Justices of the Peace in the Northwest Frontier, 1853–1889.* Westport CT: Greenwood Press, 1979.

Zemans, Frances K. "From Chambers to Community." *Judicature* 80 (September–October 1996): 62–63.

Index